COWBOY

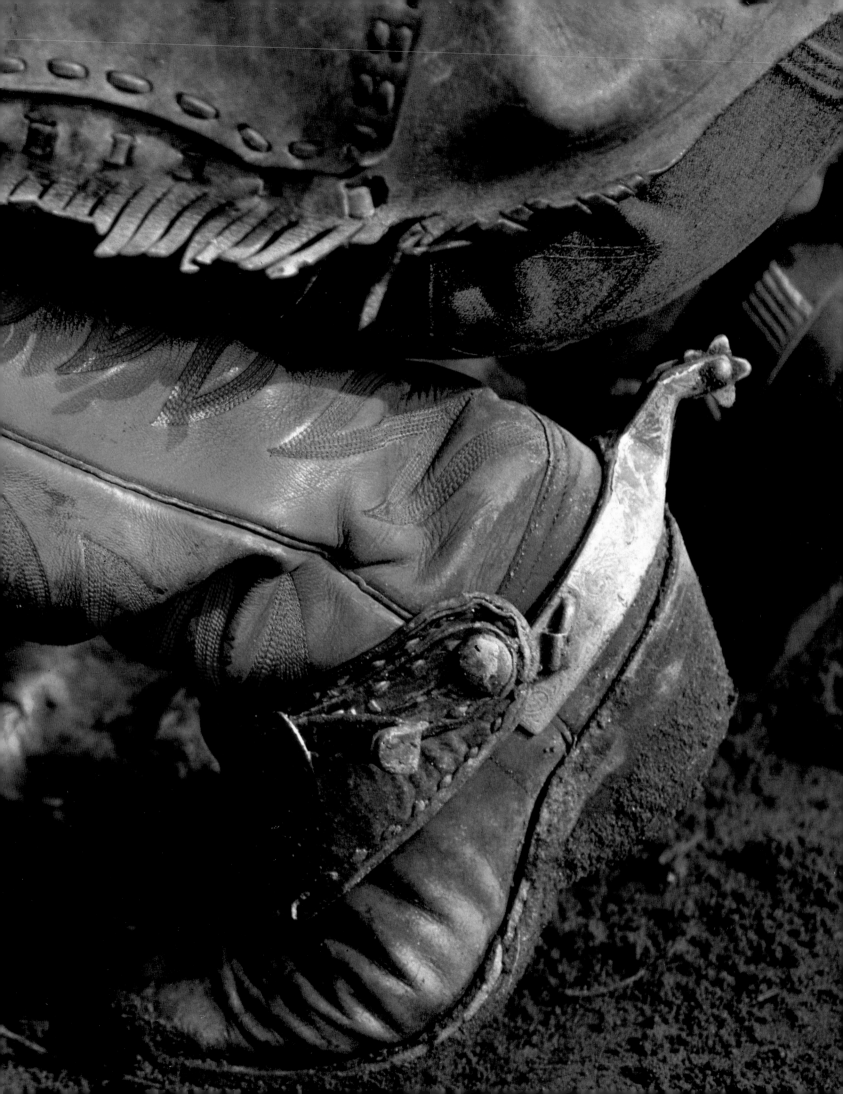

COWBOY

The Enduring Myth of the Wild West

By Russell Martin

Design and
Art Direction by
Hans Teensma

STEWART, TABORI & CHANG, PUBLISHERS

NEW YORK

I wanted—and needed—to look at America again, and it had seemed to me then that a cowboy's camp might be the proper place to start. A cowboy was, somehow, the most "American" thing I could think of.

JANE KRAMER
The Last Cowboy

My heroes have always been cowboys,
And they still are, it seems.
Sadly in search of and one step in back of
Themselves and their slow-movin' dreams.

SHARON VAUGHN

PHOTOGRAPHS
PAGES 2-3: *Kurt Markus*
PAGE 4: *Jonathan Wright/Bruce Coleman, Inc.*
PAGE 6-7: *Susan Felter*
PAGE 10: *Jeffrey E. Blackman*
PAGE 13: *David Hiser/Photographers Aspen*
PAGES 14-15: *Fred Baldwin and WendyWatriss/Woodfin Camp*

Edited by Leslie Stoker
Copyedited by Linda Reiman
Photo research by Susan Armstrong

Library of Congress Cataloging in Publication Data
Martin, Russell.
    Cowboy, the enduring myth of the Wild West.

    Bibliography: p. 414
    Filmography: p. 416
    Includes index.
    1. Cowboys–West (U.S.)   2. West (U.S.)–Social
life and customs.   I. Title.
F596.M32 1983   978   83-482
ISBN 0-941434-25-7

Text, photo, and picture credits appear on pages 409–413.

Distributed by Workman Publishing Company, Inc.,
1 West 39th Street, New York, New York 10018

Printed in Italy.

CONTENTS

Preface

From the desk where I work, I can look out the window and watch bandy-legged young cowboys in baseball caps and gray-whiskered men in sweat-stained Stetsons drive cattle down the country road near our house, and at times I wish mightily that I was riding with them. And time and again I can watch on late-night television a strapping young Gary Cooper defend the homesteaders in *The Westerner*, or listen to Jerry Jeff Walker sing "Night Rider's Lament," or read Larry McMurtry on the poignant withering-away of the brash and bucolic West, and each time I do, I am once again certain that America has carved and whittled a romantic cowboy culture that has mattered enormously and that is likely to be with us for a long time to come—a culture more alive in stories and dreams than on the land perhaps, but one that I could never tear free from even if I took it in mind to try.

I have dreamed about being a cowboy since the days when I rode stick ponies across lawns that I imagined were summer pastures, and since the Saturday afternoons a few years later when I charged out of the movie theater on Main Street and ran the seven blocks home, thrilled by the six-shooter skills of the cowboys. When I was finally old enough to ride a *real* horse out on my grandparents' sheep ranch, I knew immediately that nothing could be grander than to gaze at the whole of the wide West from the back of that swayback mare.

Decades later, I still have not seen all of the West that there is to see, and I still am not a cowboy. But I do think about being one sometimes. I imagine that a life lived out in stark and straightforward connection to the seasons of grass, to beef cattle, and to agile, quick-eyed little quarter horses must surely be enriched by important elemental truths and a lush pastoral romance. Yet I've helped brand just enough cattle, watched enough bawling heifers struggle to rid themselves of stillborn calves on desperate winter nights, and seen enough ranchers bite the cold foreclosure bullet and take to selling auto parts to understand that the truths are tempered by uncertainty and the romance is dulled by the grim familiarity of endless work. And yet, something about the sound of the word *cowboy* still tugs away at me and fosters images of a life full of purpose and pride, anchored to open country.

When I ride horses these days, I always strap spurs to my boots, not because our plug horses require them, but because the feel and the *sound* of the jangle of spurs when I walk is simply stirring as hell and strangely satisfying—a kind of mythic make-believe akin to riding stick horses, an indulgence that grown men can get away with without appearing ridiculously silly or totally self-consumed. And sometimes, when an odd need gnaws at me, I even go out in a cowboy hat, and wear it as proof that I belong somewhere, that I'm rooted in a region that, despite all its bravado and its legacy of destroying the best parts of itself, still holds buoyant hopes and still needs a few boys at work on the back of a horse.

The writing of this book, an attempt to gather the West's historical, fictional, folkloric, and contemporary cowboys into a single corral whose posts are cut out of our collective need to understand ourselves, has been a very pleasurable way for me to reconsider my own subtle cowboy connections and the ways in which the look and the lure of the West have influenced both the person that I likely am and the person I pretend to be. And perhaps it is even a book on whose pages you'll catch a glimpse of yourself as well, or a glimpse of some silk-shirted cowboy or cowgirl you once dreamed you might become.

A project like this is happily and necessarily a collaborative one, and I have been aided and assisted by many generous people. I am particularly indebted to publisher Andrew Stewart for his infectious enthusiasm and his unfailing support; to Hans Teensma, the Dutch buckaroo, and his assistant, Susan Armstrong, for the wonderful photographs and the exquisite design; to Linda Reiman for her keen eye and careful copy editing; to Leslie Stoker, who edited the manuscript and supervised every phase of the project, for her diligence, her care and insight, her remarkable good humor, and her friendship; and to my wife, Karen Holmgren, for her steadfast concern for guineas and great horned owls, harried writers, and spoiled horses. May they all always encounter clear weather in that good and open country.

R. M.
Dolores, Colorado

I

"I believe I'll run a show when I get to be a man," young Willie Cody told his sisters one day in the early 1850s while they played Indians outside their Bleeding, Kansas, home. His older sisters told him they doubted that; a fortuneteller had revealed to their mother that Willie would become president of the United States. The boy thought that prospect over briefly, then responded: *"I don't propose to be President, but I do mean to have a show."*

Twenty years later, Buffalo Bill Cody, already a nationally renowned frontier scout, formed a traveling theatrical troupe that performed melodramas about the conquest of the open West. A decade later, in 1883, he established The Wild West, a circuslike combination of pageantry and parades, feats of skill and daring, and "authentic" reenactments of frontier events. For thirty years, The Wild West played to sell-out audiences throughout the United States and Europe, forging in the minds of millions of people vivid images of the splendor of the West, of its perils and hardships, of Indians, of the mounted cavalry, and especially of cowboys—obscure and seemingly unimportant young drovers who had pushed Longhorn cattle north out of Texas—whom Cody portrayed as the heartiest, noblest, and freest of the West's historical characters.

Cody had wanted to be a showman, and he became world-famous as one. He wanted to create a cowboy that his audiences could envy and emulate and hold forever in their imaginations as a symbol of the great adventure of the West. And that too he did.

16

CHAPTER ONE

COWBOYS & IMAGES

THERE IS A DRY AND BEDEVILED CORNER OF THE AMERICAN WEST THAT HAS SEEN a lot of cowboys in its time. It is a high and rocky triangle of terrain bounded roughly by the brown waters of the Colorado, Dolores, and San Juan rivers, and it straddles the states of Colorado, New Mexico, and Utah. It is a haughty kind of country—ugly and enticing, beautiful and forbidding. It nurtures a little grass, and it engenders a perplexing loyalty.

When the Spanish explorer-priests Dominguez and Escalante passed through the region in 1776, they thought the land appeared capable of providing pasture for many cattle. The first Hispanic ranchers settled in as the nineteenth century opened. A group of Mormon stockmen followed in the 1850s. And a long and steady migration of Anglo-American cattle and sheep raisers began in the 1880s. But the region never became a cattle empire, as vast reaches of Texas, Nebraska, and Montana had become. It seemed destined instead to spawn as many kinds of cowboys as numbers of cows. After Zane Grey visited the coarse canyon and mesa country early in the twentieth century, he made the area the setting for *Riders of the Purple Sage*, a seminal Western novel and one of the most popular ever written. The sandstone spires of Monument Valley were the dramatic backdrop for John Ford's epic Westerns of the 1940s and 1950s. Novelist Louis L'Amour imagined a frontier locale called Shalako in the region's ponderosa uplands that was the setting for many of his hot-iron horse operas. And recent Westerns like *True Grit* and *Butch Cassidy and the Sundance Kid* took shape among the region's meadows and

The historical, fictional, and contemporary cowboys are characteristically men who know what they want out of life, and who are mighty glad they are cowboys. (Paul Chesley/Photographers Aspen; LEFT: Nicholas de Vore III/ Photographers Aspen)

The mythic cowboy is America's symbolic native son. He represents the ideals of individualism and courage—and he knows what has to be done. (Kurt Markus; RIGHT: John Running)

mountains, arroyos and desert ridges.

Today, cattlemen with more misery than money, and their cowhands whose lives are carefully crafted anachronisms, still do push belligerent beeves across Cowboy Wash and Red Horse Gulch, Expectation Mountain and Disappointment Valley. The region remains a place where men in sweat-stained straw hats lean long over the blades of their irrigating shovels, where Anglo, Hispanic, and Indian cattlemen and cattlewomen cut hay in the torrid summer, then feed it to cattle in the cold calamity of winter. It is a place where raucous rodeos are still the year's grandest celebrations, where men who have to ride earth-movers and oil well–supply trucks instead of horses to earn their keep dance to country swing tunes into the early morning with beer-drinking, coy cowgirls whose names are tooled onto leather belts. It is a brash and callous country where *cowboy* is a very versatile word—not just a noun but an adjective and a ubiquitous verb as well. It is a place of enduring dreams and a few pompous delusions; and it is the place where this book unfolds.

But this book is not about historical cowboys alone, or the troubles of contemporary ranchers, or the six-shooter cowboys of books and movies, or the weekend wranglers on ranchettes who struggle to sustain a personal connection to the wild spirit of the West. It is, instead, a book about all of these and especially about how these four kinds of cowboys are entwined by the rope of myth, about how the images of each one are related to, and are dependent on, the others. It is a book about how America gave birth to the cowboy, then observed him with astonishment, about how we have continually remade the cowboy, molding him to suit our needs, and about why the complex figure of that horseback boy somehow endures on the frontier of interstellar space.

The mythic cowboy, the cowboy whose image has been shaped by history, fiction, and folklore, is unquestionably America's predominant symbolic native son. His myriad images have come to represent the American ideals of individualism, strength, and courage; and his imagined role in the settlement of the West is a national metaphor for the American commitment to action, work, and achievement. Yet the mythic cowboy is not anchored in the history of statesmanship or military service. The first cowboys were not presidents or generals, explorers or philosophers. They were laborers—lower-class boys who, beginning in the 1850s, hired on to work in a saddle on the back of a horse—rounding up thousands of wild Texas cattle, branding and castrating them, then pushing them east into Louisiana and the Deep South, west toward California, and finally north to the railheads that connected the open plains to the population centers east of the Mississippi. Most of the historical cowboys—who were called *vaqueros* and *drovers* until the flow of cattle out of Texas had almost stopped—were hard-working hands who endured the caprice of weather and the crush of isolation. But they were not heroes. They were of no greater collective historical significance than the men who baled cot-

Rodeo evolved from the recreational contests held by ranch hands and from the frontier spectacles of the Wild West shows. Today rodeo is an enormously popular sport and pageant that perpetuates a symbolic connection to the cowboys of the past. (Glenn Short; LEFT: Jonathan Wright/Bruce Coleman, Inc.)

The first cowboys were vagabond boys of every race who were intrigued by the prospect of money and adventure that could be found on the back of a horse.

ton or built the railroads, the loggers or longshoremen or farmers. The cowboys became legendary figures almost by accident—and only because something in their personal images, their nomadic life styles, and their elemental connection to animals and the wide reach of the western land was intrinsically appealing to millions of Americans. The flesh-and-blood trail boys were transformed into the proud and strapping characters of the cowboy myth not because they were historically important, but because they were made *symbolically* important. The courageous and capable mythic cowboy, the footloose and unfettered man of the saddle, came to symbolize the kind of person Americans liked to believe they were, or dreamed they might become, and cowboy fantasies grew far more vivid in the public's mind than did the realities of cowboy life. When early balladeers sang

> *The winds may blow*
> *And the thunder growl*
> *Or the breezes may safely moan;*
> *A cowboy's life*
> *Is a royal life,*
> *His saddle his kingly throne,*

they weren't celebrating the truth of that claim; no, they were delighting in the fanciful notion that it *might* indeed have been so.

THE MAN WHO FIRST BEGAN TO GIVE THE COWBOY SYMBOLIC STATURE, who first presented a heroic cowboy image to an easily persuaded public, had never been a cowboy himself. If he had, he might have felt that trail hands were simply too ordinary, their jobs too mundane, and their impact too local to ever become the stuff of legend. But William F. Cody, the actor and showman who had grown up in the frontier West and had been a buffalo hunter, scout, and Pony Express rider, understood that Easterners had been fascinated by the frontier expansion into the western half of the continent and that their interest flourished even after the railroads and telegraph lines had united the regions and fences had formed an enormous gridwork across the prairies. When Cody formed the traveling Wild West show, he was aiming to make himself rich by offering reenactments of frontier adventures, struggles, and triumphs to people who had already begun to view the settlement of the West as an allegory of the whole nation's achievements and aspirations. According to The Wild West's printed program, each show would

present an exacting and realistic entertainment for the public amusement. [Cody and company's] object is to PICTURE TO THE EYE, by the aid of historical characters and living animals,... the wonderful pioneer and frontier life in the Wild West of America.

Cody presented Indians and homesteaders, stage drivers and scouts, mounted cavalry and skilled sharpshooters, performing entertaining "spectacles" that were billed as portrayals of real events from the bold frontier. In his efforts to keep his audiences captivated by the notion that something grand and transcendent had taken place when the new nation pushed westward, the showman tried to imbue every one of his frontier figures with an aura of profound significance. To complete the myth, Cody even claimed that the motley wranglers who looked after the show's livestock were stirring examples of the skill and fortitude that life in the West demanded. Cody's cowboys rode bucking broncs, bulls, and buffalos to demonstrate their talents in the saddle and to prove their daring. They "rescued" stagecoaches to show their gallantry and courage and fine moral character.

Buckaroos in remote regions of the country still look and live much like the cowboys who were at work in the West a hundred years ago. (Kurt Markus)

The audiences responded so enthusiastically to the cowboys that Cody decided to gamble on making one of his wranglers a star attraction. He chose William Levi "Buck" Taylor, a Texas-born trail hand who had worked on Cody's Nebraska ranch. Cody assured spectators that Taylor was not a ruffian, as most cowmen were presumed to be. In fact, Cody said, his handsome cowpoke was "amiable as a child," and he called Taylor, who could indeed perform impressive riding and roping maneuvers, "the King of the Cowboys." Taylor was an immediate hit, and Cody quickly began to highlight his wrangling skills; posters and newspaper ads featured Taylor and other strapping cowboys; dozens more western horsemen were added to the troupe, and the cowboys rode near the head of parades and processions, just behind the heroic figure of the long-haired showman himself.

With the publication of *Buck Taylor, King of the Cowboys* in the Beadle Half-Dime Library in 1887, the cowboy's image was well on its way to being permanently transformed. Buffalo Bill's Wild West show, and its more than a hundred imitations, played a principal role in crafting an image of the cowboy as a good and decent fellow, but it was Erastus Beadle, the successful New York publisher of mass-circulation "dime novels," who made the cowboy's life exciting enough to sustain the public's attention. Since the early 1860s Beadle had been producing cheap thrillers—stories of the exploits of pirates, rogues, detectives, and a sort of composite western character who was often called a "border man." Cody himself had been the subject of hundreds of pulp stories—more than five hundred Buffalo Bill stories were eventually published—but it was the short, sensational novel about Buck Taylor that focused immediate attention on a new kind of frontier figure—a mounted fighter and adventurer who rode nowhere without his six-shooters strapped to his hips. The fictional gunfighters in the thousands of thrillers that followed occasionally used ropes to scale cliffs or to tie up the desperadoes they captured, but their principal tools were their long-barreled revolvers. Their cows, the beasts that had given rise to their profession, had strangely disappeared.

Rodeo contests like bareback bronc riding and wild horse races are rituals that reenact the early rangeland work of taming wild mustangs. (Paul Dix; RIGHT: Douglas Kent Hall/FotoWest)

William Levi "Buck" Taylor was proclaimed by Buffalo Bill to be the "King of the Cowboys." Taylor was the first cowboy "star" and later became the fictionalized hero in a series of dime novels.

Buffalo Bill Historical Center, Cody, Wyoming.

When Philadelphia lawyer Owen Wister published *The Virginian* in 1902, the first full-length, "serious" cowboy saga, cattle were similarly missing from the scene. The Virginian was handsome, strong, and stoic. Whenever the need arose, he too could quickly fill his hands with iron; he brought outlaws to justice and won the heart of the heroine; but unlike Buck Taylor, he was often silent and essentially mysterious. Yet something about the Virginian was immensely appealing. The quiet force of his actions became a model for the thousands of fictional cowboys who followed him.

The action-filled life of the cowboy received enormous attention in the early twentieth century. Frederic Remington and many other painters discovered romantic and adventurous images in the cowboy, his horse, and the wild land he rode across. Zane Grey, Max Brand, Ernest Haycox, Clarence E. Mulford, and other novelists wrote formulaic Westerns that emphasized gunplay and hard-riding excitement. "Action, action, action is the thing," said Brand. "So long as you keep your hero jumping through fiery hoops on every page you're all right....There has to be a woman, but not much of a one. A good horse is much more important."

Action was obviously a staple in the early films as well, and cowboy stories seemed naturally suited to the cinema. Galloping horses, fiery gun battles, and the majestic sweep of a far horizon could be vividly depicted on screen. Stories about the winning of the West had an epic quality to them, and the Hollywood movie industry made the western horseman its focal heroic subject. At the same time, a new entertainment that combined the pageantry of the old wild west shows with the athletic contests that had become a common form of recreation for western ranch hands—extravaganzas variously called roundups or stampedes or rodeos—became popular across the nation. Boys and girls in stylized western dress who performed tricks and competed for prize money by riding, roping, and wrestling cattle and unbroken horses became emblematic of the early *vaqueros* and drovers. Like the cowboys in books and the cowboys who rode the ranges on the silver screen, the rodeo riders were also connected to the trail boys, but the tether was only a tenuous one. In just two decades after the last Longhorns were trailed out of Texas, the popular image of the brave and capable cowboy bore only scant resemblance to the scrappy seed stock of his breed.

Buffalo Bill and the Beadle stable of writers succeeded in transforming the cowboy from outcast to idol late in the nineteenth century. But the evolution of the cowboy into a symbolic figure of national significance has been a twentieth-century phenomenon. Although he has his roots in a poignant and specific period in the history of the nation, the mythic cowboy has been a continually evolving character, adaptable to any era and to many needs. Owen Wister's reserved Virginian gave way to William S. Hart's emotional and ambiguous film cowboy who often turned from a life of crime to one of virtue.

Then Hart's popularity was usurped by a succession of huge-hatted, handsome cowboys like Buck Jones, Lash LaRue, Ken Maynard, and Tom Mix, who were almost unimaginably good and bashful fellows, cowboys who made a booming business out of delivering women from their peril. Then cowboys who could sing as well as they could swing a rope came on the scene—Tex Ritter, Gene Autry, Roy Rogers and the Sons of the Pioneers—gaudy, silk-shirted cowboys who turned the guitar into a ubiquitous Western prop, and who forged an enduring connection between country music and the image of the cowboy. John Wayne transformed the chaste and incorruptible cowboy into a man who was happy to fight with fists and guns and anything else that was handy, who swore, spat, and swilled whiskey on occasion, the kind of cowboy who would even sleep with a lonely schoolmarm or an alluring señorita if he found the time between his fights. But Wayne's cowboy was a moralist nonetheless, a hero in common men's clothes, very different from the violent, anarchic cowboys who followed him, epitomized by Clint Eastwood's amoral drifters and anguished outlaws.

The American culture has responded with interest and affection to many other kinds of cowboys during this century, cowboys who have been angry and comic, daring and inept, handsome and homely, corral-bred boys who have never left the country, and city slickers in Lucchese boots and belts with diamond buckles. We have popularized many different kinds of cowboys because we are many different kinds of people and because the cowboy, as a mythic figure, reflects our own images of ourselves more than he reflects any verifiable truths about himself. The cowboy is, in effect, the American Everyman, and as such he is as anonymous as he is identifiable, as obscure as he is ever present. When Americans—even people who live in the cowboy-covered West—are asked to name cowboys they name figures like Buffalo Bill, the cowboy's first public relations man; or Tom Mix, one of the first Western matinee idols. They mention Charles M. Russell, a prolific painter of cowboys; Shane, a cowboy gunfighter in a book and a later movie; John Wayne, the classic film cowboy; Hoss Cartwright, a mammoth and memorable television cowpoke; Larry Mahan, a rodeo star; and even Ronald Reagan, an actor, president, and gentleman rancher of wide renown. Each is a recognizable "western" figure, a man who has presented an image that we identify in one way or another as *cowboy*, yet each is very different from the others, and none has ever earned his wages working cattle.

There are still a few of those cow-connected boys around. There aren't many of them, but they can still be found in places like Twin Bridges, Montana, and Tuscarora, Nevada, in Alpine, Texas, and Anadarko, Oklahoma. They are skilled practitioners of their craft, suffering isolation like the first cowboys, but they too have been whittled and honed by the images of our imagined cowboys. They wear wide, unwieldy hats like Tom Mix did instead

Handsome, horseback cowboys like Buck Jones were incredibly popular film stars during the 1920s and 1930s. They were heroic men—chaste, quiet, and courageous.

Women had little place in the mythic world of the cowboy early in the twentieth century, but today many women work with cattle and horses. The cowgirls at left examine the spillway of a dam. (Bill Ellzey; LEFT: Paul Chesley/Photographers Aspen)

of the flopping-brimmed felts that the range cowboys wore; they strum guitars like Gene Autry did (the early trail hands played fiddles) and listen to Porter Wagoner tapes in the cabs of their pickup trucks. They read Louis L'Amour novels at lunch breaks, watch Western movies late at night on their girl friends' TVs, and are as affected and afflicted by the romantic image of the Marlboro Man as are other Americans, perhaps even more so, because the idyllic appearance of his western way of life is something that some of them can begin to approximate in their own.

There are cowboy purists of note who swear that these modern-day horsemen are the only *real* cowboys among us, spurning the drugstore and disco varieties as phoney facsimiles of the lads who work on the land. But *real* is a dangerous word to use in connection with cowboys. It implies authenticity and a specific standard of comparison. If the historical trail ranger or drover is that standard, then there is little similarity with any contemporary figure to whom we can attach the label *cowboy*. Today's working cowboys tend beeves, as did the first cowboys, of course. But rodeo cowboys much more readily share the early trail hands' nomadic life style; the cowboys who roam the country discos and honky-tonks share the drovers' inclination to celebrate in nearly suicidal fashion; and the West's roughnecks, truck drivers, drillers, and welders are the modern-day descendants of the trail boys who worked because they had to, and who took up that dirty, grim, and grueling job because it was the only work they could get.

During the roughly one hundred years that the word *cowboy* has been in widespread use, it has as readily described fictional figures, entertainers, and laborers as bona fide boys in the saddle, and it has referred as much to a style of perceiving and presenting oneself as to a cow-centered way of life. Instead of trying to discern who is the real cowboy among the many imposters, this book assumes that each of the century's cowboys is a genuine article. It contends that whether he rides the short-grass prairies, the interstate highways, the Hollywood backlots, the decrepit small-town arenas, or the fanciful terrain of writers' imaginations, each cowboy belongs to a fine fraternal breed, to a culture of cowboys characterized by dreams of freedom and images of a western land where every man has a purposeful part to play.

John Travolta and John Wayne represent radically different eras of the film cowboy. Wayne's characters are gruff and tough, but they understand themselves and their roles in a simple world. Travolta's character in Urban Cowboy *is a country boy in the city who is trying to figure out what is important and what is ultimately worth fighting for.*

IN JOHN FORD'S 1962 FILM, *The Man Who Shot Liberty Valance*, JAMES STEWART is Ransom Stoddard, a Westerner who becomes a United States senator after he is hailed for killing a hated outlaw in a street duel. Years later, when the aging Stoddard reveals to a group of newspaper reporters that he did not actually kill Liberty Valance, one reporter stands and tells him, "This is the West, Senator. When the legend becomes fact, print the legend."

The West has provided fertile ground for the nurturing of legends since the first explorers trekked across it in the sixteenth century in search of the fabled cities of gold. Fantastic stories about the land's horror and its beauty, about the savagery of its native people, and about incredible opportunities for finding wealth began early to envelop the frontier with an aura of mystery and excitement. The people who ventured west, who endured the perils of the wilderness and who experienced its joys, appeared bolder, braver, and more full of life than those who had not tested themselves on the frontier. In the middle of the eighteenth century there were no movie stars or sports heroes to read about, to emulate, and to adore. It was the adventurers who captured the public's imagination and who held its attention.

Considering the cowboy's status as the final frontier figure, as one who experienced the demise of the wilderness and the subsequent birth of a cattle-based culture and economy, it is easy to understand why the nation was reluctant to forget him. The cowboy, once transformed by Cody and dozens of pulp writers, became vivid and vibrantly attractive to millions of people. He was envisioned as the symbolic bearer of civilization into a region that was just beginning the slow but inevitable civilizing process. Something important was under way in the West, and Americans latched on to a symbolic figure that could help make the transition comprehensible to them, that could justify the force and furor of settlement and imbue it with a sense of glory.

The cowboy, the mounted adventurer in exotic western garb, a common man with uncommon skills, was the ideal representation of the bold man of the West. But because cowboy history was sketchy, because the *facts* surrounding the trail drovers were few in number and were drab and passionless, the *created cowboy,* imbued with excitement and honor, assumed the symbolic role. The cowboy that was crafted by Cody's showmanship and the sensational dime novels began to occupy a niche in the nation's folkloric imagination even while the final trail drives were under way in the late 1880s. The cowboy as historical fact had been replaced by a cowboy as mythical force.

The examination of the myriad images of the cowboy in the following chapters is founded on the conviction that what people *believe* is real is ultimately far more important than what actually is real, if indeed what is real can ever be accurately ascertained. It is the conviction that the folkloric cowboy whom we have been told was noble and brave has become of greater significance than the historical cowboy. "Human kind cannot bear very much reality," wrote T. S. Eliot, and in the case of the cowboy it is clear that as a people we have been unable to bear the truth that the earliest cowboy was nothing special. We needed a folkloric image of him to help enliven and legitimize the history of the western expansion; we needed to revere and remember him in order to stay proud of the past. And so we transformed the cowboy and his history into myth.

But myth, in the present context, is not make-believe. It is not a fable

but a cultural force, a collectively agreed-upon way of explaining why things are the way they are and how they came to be that way. Myths are, in effect, the ways in which we agree to order the world; they are the simple and familiar stories that we use to explain the complex events of human existence, stories that bridge the gap between the actual way in which things occur and the way in which we understand them.

It is, for example, literally true that early cowboys used guns sparingly and not very accurately, but is is *mythically* true that cowboys were adept and agile gunfighters. It is literally true that range cowboys and Indian peoples had only occasional contact with each other, but it is *mythically* true that cowboys and Indians were bitter enemies. Iowa-born actor Marion Morrison appeared in over 140 films under the name John Wayne—a literal truth. John Wayne was and is America's cowboy hero—an example of the power of myth. Acknowledging that the images of all our cowboys are diverse and sometimes divergent, and admitting that cowboys are sometimes as superficial as they are widespread, this book asserts that the American cowboy is transcendent: The mythic cowboys ride out beyond the fencelines of time and place, and all of them are *true,* even if they never lived among us.

The West possesses almost as many kinds of cowboys as it does numbers of cows—wild horsemen and boys with prize-winning rabbits, stoic heroes and weathered old men. (BOTH: John Running)

THE FOLLOWING CHAPTERS EXAMINE THE EVOLUTION OF THE MYTHIC COWBOY AND his role in the American West topically rather than chronologically. Instead of investigating how we as a forming culture got from Buffalo Bill to Broncho Billy Anderson and on to Butch and Sundance or, for that matter, from Buck Taylor to Tex Ritter to John Travolta, they take a look at the movements of the myths themselves. They note that some mythic ideas assumed shape long before easily identifiable cowboy figures emerged, and they point out that although the kinds of cowboys and the media in which they have been presented have undergone constant change, the myths persist and are, in fact, the bone and sinew that support the cowboy's chameleonlike façade.

Cowboy myths fall into three basic categories. They attempt to define and explain the cowboy in relation to the land, to animals, and to the people who form his society. Chapters 2, 3, and 4 separate the mythic world of western land into examinations of the concept of wilderness, the cowboy as a nomad, and the inevitable process of settling and civilizing the land. The next three chapters deal with the cowboy's historical and symbolic involvement in the slaughter of the buffalo and other wild creatures, with the role of the horse as an animal of enormous mythic importance, and with the ironic absence of any kind of cattle mythology. The last section of the book opens with an examination of the ways in which we have always failed to understand Indians and how the mythic battles between cowboys and Indians bear little relation to the fact that Indians have become the West's most noticeable and natural

The awesome and enormous western land is the cowboy's natural environment, the place where he discovers himself and where he proves himself.
(Kurt Markus)

44

Whether he chooses an ice cream cone or a can of beer, the popularized figure of the cowboy is a man who works hard, then relaxes with relish. (Laine Whitcomb; LEFT: B. A. King)

An urban cowboy rides the mechanical bull at Gilley's, the country nightclub in a Houston suburb that played a central role in the cowboy craze of the early 1980s. (Charles Steiner/International Stock Photo)

A rodeo contestant rides an all-too-real saddle bronc. A member of the notoriously superstitious cowboy fraternity, this rider has a four-leaf clover imprinted on his chaps. (Susan Felter)

cowboys. The subsequent chapters deal with the emergence of the cowboy hero as a mythic lawman, with the amazing way in which we have transformed hideous outlaws into heroic defenders of the common man, with the cowboy's odd and uncomfortable relation to women, and finally, with the ways in which mythic cowboys have ridden beyond their own milieu and entered the culture at large.

The words and images that follow do not pretend to form an exhaustive study of the mythic cowboy's relation to the wilderness, to western expansion and settlement, to buffalo, horses, or cattle, to Indians, lawmen, outlaws, women, or the vast amalgam of American culture that lies outside the cowboy's natural realm. There is ample evidence of the impossibility of that task in these isolated facts: As many as forty thousand drovers trailed ten million cattle out of Texas. By the turn of the century over a billion words had been written about Buffalo Bill alone. More than two hundred seventy dime novels had been written solely about the outlaw James brothers. Over a million and a half hard-cover copies of *The Virginian* were sold in its first fifty years of publication, not counting paperback reprints and translations. Hollywood has produced over two thousand feature Western films. Louis L'Amour has published eighty Western novels with worldwide sales totaling more than a hundred million copies. The "Gunsmoke" television series ran for nineteen years. The Marlboro Man has sold cigarettes during three decades. The beef business in America is a multibillion dollar industry that forms the backbone of much of the West's economy. And the dimensions of two cowboy nightclubs in Texas are measured in acres rather than feet.

This book is being published on the hundredth anniversary of the opening of Buffalo Bill's Wild West, and only nine years before the five-hundredth anniversary of the arrival of cattle and horses in this hemisphere. The spare and stunning western land has felt the booted stance of a lot of cowboys in that time. And we have created thousands more who exist in the timeless world of myth—fictional and folkloric lads in love with their horses and obsessed by the women in their lives, men who are anchored to a land they treat with alternating care and contempt, who want somehow to *matter* as individuals—proud and adept, free and secure, in the saddle. This book continues the myth-making process. It also tries to gauge with some certainty what the century of cowboys, and the four centuries of cow people before them, have come to. It tries to determine whether our myriad kinds of cowboys have survived so long because they are an integral part of the American experience or whether they were latched on to by writers, moviemakers, and historical hucksters because there was no one better at hand. It tries to determine whether the cowboy and his myths provide us with any real insights into how we Americans understand and explain ourselves, or whether they are only the illusory stories of a society pretending to be something it is not.

The weathered planks of a corral fence, and a barn emblazoned with the Anchor P brand reflect the cowboy's role as a tamer of the wild and as a civilizer of the open West. (B. A. King; LEFT: Jay Dusard)

There are still cowboys at work in the modern West—riding, roping, and forever tending livestock. (Jay Dusard; LEFT: Paul Dix)

Ultimately what the following pages try to do is to celebrate the cowboy in all his guises without making the mistake of treating him as a kind of secularized American saint. They attempt to impart a sense of the pastoral romance and gritty vigor, the joy and unabashed sentimentality that have always been the cowboy's close companions. They affirm that although the early cowboy's life was far from royal, the bevies of buckaroos who have descended from him have indeed had a rich impact on the shape and style of what the world recognizes as American culture.

It is a long and complex distance from the first Hispanic hands who mounted horses to tend their feral cattle to today's boys on barstools, thumbing copies of *Western Horseman,* and grizzled old ranchmen bent over the hoods of pickups, chatting idly and listening to Willie Nelson sing on the radio about the existential predicament inherent in being a cowboy. But it has been a trip that has brought to a new nation a folklore that identifies it and begins to explain its aspirations, one that continues to lure millions to mount mythic horses of their own, and to join the romantic ride into the hopeful terrain of the West.

The strapping cowboys played by Gary Cooper not only helped keep the cowboy myth alive; they made it real and accessible to millions of Americans.

2

"All my early days," Buffalo Bill Cody remarked wistfully in old age, "I stood between savagery and civilization." As a young man he had served on wagon trains and cattle drives, had ridden for the Pony Express and been a scout and messenger for the cavalry in a western landscape that was bold and wild. It was a strange and entrancing region that drew thousands of immigrants bent on taming it and putting it to use.

When Cody organized The Wild West entertainment decades later, he understood that it was the frontier—the untamed territory—that was alive in his audiences' imaginations. Yet the only way he could offer a glimpse of the wilderness inside a circus tent was to reenact the events that led to its taming. If people were interested in Indians, he could demonstrate a cavalry and Indian battle; if they were fascinated by exotic buffalo, they could see buffalo being hunted down; but if it was the vast expanse of open land that intrigued them, he could only offer himself—the proud longhair astride a fine white horse. He had seen the wild country, had briefly been a part of it, then had helped to make it unalterably tame.

THE WILD WEST

DECADES BEFORE VAGABOND BOYS BEGAN TO PUSH LONGHORN CATTLE TO market, Horace Greeley trumpeted his advice in the pages of the 1837 *New York Tribune*: "Go West, young man, go forth into the Country." Greeley felt certain that settlement of the vast and trackless landscape of the West would be a means of alleviating chronic poverty and unemployment in the East. Yet the region that he hoped intrepid men and women would be willing to lend their dreams and their backs to was the same one he would later describe as "the acme of barrenness and desolation." And a year after Greeley's famous exhortation, as ever greater numbers were striking out for the territories, Daniel Webster rhetorically asked, "What do we want with this vast worthless area? This region of savages and wild beasts, of deserts, shifting sands, and whirlwinds of dust, of cactus and prairie dogs?"

The reports from both the Zebulon Pike and Stephen H. Long expeditions into the lands of the Louisiana Purchase early in the nineteenth century convinced Easterners that a "Great American Desert" stretched westward from the fertile heartland to the wall of the Rocky Mountains. Thomas J. Farnham, who went out from Illinois to Oregon in 1839, reported in his *Travels in the Great Western Prairies* (1843) that the gaping expanse of the plains was nothing but a "burnt and arid desert, whose solemn silence is seldom broken by the tread of any other animal than the wolf or the starved and thirsty horse which bears the traveller across its wastes." The Rockies themselves were snowbound and forbidding—largely

The cowboy's response to the wild land has always been to try to tame it, to make it productive and safe for cattle. His struggle to tame the wild has provided the cowboy with a tough and gritty purpose. (LEFT: Kurt Markus)

"Rodeo. Sure as bobcats are ornery, it's no tea party," reads a brochure for the famed Calgary Stampede rodeo. As much a pageant as a sport, rodeo symbolically reenacts the taming of the wild, and rodeo cowboys are portrayed as being strong and mean enough to tame it. (BOTH: Susan Felter)

impassable—and the dry basins beyond them seemed to cradle desolation in every corner.

Yet the land—beguiling open space—was *out there,* full of mystery and danger. The journals of the explorers and the tall tales of trappers and traders, the paintings, engravings, and early photographs reflected a terrain full of bizarre topography and natural wonders. It was a land that was rich with surprises, unlike anything in Europe or the Atlantic states, a landscape that generated romance, intrigue, and a fledgling pride founded on the notion that the new land had been blessed by a benevolent God.

These two myths, the forbidding myth of the desert wasteland and the romantic myth of Western grandeur and opportunity, existed separately until late in the nineteenth century, when the cowboy—once seen as a lowly mounted herdsman—began to be perceived as a kind of universal frontiersman. Through the stories of the dime novelists and the exploits of the showmen, coupled with the young nation's passion for grand and exotic images of itself, the figure of the cowboy succeeded in incorporating the two myths. The images of the cowboy seemed to prove that the western lands were indeed made up of searing plains and treacherous deserts, but that those same lands imbued the hard lives lived out upon them with adventure and joy. The popularized cowboy rode out into the desert, drew his livelihood from it, and made it habitable. He lived amid the grandeur and made it believable.

As the young nation imagined him, the cowboy lived within the wild lands, but his work was to tame them, to make them safe and prosperous. And as his mythic stature grew, the ambivalent attitudes toward the cowboy's country became stronger and in many ways more complex.

That tension between the wild and the tame has always been central to the multifaceted myth of the cowboy—it is present in his portrayals in paintings, books, advertisements, movies, and television, as well as in contemporary cowboys' perceptions of themselves. When the cowboy does battle, be it against rattlesnakes, cattle rustlers, hailstorms, or bellicose Brahman bulls in a rodeo, he is figuratively pitted against the wild. In every image of a cowpuncher struggling to halt a stampede, breaking a wild horse, heading the outlaws off at the pass, setting coyote traps, or patching a line of fence, the mythic figure is at work taming the territory.

Without that tension between the wild and the tame, the cowboy myth would probably have had little of its amazing vitality and longevity. The cowboy has helped explain our settling, our husbanding, and our spoiling of the western terrain; he has imparted to that process romance and a collective sense of purpose. But for the mythic image of the cowboy to survive, some notion of the frontier has to survive as well. If the cowboy is ever left with no open, empty land to head into, to test himself against, our

mythic horseman may well have to dismount and unsaddle his horse, never to ride again.

"All my early days, I stood between savagery and civilization," said Buffalo Bill. In the public's imagination, Cody symbolized the courageous frontiersman who was willing to battle the wild.

EARLY AMERICANS WHO HAD GROWN UP IN THE SHADOWS OF THE continent's eastern hardwood forests were stunned when they discovered that west of the Mississippi the timber dwindled, then disappeared. Trees, of course, were easy evidence of rich ground, and the absence of trees must have meant the absence of fertility. Even the lush, well-watered prairies of Illinois at first seemed strange and repellent. Farther west, as the ground grew drier, the grasses turned stubby and yellow, and the landscape appeared sadly forsaken.

Zebulon Pike was among the first to herald the existence of a vast and horrible western desert when the journal of his expedition was published in 1810. Pike claimed that the plains were a wasteland similar to the sandswept deserts of Africa, and he warned that they just might be forbidding enough to form a barrier against further westward expansion.

Henry M. Brackenridge became a prophet of sorts when he wrote in 1817 in his *Views of Louisiana* that "there is scarcely any probability of settlers venturing far into these regions. A different mode of life, habits altogether new, would have to be developed." Although he was blatantly wrong on the first count, Brackenridge correctly sensed that a drastically different kind of society would emerge from settlement of the prairie. Washington Irving worried in 1836 that the great desert might spawn some strange and wild race of people made up of "the remains of broken and almost extinguished tribes, the descendants of wandering hunters and trappers; of fugitives from the Spanish and American frontiers; of adventurers and desperadoes of every class and country yearly ejected from the bosom of society into the wilderness." Irving's concern was shared by many. And even if the region remained largely unpopulated, it would still be possessed by vicious animals, killing droughts, violent storms—and the oppressive force of space itself. Buffalos, coyotes, and wolves were said to rule the spare grasslands; the summer sun heated the land anvil-hot; rain refused to fall for months at a time, and when at last it came, hail and black funnel clouds often accompanied it, battering and ripping the ground apart.

But perhaps most sinister was the prairie's dry, barren enormity. It was an ocean of desolation, and it possessed a sense of despair and doom that seemed impossible to wash away or to run free from. A New Mexico rancher said that he had spent his whole life "in a land that seemed to be grieving over something—a kind of sadness, loneliness in a deathly quiet. One not acquainted with the plains could not understand what effect it had on the mind. It produced a heartache and a sense of exile."

Place names often reflected the heartache the land induced: the Badlands, Disappointment Valley, Death Valley, Poverty Flats, Stinking Water, the Dismal River, the Crazy Mountains. The Fruitvales and Pleasant Valleys of other regions were impossible to find among the adobe hills and the dry gulches or on top of the burning hardpan.

The myth of the desert was nurtured by the bleak names and the bizarre accounts filtering eastward that told of wild lands and wilder men. It was a potent myth that survived even after the open West had been peopled and plowed, and it survived because it affirmed the mystery and adventure that people assumed were inherent in the wilderness.

Aspects of the desert myth were principal elements in the melodramatic formula of the dime novelists, whose work began to proliferate in the 1870s. In countless sagas, like *Mustang Sam; or, The Mad Rider of the Plains, Red Renard, the Indian Detective; or, The Gold Buzzards of Colorado,* and even *The Doomed Dozen; or, Dolores, the Danite's Daughter,* the western landscape was portrayed as a vile place where danger lurked behind every boulder and where virtue and decency were always at peril. Just as Washington Irving had done decades before, the dime novelists linked the hard terrain with crafty and corrupt characters. Unpredictable territory was the perfect melodramatic backdrop for skullduggery and mischief, murder and mayhem. As the pulps portrayed it, the frontier West would have been in a dire fix indeed if not for the strapping men (and the occasional woman) of courage and correct breeding who were willing to go into the region to ferret out trouble and to battle the elements and the purveyors of evil.

The lurid Western sagas cast a spell over millions of Americans, young and old, who had never seen the wide prairies, high mountains, or stalwart desert buttes. To their minds the West was as exotic as India, a truly American place that nevertheless seemed like it was worlds away.

A Cheyenne, Wyoming, newspaper carried a story in 1885 of a New York banker who was offering a $10,000 reward for the safe return of his eleven-year-old son, Fred Shepard. A voracious reader of Western sagas, the boy had scrawled a note at the bottom of the page of a story in which a "cowboy detective" successfully carves an awful murderer "into mincemeat." The note read simply: "I'm goin' West to be a cowboy detective." Young Fred took his tin savings bank and a few clothes, climbed out of his window, and struck out for the wastelands in search of unimaginable sights and high adventure.

THE SAME WESTERN REGION THAT HAD REPELLED AND FRIGHTENED MEN LIKE Daniel Webster and Washington Irving, and had seemed the perfect place to right the world's hideous wrongs to boys like Fred Shepard, was conversely conceived as a miraculous and splendid place by others. It was the West's gran-

Riders of the Purple Sage
By **Zane Grey**

HARPER & BROTHERS · *Publishers* · Established 1817

In Zane Grey's seminal Western novel, Riders of the Purple Sage, *the land is portrayed as being both menacing and beautiful. Grey's characters can appreciate the beauty, but their principal concern is battling its many dangers.*

Explorer Zebulon Pike reported in 1810 that a "Great American Desert" covered much of the West, and millions of Americans assumed for decades that the West was composed of only emptiness, desolation, and death. (BOTH: Hans Teensma)

Photographers of the early West like William Henry Jackson often focused on the colonizers' first attempts to tame the immense and primeval terrain, rather than on the land itself.

deur that caught their eyes and held their attention—its snow-wrapped peaks and sheer canyons, its proud monoliths and raging rivers. No European or colonial American had ever seen terrain so strange. Yet, instead of reacting to the wilderness with caution, many painters and chroniclers reacted with awe. The western lands they explored were stunning and exciting. The landscape shaped a continent that indeed was a New World, a primeval place full of wonder.

Those who were convinced that America was carving an entirely new social order had often lamented that the eastern American landscape somehow didn't reflect the stature and uniqueness of the society that it bore. "As a whole it must be admitted that Europe offers to the senses sublimer views and certainly grander, than are to be found within our own borders," conceded James Fenimore Cooper, "unless we resort to the Rocky Mountains, and the ranges in California and New Mexico."

Painters like Albert Bierstadt and Thomas Moran were quite willing to resort to vistas of the western mountains for subject matter. But Bierstadt, who first ventured west in 1859, and who had spent the four previous years studying landscape painting in Germany, perceived the West not as a fresh new country to examine and to record in paint, but as a mirror of Europe. He wrote of Utah's Wasatch region: "The color of the mountains and of the plains, and indeed, that of the entire country, reminds one of the color of Italy; in fact, we have here the Italy of America in a primitive condition."

Bierstadt, Thomas Moran—who accompanied the 1871 Hayden Survey into Yellowstone—and predecessors like Alfred Jacob Miller, were enthralled by the West's physical grandeur, and their paintings, perhaps because of the inevitable instructional purposes they would serve in the East, often appeared grander than did the land itself. Theirs was a romantic realism that was intended to be more inspirational than representational. Bierstadt's huge canvas *A Storm in the Rocky Mountains* is certainly grounded in the visual reality of the craggy Rockies, but it is much more a dream than an artist's vision. Miller's *Trappers Saluting the Rocky Mountains* is wonderfully evocative of the awe the first immigrants to see the Rockies must have felt. And Moran's work, although generally less maudlin than Bierstadt's or Miller's, is nonetheless rooted in the same romantic traditions. "I place no value upon literal transcripts from Nature," Moran wrote. "My general scope is not realistic; all my tendencies are toward idealization."

The myth of grandeur, the conception of the western lands as an ethereal realm separate from humankind, free of its corruption, probably did little to lure immigrants into the region. People initially went west for economic reasons, drawn by the promise of riches or the meager hope of survival. Few made the arduous move simply because the land seemed beautiful or inviting.

The most important legacy of the myth of grandeur—what historian Henry Nash Smith called the "garden myth" in his often-cited book, *Virgin*

Land—was the formation of a fledgling conservation consciousness. Federal protection for Yellowstone and the Yosemite Valley came in direct response to Bierstadt's and Moran's paintings and began an enduring national interest in preserving natural wonders and fragile landscapes. Long before the nation's citizens began to visit the western "treasures" in great numbers, the painters and early photographers like William H. Jackson, T. H. O'Sullivan, Edward S. Curtis, and others, had convinced them that those locales were immensely important in and of themselves—unimproved, untouched, and empty. The Grand Canyon, Yosemite, the Black Hills, Yellowstone, Canyon de Chelly, and the towering redwoods were collectively deemed precious and had become sources of national pride long before moves toward exploiting or taming them were ever considered. The power of the myth was never great enough to leave all of the West untouched, of course; there were far too many other westering imperatives at work to allow that to happen. But pieces of the primeval and grand land did survive, heroic landscapes that alluded to heroic human possibilities.

Ben Cartwright, played by Lorne Greene in the television series "Bonanza," epitomized the cowboy who believes he can create a beautiful land out of the wilderness only by making it productive and profitable.

"PONDEROSA WAS HIS HOME," WROTE WILLIAM COX IN A 1969 WESTERN NOVEL that brings back the same characters from the renowned "Bonanza" television series. "The spreading loveliness of it, reaching to the edge of Lake Washoe, was part and parcel of [Ben Cartwright], as much as his bones, his marrow. This was something the Cartwrights had built, great and profitable and beautiful."

Beauty and profit: It would be hard to express more succinctly how the cowboy culture fused the myths of the desert and the idyllic garden into one myth with far more might and meaning than either had had alone. Ben Cartwright, the proud patriarch, cut from the classic mold of the powerful but gentle ranchman (silver-haired Lorne Greene sitting tall in his ornately-tooled saddle), surveys his kingdom and pronounces it good. There is loveliness in what Ben and the boys have built, the land has been shaped by human hands to meet human needs. And the Ponderosa is beautiful, not just because of its towering pines and lakes, but because it makes money. It is land that has a job to do, that earns its keep.

This hybrid myth, the view of land as a wasteland that humankind—cowboy kind—can bring under control and make productive and beautiful, is the essential cowboy conception of land. As horticulturists tend to favor nature nurtured over nature in the raw, so do pastoralists, people who raise animals, seem to prefer, and work to produce, land that looks as though it's been husbanded—enclosed by fences, stock water imported, feed supplements and salt provided, rattlesnakes and coyotes removed. The process of taking a reach of land that "looks rangy," and "kinda sorry" and turning it into "a pretty fair piece of ground" is the work that principally characterizes a cowboy's image of him-

If the fickle and frightening weather could be harnessed, and if the land's danger and unpredictability could be controlled, the cowboy would lose much of his purpose, and little would still seem wild about the West. (Nicholas de Vore III/Photographers Aspen; LEFT: Bill Ellzey)

The trail cowboys were charged with protecting their Longhorns from stampedes, prairie fires, and the predations of wolves on the long journeys to the Kansas railheads. (Jim Richardson)

self. He's a man of the land who is smart enough to know that the land wouldn't be worth a damn without him.

This potent yet rather prosaic way of looking at western land had its beginnings in the late 1860s when hundreds of defeated Confederate soldiers headed to Texas and began rounding up the hearty and prodigious Longhorn cattle that had gone feral during the Civil War. The cattle roamed the cedar and oak savannahs of the Texas hill country, the hot and humid lowland grasses, and the brittle prairies that reached westward as if they went on forever. The herders discovered that those broad-horned animals had fared remarkably well. All they needed was to be rounded up, claimed (often one could claim as many as one could round up), branded, and put back on the grass again. The empty land that was available to range cattle was vast and, to the surprise of many, perfectly capable of sustaining them. What the early ranchers lacked was a market for their cattle, a hungry populace with a newly developed taste for quantities of fresh meat.

Working cowboys, and the cattle industry they were a part of, helped dispel the myth of the Great American Desert by proving that the land was capable of producing bounty. (Kurt Markus)

Texas cattlemen hired scrappy and impoverished but game young men to help them drive cattle into Louisiana, to New Orleans. Some drives were destined for St. Louis, and a few even went westward into California. But it was when the first long drives north to railheads in Kansas began in 1866 that the rangeland attitudes that still persist were firmly battered into the soil. The range was free for the using; it belonged only to a government too far away to be concerned about it and native tribes already too broken by battles with the immigrant whites to be able to put up more than token resistance. The miles of bleak prairie that were once considered absolutely worthless became feedlots for moving cattle, wide highways that led the animals northward. The Great American Desert was redeemed by the cattle it nourished; and the idyllic wilderness was made accessible by those bandannaed boys who rode out into it.

The great nineteenth-century cattle culture, a business rooted in the conversion of scrub grass into muscle fiber, spread north out of Texas onto the high plains of Kansas, Nebraska, and the Dakotas; west to New Mexico and Arizona and on into California, where it met an already established, heavily Spanish-influenced cattle industry; and northwest to the Rockies regions of Colorado, Utah, Wyoming, and Montana. Cows quickly became the ubiquitous western animal, lumbering across the Staked Plains of Texas, bawling for their calves in Nebraska's Sand Hills, chewing clover and timothy grass on the foothills of Montana's high Absaroka Range.

But the cattle couldn't tame the wild. In fact, the cowboys' real work revolved around protecting their beeves from the wilderness, from sudden blizzards that could kill hundreds of animals and strand thousands away from their feed, from prairie fires and the predations of wolves, from bloat and colic and mastitis and pinkeye, and from the mysterious and often dangerous business of giving birth. Cows simply lent the promise of profit to the wilderness. And

Like the battering of a prairie dust storm, the wildness of the West is the cowboy's persistent adversary. (Ernst Haas)

A cowboy herds his horses across A Deep Ford in this Frederic Remington engraving. The first artists and writers to depict the cowboy focused on the danger and difficulty of his work.

their presence within it demanded that the herders do what they could to subdue it, to hold the wilderness back and make it safe for the high-hipped critters with brands burned into their hides.

ONE OF THE GREAT IRONIES OF THE COWBOY MYTH IS THAT ALTHOUGH VIRTUALLY every cowboy attitude or activity bears some relation to the taming of the wild, it is essential that that job never get done. For if the land were no longer capable of inducing hardship and surprise, if the fickle weather could be harnessed, if predators and varmints could be corralled once and for all, if horses could truly be trusted and if cows had a lick of sense, then there would be nothing wild about the West at all and nothing special about being a cowboy. The fictional and the literal cowboy have to straddle the tenuous territory between the wild and the controlled, and that ambiguous stance is much of what has made both figures intriguing and appealing. Yet it is a stance that makes the cowboy appear often contradictory in attitude.

Wilderness, with its potential for danger, is the fundamental setting for the cowboy story; the unpredictable terrain becomes the cowboy's principal foil. Bandits hide out in the boulder-strewn badlands; feverish horseback chases thunder through the grassland. The scattered towns are "carved out of the country," reflecting its rawness and its potential for violence.

But the land holds both loveliness and danger; it offers romance and a sense of nature's balance and order—as well as nature's potential for chaos. Listen to Zane Grey, master of the horse opera, treat the cowboy's ambigious attitude toward the land in his monumentally successful 1912 novel, *Riders of the Purple Sage:*

> The crushed sage resembled the path of a monster snake. In a few miles of travel he [Venters] passed several cows and calves that had escaped the drive. . . . The opening of the cañon showed in a break of the sage, and the cattle trail paralleled it as far as he could see. That trail led to an undiscovered point where Oldring drove cattle into the pass, and many a rider who had followed it had never returned. Venters satisfied himself that the rustlers had not deviated from their usual course. . . . The sun sank. There was an instant shading of brightness about him, and he saw a kind of cold purple bloom creep ahead of him to cross the cañon, to mount the opposite slope and chase and darken and bury the last golden flare of light.

In that one scene the land resembles a snake, harbors fugitive cattle and rustlers and crannies from which some riders never return, and at the same time shapes marvelous vistas and sunsets, full of color and intensity and emotion.

Landscape has played an important role in Western films, of course. Directors have often used land symbolically to represent both evil and virtue, danger and refuge. Early D. W. Griffith silent Westerns often underscored the enduring qualities of both the land itself and of human conflicts and conditions. William S. Hart films characteristically featured the dominance of the land, its size and its power. John Ford, on the other hand, focused on the cowboy's attempts to conquer the land. Ford was the first director to bestow star status on a specific terrain—the bold red sandstone bluffs, buttes, and spires of southern Utah's Monument Valley. Horizons are low in Ford films, creating skyscapes of enormous breadth and depth, silhouetting his characters in heroic poses against them. Ford's landscapes in such films as *The Searchers, Stagecoach,* and *Fort Apache* reflect power and are imbued with a sense of wild possibility, but his heroes are always capable of confronting the land; they are equal to its demands, strong enough to survive its misery.

In Howard Hawks's 1948 classic, *Red River,* the land is a testing ground for dedication to purpose, friendship, and maturity. Cattleman Tom Dunson, a dictatorial cowboy Captain Bly played by John Wayne, wants to supply beef to the midwestern heartland—"good beef, good cattle to make the country grow." But to do so, he and his men must endure a thousand miles of tribulations brought on by their own foibles and by the land itself. By the time they cross the Red River and push their cattle into Abilene, Kansas, each of the men has undergone an elemental transformation: Each man is now surer of life's hardships, each has had to deal with his own and his comrades' weaknesses, and each knows that shared danger can be as intimate as shared love. Hawks's *Red River* teaches a hard lesson: The land can't be controlled, but it can be endured.

The truth, of course, was that the western land could be and was conquered; it was plowed under, pushed apart, strip-mined, bulldozed and bombed, and filled with cities and suburbs. As the West has increasingly suffered "civilization," it has curiously become more important for many Westerners to assert the existence of wilderness within the mythic framework. It now seems to be more important than ever to insist that life's tough out West, to glorify the wild as it shrinks out of sight.

Rodeo, in many ways much more a pageant than a sport, plays a vital role in affirming that the West is still wild and potentially violent. "Rodeo. Sure as Bobcats are ornery, it's no tea party," reads a brochure for the famed Calgary Stampede rodeo. "Ask any cowboy who explodes out of a chute biting off a sunfishin' chunk of fury . . . and then chews it. That, though, is his life . . . skinned raw from the living flank of adventure. He takes it, tames it and loves it."

At small-town rings and city arenas throughout the western half of the United States and Canada, billed as a "Legend Walkin' Tall," "An American Legend in Action," and a rip-snortin' wild time, rodeo reminds its fans that there's a mean country out there. Bucking horses and ornery bulls are compared with grizzlies and lions and snakes. Announcers stress the incredible dangers that rodeo cowboys expose themselves to; they banter continually about the

The land in Westerns like Howard Hawks's 1948 film, Red River, *is a testing ground for the cowboys who are pitted against its obstacles.*

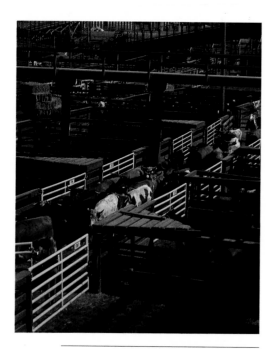

Much of the wild West had been unalterably tamed. Oil and gas wells cover the range lands, lazy cow towns have become frantic cities, and cattle are now tended inside the metal fences of enormous feedlots instead of out in the open spaces. (James Cook/The Stock Market)

bad tempers and the treachery of the bucking stock. Even when a cowboy completes his mandatory eight-second ride without getting bucked off—effectively conquering the animal—fans are reminded that the critter can hardly wait to try to kick another cowboy off his back.

At a Cortez, Colorado, rodeo, after a huge gray Brahman bull had pitched its rider into the dirt, kicked at him, and thrown his horns into an arena clown, he began to circle the high perimeter fence, charging into it whenever anyone appeared momentarily close enough to gore. While wranglers tried to herd the enraged bull out of the arena, the announcer commented that the action in the ring "had got a little Western." The message in every rodeo's action-charged and colorful spectacle is rather explicit: cowboys are tough as nails and determined as hell, but things are still pretty wild out West.

When Emerson Hough described the "true cowboy" in 1923 as a "product of primitive, chaotic, elemental forces, rough, barbarous, and strong," he meant that the cowboy was whittled into shape by the hard might of the land he lived on. And when we realize the rough, primitive truth about the cowboy, Hough claimed, "then we shall all love him; because at heart each of us is a barbarian, too."

Perhaps it is the barbarian in the cowboy that we've long found so attractive. Nocona-brand cowboy boots are advertised in a series of scenes in which a fancy-booted Westerner wars against wolves, rattlesnakes, and scorpions. In a song called "The Dalharted Cowboy," the hero claims:

I'm a wild raging stallion
In a race with the wind—. . .
Don't rein me too tight.

Modern-day cowboys hang rifles in their pickups as if some terrible primeval danger lurks around every S-turn in the highway. They nickname themselves "Wildman," "Sidewinder," and "Hoss" and call their horses "Lightning," and "Blizzard." And a western poet declares that a cowboy is finally corrupted by the wild he hopes to tame:

Of rough rude stock this saddle sprite
Is grosser grown with savage things.
Inured to storms, his fierce delight
Is lawless as the beast he swings
His swift rope over.

Even if cowboys sometimes become "wild" themselves, they are still tied to the romantic and sentimental images of wild terrain and wild animals that are used to describe the idyllic western life. During the singing-cowboy era of the thirties and forties, when Roy Rogers, Tex Ritter, and Gene Autry were making happy, lighthearted movies and crooning about the good old West, it was hard to believe that the bad guys served any purpose other than to give

A series of ads by the Nocona Boot Company pits a cowboy against rattlesnakes and other animals that symbolize the wild. But the wildness and brutality of rodeo is far from merely symbolic. (Bruce Benedict/The Stock Market)

A sign at a Texas rodeo arena explains that cowboys are liable for their own injuries. Broken arms, legs, and even necks are frequent occurrences. (Bill Ellzey)

the cowboys something to do between songs; and images of the land itself were benign and, oh, so inviting:

> Ridin' down the canyon, just to watch the sun go down,
> A picture that no artist ever paints.
> White-faced cattle lowin', across the mountain trail,
> I hear a coyote howlin' for its mate.
> Cactus plants are blooming, sagebrush everywhere,
> Granite spires are standing all around.
> I tell you folks it's heaven to be ridin' down the trail,
> To watch the desert sun go down.

A 1975 song by Mike Burton, "Night Rider's Lament," also revels in the glories of the western land, but in a much more poignant way it attempts to explain why someone would willingly endure the lonely, isolated, hard life of a cowboy. As it begins, a cowhand who is out on night herd reads a letter from an old friend who has seen the cowboy's former sweetheart. The sweetheart has rhetorically asked:

> Why does he ride for his money
> Why does he rope for short pay
> He ain't gettin' nowhere
> And he's losin' his share
> He must've gone crazy out there.

The cowboy answers the question into the night, explaining to himself that it's the land that holds him:

> . . . they never seen the Northern Lights
> They never seen the hawk on the wing
> They never seen spring hit the Great Divide,
> They never heard ole camp Cookie sing.
>
> Well, I read up the last of my letter
> Tore off the stamp for Black Jim
> When Billy rode up to relieve me
> Just looked at the letter and grinned.

The two cowboys don't even have to talk about it. They implicitly understand that while for some open terrain may be just too wild or barren or boring, for them it is full of meaning; it's the only place they can imagine being.

DURING THE DECADES OF THE TWENTIETH CENTURY, THE COWBOY CULTURE AND the mythic horseman in all his guises have become removed from the wild frontier. The era of the cattle drives is just a dim memory, yet the work of taming the wild continues. A variety of symbols have emerged that now represent the unfettered and violent wild of the past and that imply the need for continued work at taming it. The West is a safe and secure place today, but the cowboy nonetheless has to try to keep it under control because that is what he has always done.

Ranchers have latched on to the coyote, the intrepid little canine some tribal peoples called "god's dog," as their archetypal wild nemesis, claiming that he terrorizes and kills calves and sheep as much for sport as for sustenance, that he eludes baits and traps and reproduces at astonishing rates. They grouse about the federal government's poison control regulations and argue that a major extermination campaign is the only action worth taking. "The coyote is nothing but a killer," claims a Montana rancher. "The bleeding hearts put out propaganda about coyotes killing only mice and rodents, but really they are like humans or dogs, they will not eat a mouse if they can get steak—like deer, lambs, and calves. The reason people think coyotes are scarce is that they are pretty slippery; they hear you coming and slide off into the brush.... The dudes drive down the road and if they don't see them, they think they are extinct. If they ever get that thick, they will eat people."

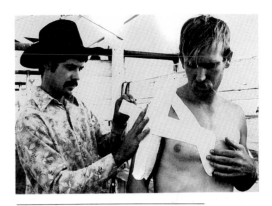

"Cowboys are rough, barbarous and strong," wrote historian Emerson Hough, and we love them "because at heart each of us is a barbarian, too." (Craig Aurness/West Light)

Biologists, ecologists, and wildlife officials often disagree about the coyotes' numbers and the harm they cause. Some insist that no eradication measures are likely to significantly reduce coyote populations, and one ecologist claims that "predators [including coyotes, eagles, bobcats, and cougars that prey on stock, and elk, prairie dogs, and assorted varmints that feed on rangeland grasses] are a scapegoat for all the problems inherent in making a living from livestock in the West."

Although sentimentalized in songs as essential to the flavor and character of the West, predators—in many respects the last vestiges of the primeval terrain—still have to be rubbed out, and people imagine the killing as another elementally western experience. Witness a paragraph in a recent Montana vacation guidebook:

Hunt Varmints Year-Round!

With a long list of varmints and predators, from coyotes to small ground squirrels, you can hunt anytime you can visit.... Sharpen your skills on mountain roaming marmots and squirrels. Hunt cottontails (yessir) and jackrabbits at will, even at night. Call coyotes and fox, or run coon and get ranchers' thanks. Practice on crows and magpies, the tricky pests of the west.

The stockmen may never be rid of all those pests of the West, but they symbolically continue their struggle. Coyote carcasses hang from roadside fence posts like dire warnings to others of their kind. Elk antlers adorn gates, hang above doorways, and are sometimes stacked in great piles in yards and town squares. Rattlesnake hat bands abound, a few expensive ones featuring the varnished heads of the snakes, fangs agape, jutting out from the brim of the hat, ready to strike. Cowboy boots are available in every kind of exotic leather—

from anteater, eel, and elephant to water buffalo, lizard, crocodile, and the more prosaic antelope and calfskin. Whatever the leather, the symbol is the same: cowboy culture at work and in image pitted against the wild, subduing it, making the West safe for cattle and kids, schoolmarms and shopping malls.

As the cowboys struggle with the myths of their own making, as well as with those imposed on them from outside, the dichotomous demands of the land still pull at their shirttails and fly in their faces like prairie winds. There's a lot of taming left to do—much of the world that surrounds them is capricious and cruel and full of confusion. But lots of the open land they knew is gone now. Oil and gas wells pockmark the rangelands; coal outfits tear into the bare shoulder of the earth; lazy cow towns have become cities frantic with enterprise, and cattle—the genesis of it all—are fattened inside the metal fences of enormous feedlots. In *The Modern Cowboy*, cowboy author John R. Erickson describes a visit to a contemporary hand at work in a Texas feedlot:

> He rode his horse through acres of steel pens and looked at corpulent steers that had forgotten how to run and fight. There was no silence here, but instead the constant roar of the feed mill and the hay grinder. The mountains behind the cowboy were not the Rockies, but hills of dung that had been pushed up by front-end loaders. He sat in a new saddle, with a big dally horn wrapped with strips of rubber, a breast harness and a roping cinch. But he carried no rope. Neither did the other men on the crew. And I thought to myself: "Well, cowboy, they've taken away your rope. Tomorrow, they'll take away your horse and issue you a Honda motorcycle. Horseman, pass by."

In the 1979 film *Electric Horseman,* the alcoholic cowboy hero, Sonny Steele, played by Robert Redford, refuses to dismount, refuses to succumb to the numbing trappings of the modern world. *Electric Horseman,* in many ways a vehicle for the expression of Redford's own environmental concerns, reverses the standard wild and tame valuations of the old Western movies, requiring Sonny to escape the tame and tainted world and head out into the mountains, the sane and primal place. Sonny is a has-been rodeo cowboy reduced to doing demeaning advertisements for a breakfast cereal. When he discovers to his disgust in Las Vegas that the renowned race horse he is scheduled to ride in a promotion has been drugged, Sonny plugs in his gaudy lighted uniform and rides the horse out of the bowels of Caesar's Palace, down the glittering Strip, and away into the night.

In the ensuing hunt for Sonny and the horse, the classic cowboy-movie formula is turned on its head: The chase scenes take place on the blacktopped streets of St. George, Utah, instead of out in the dangerous spaces; the bad guys are slick city men in three-piece suits, and the faithful friend is a backcountry hermit. Civilization is riddled with corruption and greed and the drab diminishment of self. Only the land is noble and grand. In the end, even freeing the horse from its cruel owners isn't enough for Sonny. The redemption of the

As Sonny Steele in Electric Horseman, *Robert Redford portrayed a has-been rodeo cowboy who refuses to succumb to the corruption and greed of "civilization" by escaping with his horse into the Utah wilderness. (Stanley Tretick)*

Rodeo announcers sometimes claim that the action inside the arena "has got a little Western," implying that mayhem and danger are integral parts of the West. (Lewis Portnoy/Spectra-Action)

proud stallion and of Sonny himself comes only when the horse is freed to run with a band of mustangs, let loose into the gaping wilderness, into a remnant of what the West used to be—a land of possibility and strength and the few horseback men who tried to match it.

Nostalgia has always been vital to the cowboy experience—nothing quite as good as it once was, the land filled with people and plundered and few eagles climbing thermals into the sky. The wide West has withered today, and the epic cowboy, at work taming the wild, has to hunt around for a patch of wild to tame. There isn't much to find on the face of the land itself. Huge country discos like Gilley's near Houston and Billy Bob's in Fort Worth make much of their size and the wide-ranging, hot-dogging good times they provide, trying to preserve some vestige of the wild and wooly under their steel-raftered roofs. Neither succeeds in recapturing the rough life, of course. It's gone forever. But so much of the cowboy mystique is bound up in battling the wild that even paltry symbols of it become important.

Rodeo, more popular than ever, enlivens the myth of the wild, employing carefully selected bucking stock to represent the flared-nostrilled fighters of the old days. The eight-second rides of the cowboys are ritual reenactments of the taming of the West, and they will continue to excite audiences as long as the West retains its vitality and appeal.

Cowboys will continue to dream about a home on the mythic range, imagining they can get back some day to a deliberate life in which they battle the land alone, in which they can grab hold of it, work it, shape it, and finally improve the land, making it better because of their presence. Some have found their remnant piece of the wild West and are anchored fast to it. Most others are still searching, keeping a wary eye out for rattlers and kindred symbols of the wild, listening cautiously for a chilling howl in the tame and settled night.

3

William F. Cody succeeded in making the West mythic, then made the myths mobile. The first immigrants into that region had been willing to uproot their lives and to strike out for something strange and unknown; the first cowboys were true nomads, at home wherever they pushed their cows. In that same tradition, Cody's Wild West was always on the move, traveling throughout the United States, and regularly touring Europe from 1887 until 1906.

Cody exploited the history of the westward migrations and portrayed himself as one of the riders at the vanguard of the movement into the West—and out into the world. A Wild West poster depicting a proud Buffalo Bill on horseback declared him to be: "The Man on Horse of 1898. From the Yellowstone to the Danube. From Vesuvius to Ben Nevis."

When American artist Frederic Remington passed through London in 1892 on his way home from Russia, his spirits were buoyed by the sight of Cody's Wild West tents on the plush lawns of Earl's Court. It was almost as if the wide spaces themselves had been transported across the Atlantic. "One should no longer ride the deserts of Texas," Remington wrote, "or the rugged uplands of Wyoming to see the Indians and the pioneers, but should go to London."

CHAPTER THREE

RIDING TOWARD THE SUNSET

FROM THE TIME OF THE SPANISH EXPLORER CABEZA DE VACA'S INCREDIBLE AND arduous trek early in the sixteenth century up to the present, immigrants to the West have roamed its spaces in search of new wealth, new land, new sights, and new adventures. The enormous western territory has always held a grand sense of possibility. Something better has always been waiting just beyond the horizon, in the next valley, in any locale not yet soured by the grim realities of the present place. After eight years of suffering and starvation, enslavement and fear, desperate wandering from the Texas coast into the uncharted American Southwest and finally safely into Mexico City, Cabeza de Vaca was still able to say of his and his comrades' quest to survive: "We held it certain that going toward the sunset, we would find what we desired."

This process of moving toward the sunset and the promises it holds has been an integral part of the western experience—in history, in fiction, and in myth. Initially, people moved west because the western terrain was empty and full of promise; it was unexplored, unsettled, as yet unexploited. Moving west became synonymous with starting over, with trying something new. And eventually, westering was directed not only in a specific direction but also toward a dimly defined idea of prosperity and a better life.

Westering began with the Spanish conquerors of the New World who brought the cow and the horse to the American continent and then headed west with them. Anglo-American settlers then pushed west from the Atlantic colonies, driven by economic necessity, by curiosity, and by the belief that their

Cowboys have always been wanderers, whether in search of cattle like Frederic Remington's trail cowboy in Cruising for Stock, LEFT, *or simply in search of new places and possibilities. (Kurt Markus)*

97

The vaquero *was the first figure in the western hemisphere to herd cattle from the back of a horse. He is the ancestor of all of North America's cowboys. (William Albert Allard)*

new nation was destined to occupy the whole continent. When colonial American cattle herders encountered the mounted Spanish and Mexican *vaqueros* in what is now Texas and New Mexico, they adopted their methods, equipment, and dress, and slowly the American cowboy emerged—a figure that eventually became the perfect embodiment of westering man.

The cowboy was defined as much by his movement, his lack of roots, as by his methods and dress. His was a life on the hoof, pushing cattle north and west across Texas and into the whole western half of the continent, riding from one cattle outfit to another, riding roundup and fence lines, traveling light and always on horseback—an anonymous man characterized not by where he came from but by the fact that he was always on his way to someplace else.

When the weavers of fiction discovered the cowboy, they made his westering habit, his determination to roam, his prime attribute. By always being on the move, he could continually find new adventure and provide dramatic action. A single cowboy—whether it was Buck Taylor of the dime novels, William S. Hart of the silent screen, or Richard Boone as Palladin on television's "Have Gun, Will Travel"—could fight Indians in Arizona, catch horse thieves in Montana, and then trail desperadoes on the Texas border. And at the end of each story, this mysterious man who was "just passin' through" could ride into the sunset, toward new places, new dangers—and new plot lines.

The horseman *had* to be on the move; according to the Broadway musical *Paint Your Wagon,* he was "born under a wandering star." Or, as the hero explains in the 1946 film *Buffalo Bill Rides Again:* "If I was to settle down, then I wouldn't be Buffalo Bill."

Today's cowboy is still a wanderer, still someone who expects to find something better, newer, truer. The mythic image of the cowboy, nurtured in songs and advertisements and by the life styles of thousands of worn-booted, restless young men, is one of a seasoned loner who soon has to be on his way. He is described in Sam Peckinpah's 1972 movie, *Junior Bonner,* as "nothin' but a motel cowboy," rootless, wandering westward toward the sunset, afraid perhaps that if he settles down he won't be a cowboy anymore.

WHEN HE LANDED ON THE ISLAND OF HISPANIOLA IN 1494 on his second trip to the New World, Christopher Columbus and his men unloaded thirty-four Andalusian horses and an unknown number of domestic cattle, introducing to the Western Hemisphere the animals that would direct its future for hundreds of years to come. The horses and cattle thrived on the lush Caribbean island, and a few of them were shipped in 1519 to the Mexican mainland, which became known as New Spain. That was the year that Hernán Cortés began his conquest of the Aztec capital of Tenochtitlán with the aid of sixteen

Vaqueros *wore wide-brimmed hats to shield them from the sun—hats whose utilitarian function and imposing size made them, over the centuries, the dominant symbol of the continent's nomadic horseman. (Rich Clark)*

Remington called this vaquero *a "buc-caro." Some modern cowboys still prefer to be called "buckaroos," a bastardization of the Spanish word for "cowman."*

prized horses, the year that Gregorio de Villalobos and his expeditionary party landed near present-day Tampico with several head of cattle.

Villalobos was soon named lieutenant governor of New Spain. He oversaw the arrival of Spanish immigrants—lifelong European herdsmen who quickly recognized that this new land was rich with pastoral resources. In numerous accounts the settlers commented about how the interior of the mainland reminded them of their Iberian homeland. But the New World was perhaps even better suited than Spain to support huge numbers of cattle and the horses that were used to tend them. Villalobos's cattle quickly multiplied, and Spanish *ranchos* were steadily staked out westward toward Zacatecas, Compostela, and Guadalajara, and northward to Durango and the valley of the Rio Grande. When Francisco de Coronado left the small settlement at Compostela in 1540 in search of the fabled Seven Cities of Cibola somewhere north of the Rio Grande, he took five hundred head of cattle with him on long expeditions; all were slated for eventual slaughter, but many strayed away, and feral herds were established throughout what is now northern Mexico.

When Juan de Oñate established the settlement of San Gabriel in the upper Rio Grande valley of present-day New Mexico in 1598, he supplied it with seven *thousand* head of cattle. That same year cattle had become so plentiful to the south that a fleet of ships carried 150,000 New World cattle hides to Spain.

Cattle were everywhere. "You can not exaggerate their numbers or imagine the spectacle before your eyes," wrote Spanish chronicler Muñoz Camargo. The huge numbers of Spanish-bred beeves had to be trailed and watched over on horseback, a grueling job that the wealthy Spaniards disdained. There was no honor in herding cattle. The friars in charge of mission outposts, virtually all of which had herds of cattle, similarly hated the work the cattle imposed, and they seem to have been the first to have trusted their herds to mounted Indians and the immigrant African and European lower classes and slaves. These *vaqueros,* cowmen, outcasts, gradually developed their own customs and costumes and life styles. They wore wide-brimmed hats to shield them from the sun and bright scarves and sashes to protect them against the wind and the dust. They tied heavy iron *espuelas,* spurs, to their often bootless feet. And they used huge saddles with large horns to which *las reatas* and *los lazos* could be tied—the same ropes whose bastardized names became lariats and lassos in the jargon of the American cowboy.

The territorial limits of New Spain spread steadily westward to the Pacific, northward into California, where a permanent string of missions was established along the coast, and northward to the unexplored lands of New Mexico and Texas. Spanish immigrants continually headed cattle into those remote regions, and wherever the cattle went, they were accompanied by the skilled *vaqueros*—itinerant young men for whom cattle became an opportunity and for whom horses offered a position of responsibility and self-esteem. The *vaqueros* were proud and adept on horseback; they were mobile and unfettered; yet their purpose was precisely defined. They adapted clothing and equipment to suit the demands of the rangelands—much of which is still used by western cowmen today.

The *vaquero*'s woven *chaqueta* was the forerunner of the cowboy's indispensable denim jacket; the leather *chaparejos* that protected his legs from brush became the cowboy's chaps. *Vaqueros* used *cinchas* to secure their saddles, *jáquimas, mecates,* and *bosales* to bridle their horses—the same tack that American cowboys would eventually call cinches, hackamores, McCartys, and bozos. When a *vaquero* would wrap his *reata* around the saddle horn to hold a cow tight, he would *da la vuelta,* the same technique, used thousands of times over hundreds of years, that was finally called, simply, dally by the cowboys. Rodeo, the name for the spectacle that still dramatizes the cattle culture's ties to its Spanish origins, comes from the verb *rodear,* which means to encircle or round up. And buckaroo, the lilting sobriquet that's synonymous with cowboy (and that is actually preferred in some parts of the Far West) is nothing more than the word *vaquero,* pronounced by a thousand wide-eyed boys from Cornwall, County Kildare, and Kentucky.

Spaniards, and subsequently Mexicans, didn't enshrine the early figure of the *vaquero* in the same way that Americans came to revere the image of the cowboy. The *vaquero* remained a laborer, albeit a skilled and colorful one. By the time the mounted horseman became an important folkloric figure in Mexico, he had already traveled north across the Rio Grande, had been imbued with a bit of gallantry and mystery in books and movies, and had returned to Mexico in many ways more a cowboy than a *vaquero.* Today young Mexican men in that country's northern cattle-ranching states wear broad-brimmed straw hats with bright cloth bands and long sashes that hang jauntily down in back—a uniquely Mexican style, to be sure, but ironically one influenced as much by images of celluloid buckaroos in ten-gallon hats as by the *sombreros* of the early *vaqueros* who tended the Spaniards' cattle.

The chaps worn by the trail cowboys were fashioned after the chaparejos *worn by Mexican horsemen.*

THE HISPANIC CONQUEST OF THE NEW WORLD, OUTWARD AND UPWARD FROM the Gulf of Mexico, was aimed at increasing the size and power of the Spanish empire, at glorifying God and converting the heathen, and, somewhat more entrepreneurially, at securing grasslands for the fattening of cattle. Anglo-American westward migrations, on the other hand, were spurred by circumstances that were philosophical and less precisely defined. Long before the American Revolution, Great Britain worried about the growth of a huge and potentially unruly American colony; the conquest and acquisition of new territories wasn't universally favored. As for the Indians—the dominant Protes-

The vaqueros *were proud and adept
on horseback, unfettered and mobile
men at home on the desert ranges.*
(William Albert Allard; LEFT: J. Peter
Mortimer)

When the long cattle drives north out
of Texas began in 1866, unattached
young men of every race were anxious
to mount up, to chase after feral cattle,
as shown in Remington's The Cowboy.

tant attitude in Great Britain and the American colonies was that annihilation
of the heathens might be more practical than conversion. And farming, not ranching, was the chief colonial agricultural pursuit. Rich and plentiful farmlands
rolled away from the eastern shore, and few farmers were interested in going
out into the fearsome wilderness to plant their crops.

But there were persistent discussions about the *inevitability* of westward expansion. British bishop George Berkeley had written somewhat sadly
in the 1720s that "Westward the course of empire takes its way." Berkeley
noted that the Grecian empire had given way to Rome, that Rome had yielded
to the power of Northern Europe, and that the might of the French and
Spanish empires waned as English power increased. One day, he feared, the
seat of world power and prestige would inevitably rest in the Western
Hemisphere.

Following the American Revolution, Thomas Jefferson stated that the
"original nest" of the new nation would have to be quickly expanded westward.
He noted in 1786 that the population of the inhabited regions of the United
States had reached an average of ten people per square mile, and "wherever we
reach that the inhabitants become uneasy, as too much compressed, and go off
in great numbers to search for vacant country."

During the first half of the nineteenth century, numerous proponents of
a notion that became known as "Manifest Destiny" spoke loudly, and a little hy-
perbolically, that the American people were, in the words of politician William
Gilpin, destined to "subdue the continent—to rush over this vast field to the
Pacific Ocean—. . . to cause a stagnant people to be reborn—. . . to absolve
the curse that weighs down humanity, and to shed blessings round the world!"

Poet Walt Whitman became fascinated with the concept of Manifest
Destiny because it complemented his own conviction that America's ancestral
ties to Europe were far less important than the new social order that was
springing up from the American earth. He declared in 1860 that he looked to
the West for inspiration, for the fulfillment of promise, and for readers: "I depend on being realized, long hence, where the broad fat prairies spread, and
thence to Oregon and California inclusive." The people of the West, he said,
possessed "a free original life there . . . a simple diet, and clean and sweet
blood, . . . litheness, majestic faces, clear eyes and a perfect physique."

While it is certain that the western lands gave rise to far more severed
limbs and broken backs than perfect physiques, Whitman's words do echo the
fervent hope that many Americans held out for the western wilderness. It had
to be a place of grand possibility if for no other reason than the fact that it lay
there untouched, stretching away to the Pacific, ready for its destiny to be
gloriously fulfilled.

Numerous guidebooks appeared in mid-century that offered glowing
descriptions of the western lands, successful accounts of the brave journeys

105

Early cowboys often looked like Americanized versions of their Mexican counterparts. (Jay Dusard)

already undertaken, and "all necessary information relative to the equipment, supplies and the method of traveling." The canvas-covered Conestoga wagon, the "prairie schooner," became a symbol of the westward march, of the willingness to endure incredible hardship for the promises ahead. The hard-packed tracks of the pioneer trails stretched away from the Mississippi across the grasslands, through the few secure passes in the Rockies and the Sierras, connecting the civilized worlds of St. Louis, St. Joseph, Independence, and Council Bluffs with the wilds of Wyoming and Oregon, the golden lure of California, the Mormon haven of Utah, and the rugged ranges of Texas.

"Westward Ho!" was the collective cry; and the wagon trains that rolled during the last half of the nineteenth century succeeded in "the formation of a composite nationality" from the diverse backgrounds of the pioneers, according to historian Frederick Jackson Turner. The shared struggles and singleness of purpose forged a citizenry that was uniquely American, he contended in his famous paper, "The Significance of the Frontier in American History," delivered in 1893 in Chicago—ironically just across town from the arena where Buffalo Bill's mythic reenactments of the frontier were playing to sell-out audiences.

Turner argued that the western frontier had been vital to the shaping of the American character. The wild land itself had spurred the growth of American democracy because frontier conditions bred antipathy to control and had instilled ideals of strength and self-reliance in the pioneers. Turner's thesis had a profound influence on the interpretation of American history well into the twentieth century, yet many of its central tenets were fundamentally flawed. His contentions that western pioneers sought to escape from civilization, that the wilderness caused them to revert to "barbarism," then to slowly rebuild a society shaped by hearty individualism, simply weren't supportable. The pioneers, in fact, sought to bring some vestiges of civilization into the wilderness with them, and many facets of frontier life were characterized much more by collective efforts than by individual action.

But Turner was somehow *mythically* accurate. He understood that in the process of westering, Americans had discovered a means of self-identification and self-explanation. In the reflections of themselves and their still adolescent nation offered by historians like Turner and showmen like Cody, they saw images they could be proud of, images that made going west seem grand.

THE HISPANIC AND ANGLO-AMERICAN CULTURES CLASHED HEADLONG IN THE Texas Revolution of 1835–1836 and again in the Mexican War of 1845–1848, which ended with the signing of the Treaty of Guadalupe Hidalgo, which ceded the regions of California, Arizona, and New Mexico to the United States and established the Rio Grande as Texas's southern border.

During the years of fighting, groups of mounted "Texians" had often ridden south of the Nueces River to raid cattle from Mexican ranchos to supply meat, hides, and seed stock to Texas settlers and the soldiers who were fighting for them. These raiders became known as "cow-boys." Although the term wasn't applied derogatorily, it did imply a certain craftiness, a willingness to employ any means necessary to accomplish the task of stealing cattle.

The term *cow-boy* had first appeared in Ireland as early as 1000 A.D., when cattle herders began to be known by that name. Colonial English stock raisers in America associated the term with the Irish and preferred the English *drover* as their occupational title, especially after loyalists who called themselves cow-boys began stealing American cattle during the Revolutionary War.

Perhaps Irish immigrants to Texas first began to make the word cowboy somewhat familiar out West. Or the Texian raiders may have been reminded of tales of cow-boys from the American Revolution. Whatever its origins, the appellation remained far less common than *vaquero*—applied to Hispanic, Irish, and American herders alike—until after the Civil War.

"The Texas cowboy's mode of speech and dress and actions set the style for all the range country," wrote cowboy Teddy Blue Abbott. "And his influence is not dead yet." (Jay Dusard)

When the first of the long drives to northern railheads and cattle markets began in 1866, an amalgam of young men—whites, blacks, and browns, universally poor, unattached, and anxious to sit in a saddle—had already been at work on the Texas ranges for a couple of decades, engaged in the early roundups that were called "cow-hunts," branding, roping, and riding herd. Their techniques were remarkably like those of the Mexican *vaqueros*; they even looked like Americanized versions of their Mexican counterparts. "They wore wide-brimmed beaver hats, black or brown with a low crown, fancy shirts, high-heeled boots, and sometimes a vest. Their clothes and saddles were all homemade," wrote E. C. "Teddy Blue" Abbott, an early range cowboy, in his fine and lively 1939 memoir, *We Pointed Them North*. "The Texas cowboy's mode of speech and dress and actions set the style for all the range country," Teddy Blue wrote. "And his influence is not dead yet."

The figure of the Texas cowboy was without question responsible for the emergence of an identifiable "range cowboy," who in turn led the way for the appearance of the "western cowboy" and the multifaceted image of the "American cowboy," who followed him. Thousands of scrappy Longhorns were driven out of Texas to Kansas, Nebraska, Colorado, Wyoming, Montana, and throughout the West. The exotic young men who arrived with them, dressed in strange and flamboyant garb, their long hair flapping in the wind as they rode, were striking figures. They were rough and a little uncivilized, silent and secretive at times, yet invariably willing to take part in raucous parties they called "blow-outs" that helped erase some of the range's isolation from their minds.

The drives were long and grueling. An adolescent who left Texas lighthearted and full of vigor often arrived in Wichita or Denver or Miles City a grizzled veteran possessed of deep sadness and wind-whittled loneliness. Wit-

Whether trekking through snow, as shown in this James Reynolds painting, Red Rock Country, or crossing an anvil-hot desert, hardship and isolation were the early cowboy's constant companions.

109

"The cowboy's life is a dreadful life,"
said an early camp song. But thou-
sands of scrappy boys mounted up
nonetheless for the arduous and adven-
turous drives. (Kurt Markus)

ness these excerpts from cowboy George Duffield's 1866 diary:

> April 6th: Everything wet… Hard wind & rain. Cold.
> May 1st: Travelled 10 miles to Corryell co. Big stampede. Lost 200 head of cattle.
> May 2nd: Spent the day hunting & found but 25 head…. These are dark days for me.
> May 3rd: Day spent in hunting cattle. Found 23… lots of trouble.
> May 13th: Big thunder storm last night. Stampede. Lost 100 beeves. Hunted all day. Found 50. All tired. Everything discouraging.
> May 26th: Hunt beeves is the word—all hands discouraged & are deter-mined to go. 200 beeves out & nothing to eat.

An early range camp song called "The Kansas Line" cynically asked:

> *Come all you jolly cowmen, don't you want to go*
> *Way up on the Kansas Line?*
> *Where you whoop up the cattle from morning till night*
> *All out in the midnight rain.*
>
> *I've been where the lightnin', the lightnin' tangled in my eyes,*
> *The cattle I could scarcely hold;*
> *Think I heard my boss man say:*
> *"I want all brave-hearted men who ain't afraid to die*
> *To whoop up the cattle from morning till night,*
> *Way up on the Kansas Line."*
>
> *The cowboy's life is a dreadful life,*
> *He's driven through heat and cold;*
> *I'm almost froze with the water on my clothes,*
> *A-ridin' through heat and cold.*

Cold and wet though they were, or hot and dry, lonely or sad or sick, the thousands of range cowboys rode from the first drives of 1866 until they ended in 1890, spurring their reticent ponies, spurred themselves by the pro-mise of meager pay, by the bawdy delights in the cow towns at the end of the line, by the strange security the saddle provided, at times by the quieting com-fort that came in simply being on the move.

LOUIS L'AMOUR, DEAN OF THE WRITERS OF CONTEMPORARY WESTERN ROMANCE and author of more than eighty horse operas set in the gun-blazing frontier West, contends that the life styles and self-images of the first cowboys were directly influenced by a "code of the cavalier" that was espoused in the works of such popular nineteenth-century writers as Sir Walter Scott. According to L'Amour, it was from Scott and other romantic writers that young men with an inherent wanderlust acquired a sharp sense of pride and honor, commitments to duty and independence that eventually were recognized as integral to the character of the western man. L'Amour wrote:

> This same code of behavior was carried along in the dime novels read by many a boy on the farm or in the city before coming West and helped create some of the ideas as well as situations that developed later.... The boy or man who came West to become the cowboy rode into a land empty but for occasional Indian villages, and while learning much from the land itself, he brought with him a baggage of folklore, song, story and remembered history, and from this was created a new folklore, a new literary tradition.

Sometimes there was a quiet comfort in simply sitting alone amid the empty space. (Kurt Markus)

Perhaps the biggest obstacle to the creation of this new literary tradition was that except among the lads themselves, the general impression of the cowboy late in the nineteenth century was that he was a shiftless and unsavory character, rough-hewn and unkempt, a brash sort of boy always on the move—but one you wouldn't want sticking around for long anyway. In his annual message to Congress in 1881, President Chester A. Arthur denounced a group of bandits who were menacing the Arizona territory as "armed desperadoes known as 'Cowboys.'" That same year a Las Vegas, Nevada, newspaper editorialized that "there is not a wilder or more lawless set of men in any country that pretends to be civilized than the gangs of nomads that live in some of our frontier states and territories and are referred to in our dispatches as 'the cow boys'... most of them merit the gallows."

It was, in fact, nothing short of a public relations miracle that the image of the cowboy as footloose and irresponsible was so quickly and completely transformed into the heroic image of the wandering do-gooder, a man who couldn't be considered a shameful vagrant because he roamed in pursuit of noble goals.

Following his vacation in the west in 1883—an experience he later remembered as the time when the "romance of my life began"—Theodore Roosevelt defended the western cowboys he had encountered as fine, brave, and dependable men. They possessed, he wrote, "few of the emasculated milk-and-water moralities," but instead "the stern, manly qualities that are invaluable to a nation."

Then in 1884, Colonel Cody, who had already given virtually every other western type a turn in The Wild West's ring, introduced William Levi "Buck" Taylor, the "King of the Cowboys," to enthusiastic audiences across the country. It was a risky maneuver—much like some modern entrepreneur trying to sell a heroic image of the "King of the Motorcycle Gangs"—but it worked. Cody was careful to portray Taylor as "a typical Westerner by ancestry, birth and heritage of association." He assured audiences that Buck possessed "sturdy qualities" that made him capable of dealing with "privations, hardship, and danger... excitements and adventure."

111

Flying out to check on the cows on their summer ranges, or bucking bales of hay in a remote pasture, the contemporary cowboy knows the same urge to be moving that afflicted the early-day hands. (Paul Dix; LEFT: Timothy Eagan/ Woodfin Camp)

Fictional cowboys—like television's Bret Maverick, played by James Garner— have been roaming for nearly a century, assuring us that moving on is the American thing to do.

Cody's friend Prentiss Ingraham latched on to Taylor's valuable star in 1887 when he published *Buck Taylor, King of the Cowboys; or The Raiders and the Rangers: A Story of the Wild and Thrilling Life of William L. Taylor* in Beadle's Half-Dime Library—the first appearance of a cowboy hero in fiction. Numerous additional Taylor adventure yarns followed, all portraying Buck riding throughout the West saving the day and punishing evil—and having absolutely nothing to do with cows.

When *The Virginian* appeared in 1902, author Owen Wister presented the story of a strong, silent, anonymous man "who had plainly come many miles from somewhere across the vast horizon, as the dust upon him showed." Although the hero—who hangs the villain and wins the heart of a young schoolmarm—never reveals his name, he is, according to one critic, "the best visualized cowboy in fiction." Hundreds of literary cowboys who followed him were shaped directly or indirectly in his image; in fact, few popular Western writers ever went beyond the Virginian, beyond the stoic man who endlessly rode the trails.

Zane Grey's action novels became readily identifiable by the scores of miles their heros galloped. Jack Schaefer's *Shane* "rode easily relaxed in the saddle, leaning his weight lazily into the stirrups. Yet even in this easiness was a suggestion of tension. It was the easiness of a coiled spring, or trap set," always capable of action. Louis L'Amour's *Shalako* was a "lone-riding man in a lonesome country—riding toward a destiny of which he knew nothing, a man who for ten long years had known no other life than this, nor wished for any other." In countless films, such as *The Westerner, The Gunfighter, My Darling Clementine, Lonely Are the Brave, Will Penny,* and Sergio Leone's several "spaghetti Westerns" in which Clint Eastwood played the "Man with No Name," the hero was a wanderer, sometimes willing to reveal his past, sometimes not, always ready to ride. (And the bad guys of the films, the vermin who knew when they'd been licked, shouted, "Let's get outta here!" and rode away just as the marshal arrived.) Television's early heroes like Hopalong Cassidy and the Lone Ranger, and latter-day vagabonds like Palladin and Maverick and the "Rawhide" cowpunchers slept on new ground every night.

The Sons of the Pioneers, considered by many to be the best singing cowboy group of the 1930s and 1940s, sang their way right into the heart of the matter:

If you like a lot of room around to roam in,
Where any place you stop your heart's at home in,
If you like to see a campfire in the gloamin',
There's an open range ahead.

If you like the sound of lazy cattle lowin',
Where miles of sage and tumbleweeds are growin',

Then it's time you knew the only place for goin',
Is an open range ahead.

The fictional cowboy has been on the move now for nearly a century and may keep riding a while longer. With his horse and his saddlebags, his creators have been able to keep him mobile; they have thrown him into the clatter and danger of ever new predicaments and have changed the scenery a little without having to sculpt new characters or abandon the ones their audiences have come to love. But perhaps as important, their characters have gleaned some measure of purpose from the roaming itself. They have helped assure the immigrant inhabitants of a New World culture once bereft of tradition and a sense of belonging that they can be at home anywhere, that *moving is the proudly American thing to do.* Remember when Roy Rogers and Dale Evans sang:

Happy trails to you, until we meet again;
Happy trails to you; keep smiling until then.

It was as if they could have wished nothing better for us than to be simply going, riding west toward the land of promise.

In a series of Italian-made Westerns, Clint Eastwood played the "Man with No Name," a mysterious wanderer who belonged to no one and to no place.

WHEN HE WAS ASKED TO EXPLAIN THE RATIONALE BEHIND THE DESIGN OF HIS renowned cowboy boots, the late Cosimo Lucchese, founder of Lucchese Boots of San Antonio, said, "We used to make them fit a stirrup. Now we make them fit the gas pedal of a Cadillac." The cowboy—whether he's the ranch or rodeo variety or a rhinestone cowboy riding the range in the comfort of his Caddy—is still a man on the move, still under the spell of the wandering star, yet he doesn't head west anymore. The frontier is history, the rangelands are filling up. You could still ride a horse from the *brazada* of south Texas to the Missouri Breaks of Montana, but you would cross far more fences and freeways than rivers and creeks today, and it's hard to imagine why anyone would want to try it. Contemporary cowboys ride instead into a hazy but nonetheless compelling *idea* of the West, driven by a measure of nostalgia and the need for security that lies in strong traditions.

Among the few hands who still cowboy for the huge outfits in Nevada, Montana, and Texas, you can sense the same streak of itinerancy that steadily gnawed at the boys on the range a hundred years ago. The work is still hard, the pay is still poor, and the living conditions are still far less than comfortable most of the time. Cowboys like the buckaroos in Nevada's Paradise Valley are prone to work on the same ranch for a year or two or five, then to move on to another outfit in an adjacent valley or to some spread they've heard about in Arizona's Verde Valley, or a cow-calf operation down on the Beaver River in

Whether reading road maps or shaving beneath a cottonwood tree, the vaga-bond boys are at ease with their itinerant lives. (BOTH: Melinda Berge)

Many rodeo cowboys fly their own planes between contests scattered throughout the West in an attempt to improve their odds of winning by entering as many rodeos as possible—at times traveling a thousand miles or more in a week. (Douglas Kent Hall/ FotoWest)

Oklahoma—places where the labor and the loneliness and the occasional exultation of the open spaces are the same, but where the horizon lines are different, where there are new horses to ride and new hills to ride them on, and where the bars have different names.

Today's rodeo cowboys, most of whom have never trailed a cow or put a brand on one, ride the wide highways that cut through the country. Riding the circuit that keeps them shuttling between rodeos for eleven and a half months each year is what they call "goin' down the road." But the circuit isn't a trail, and the conveyance is no longer a horse but a motor home. In order to improve their odds, some cowboys enter as many events in as many rodeos as possible—at times traveling a thousand miles or more in a week, and occasionally riding broncs in Scottsbluff, Nebraska; Dalhart, Texas; Elko, Nevada; and Casper, Wyoming, on four successive nights.

In a song written by Steve Davis, himself a circuit rider, a rodeo cowboy muses:

> I'm in a bull ridin' tonight in Jackson
> Got a bronc tomorrow in San Antone;
> And you know just sitting here thinkin' about it,
> It wouldn't take but about four hours to get home.
> You know I'd love to see you,
> And God knows how much I'd like to tell the kids hello,
> But I could only stay for about a day,
> Then it's back down the road to the rodeo.

Many professional rodeo riders who can afford to, fly small private planes between rodeos, leaving the romance of the road behind for the speed and efficiency—and romance—of the sky. In Bob St. John's book about modern rodeo, *On Down the Road*, cowboy Don Gay talks about flying late at night: "This is my favorite time. . . . The stars are out, everything's so vast. It's like up here you can hear your own thoughts."

Cowboys have been hearing their own maudlin thoughts for over a hundred years, of course, sentimental thoughts that at once keep them company and emphasize their solitude, that over the decades have given reason to the going, that still link a lonesome rangeland boy riding night herd with a cowboy pilot alone in a blackened sky.

And if the horseman has given way, in part, to the wealthy rodeo man behind the controls of an airplane, the West itself has evolved from a palpable place to a mythic region where the force of ideas is often more potent than fact. Just before the Federal Communications Commission banned television cigarette advertising in 1970, Marlboro-brand cigarette commercials could claim that "Today, the West is everywhere," and, in a way, almost mean it. The West, by then, had become something of a state of mind, a place that was conjured up in images of freedom and adventure—just the sort of place where a man would want to light up a smoke. Today the Marlboro Man, who happens to be a flesh-and-blood Wyoming ranch cowboy, still rides across the pages of magazines, and the ads urge us to "Come to Marlboro Country." Many of us have gone, it seems, either in reality or riding a horse named fantasy.

The rise of what has been called "Western chic" early in the 1980s, no doubt part fad, was also in part a symbolic westering experience. In the midst of national economic and political uncertainty and as the West gained the attention of the nation with its booming population, its vast resources, and the election of a western president who had once been a movie cowboy, "going western" in fashion, in art, and in music was a collective ride into the mythic world of the cowboy, a quest for something different, something true. If the world was rotten to the core, if few things made sense and fewer things were dependable, we did at least have that long cultural tradition that centered around saddling up and moving on to better things. "Well, the country ought to turn to the West," said Neal Gay, rodeo stock contractor and father of the champion bull-riding pilot, "it's the only history we have." Designer Ralph Lauren seemed to agree when he previewed his "western" clothing: "The look and feel of the West," he said, "represents honesty, integrity and naturalness."

Lauren could have included the freedom to roam in his description of Western attributes. Without his free-spirited image, himself sitting tall in the saddle, the cowboy might never have caught our eye. He might have remained just a poor laborer, a crude cowhand in Mexican dress; he might never have become ennobled. The evolution of America's Western Man in history, in fiction, and in myth has been shaped by movement, by the multifaceted character of the cowboy who can't stay put because like Cabeza de Vaca he believes that if he just keeps riding toward the sunset, he'll find what he desires.

Although many cowboys ride pickups instead of horses, the freedom to roam remains essential to the image of the cowboy. (Douglas Kent Hall/FotoWest)

4

Buffalo Bill began to invest a considerable portion of his Wild West earnings in a land development scheme in northern Wyoming's Big Horn basin on the eastern flank of the Yellowstone plateau in 1895. Cody and his partners dammed the Shoshone River, built the Cody Canal, and began selling shares of water to immigrant farmers and ranchers. They laid out a town, called Cody, succeeded in getting a post office established in 1896, and started a newspaper in 1899. Then the great showman persuaded the Burlington Railroad to extend a branch line into Cody, and convinced the U.S. government to construct the "Cody Road" into Yellowstone. There was opposition to the plan among those in Congress who didn't see the need for an enormously expensive road connecting a tiny remote village with an even more remote national park. But President Theodore Roosevelt approved the plan, declaring: "My old friend Buffalo Bill has hit the trail up there, and if he was good enough to guide such men as Sheridan, Carr, Custer and Miles with their armies through uncivilized regions, I would take chances on building a road into the middle of eternity on his statement."

The settlement of the Big Horn basin was formally celebrated with the opening of Cody's Irma Hotel in 1902. It was a grand affair, with hundreds of invited guests and the gentleman himself appearing in white tie and tails. But Cody was outraged later when he read the account of the gala in the Boston Globe. The reporter had given detailed descriptions of the cowboys who wore chaps and spurs in the grand ballroom, but he didn't even mention the swallowtail coat worn by Cody. Always a man of symbol, Cody felt his formal attire exemplified the degree to which Wyoming had been civilized, and he wanted the world to know about it.

120

CHAPTER FOUR

THE SETTLING IN

AT NOON ON APRIL 22, 1889, FEDERAL TROOPS STOOD READY TO FIRE THE SHOTS that would signal the start of the rush to claim two million acres of unassigned land in Indian Territory. Fifty thousand settlers on horseback or driving teams pulling wagons had been assembled for days along a starting line that stretched for miles at the edge of the coveted land that the federal government had purchased from the Creek and Seminole tribes. Troops guarded against "sooners"—those who attempted to steal in ahead of time to claim choice parcels—and they tried in vain to control the restless throng waiting to charge ahead. When the guns cracked and bugles began to blow, the race was on; prairie dust billowed into the sky, horses bolted, people shouted and cursed and barreled into the last region of the West still empty of immigrant settlements. By nightfall, 1,920,000 acres had been claimed; 10,000 people had set up camp in a tent town that would become Oklahoma City; 15,000 slept at the site of nearby Guthrie.

Congress soon created Oklahoma Territory out of the former Indian nation; additional Indian lands were later annexed for settlement; and by 1907, the year Oklahoma became a state, more than a million and a half people lived inside its borders. The last frontier had been settled, the West was won.

In 1890, the U.S. Census Bureau reported that the western frontier no longer existed. It was as simple as that. The wild and wooly West may have still been alive in millions of imaginations, but the Indian Territory had been settled; cow towns were scattered throughout the rangelands; telegraph poles stood beside the straight steel tracks of the railroads that spanned the conti-

Windmills and silos—symbols of the settlement of the West—are evidence of the cowboy's role as one of the rangeland's many determined settlers. (Bill Ellzey; LEFT: Paul Dix)

The cowboy has alternately cheered and cursed the settlement. It has provided him with a purpose, but at times it has simply gotten in his way. (Craig Aurness/West Light)

nent; and barbed wire—the devil's hatband—was strung from the Rio Grande to the Columbia River.

The development of the West had been sudden and certain. From the time of the first journeys of Europeans into the interior West, the region had been compelling in its immensity and its emptiness. Yet it somehow seemed to offer tantalizing pleasures and riches. And it seemed also to invite exploitation; it lured civilization like a sorceress. The work of the horseback immigrants had from the outset been the work of settlement. "The opening of the West," was what the inevitable introduction of civilization was sometimes called. But it was much more a filling up than an opening—filling the West with people and paraphernalia that made it soon begin to resemble the Midwest and the Atlantic states. It was a civilizing procedure that induced a nagging sense in the settlers that something was being inexorably lost in the process.

"The West is dead, my friend," said cowboy artist Charles M. Russell as early as 1917. Russell mourned the disappearance of the open range, the coming of the roads and tracks that now cut across it, and the end of trailing cows. But Russell's melancholy wasn't really much different from the sadness and sense of loss that had always seemed to hang like smoke in the western air. Trappers and mountain men bemoaned the coming of settlers into regions they had helped explore; plains cattlemen decried the tyranny of the western railroads that had given purpose to the trail herds in the first place; stockmen on the northern ranges began to search for grazing lands in South America as early as 1880 because they thought that their northern grass was gone.

When oil was discovered in Texas in 1901, the region's industrial age was born. Tall latticework derricks, pipelines, and persistent pump jacks dotted the prairies, and the cattle culture reeled: The western land hadn't undergone such a fundamental shift in use since the cattle themselves were shipped there from Spain. Towns and cities sprang up, then spread out; horsepower became more important than horses, and a citified cowboy emerged—a fellow in Levi's and Tony Lamas who dreamed that by God he'd get back to the land someday. But he really knew more about sidewalks and blacktop than he did about grama grass or bluestem; he headed a ¾-ton pickup out onto four-lane ranges every morning; his bunkhouse was a mobile home, 12 feet by 40 feet and aluminum-sided, set down in a desolate trailer park like a covered wagon in a vigilant early-day circle.

It may be surprising that the cowboy has survived the settlement of the West at all, but he has, in fact, been one of its foremost settlers. And whether he still works on horseback or drives the dusty roads that interconnect the well-sites out in the oil patch, he remains at bottom a working man, a good hand, who is nonetheless a little saddened by all the changes he's wrought, wondering how much his West can ultimately withstand.

The fictionalizers and portrayers of the cowboy have had an awkward

Immigrants poured into the vacant western lands in the last quarter of the nineteenth century, spurred by the promises of freedom and prosperity. (ABOVE: David Hiser/Photographers Aspen; LEFT: Tom Stack & Assoc.)

The cowboy—and his paraphernalia—often seems indigenous to the land; but he has been as much a civilizer of the West as the railroader, the highway builder, or the oilman, and has brought as many changes. (Bill Ellzey)

A father passes a wire-stretching tool to his son. Early cowboys were outraged when farmers fenced off their lands, but before long ranchers were also using the newfangled barbed wire to corral their stock. (Nicholas de Vore III/Bruce Coleman, Inc.)

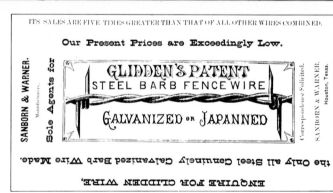

time with the settlement of the West. The steady march of civilization has alternately bored them, preoccupied them, frustrated and confused them. The first fictional cowboys cavorted in a West that civilization had barely touched, and pulp novelists like Ned Buntline and Prentiss Ingraham treated the settlement of the West by paying no attention to it. The writers of the Western sagas that followed in the twentieth century knew that blazing six-guns could attract more readers than could accounts of "nesters" settling into the range.

Although early moviemakers quickly discovered as well the value of gun-play to their stories, they were the first entertainers to try to portray the process of settlement. During the heyday years of the Western in the 1940s and 1950s, the settlement of the West became a focal theme; but it wasn't until the 1960s that Westerns began to consider whether the civilizing of the West might have brought destruction as well as progress. And recent films like *Urban Cowboy* have completely abandoned the theme of the filling up of open space and have placed their cowboys in the chaotic heart of "western civilization," where a man still has to defend himself and his honor, but where his enemies are very different from those of the old days, and where he can no longer elude the turmoil by saddling up and lighting out for solitude. Solitude, like the empty land itself, is gone and almost forgotten.

The kitchen of a ranch house out in the back of beyond is a warm island of civilization. (Nicholas de Vore III/ Bruce Coleman, Inc.)

THE STREETS WERE NEVER MUDDY IN THE FALSE-FRONTED TOWNS IN the early Western movies, the paint was always fresh, the saloon was well swept, and the faces of the curious young boys were scrubbed. But the real Dodge Citys, the Abilenes, the Cheyennes, and the Tombstones were far different places. They were unusual curiosities, cow camps that evolved without plans, spurred by obsessive entrepreneurial ambition. They weren't so much communities as jumbled collections of people, and they teemed with the clatter of the mercantile trade. But they were important nonetheless. They were the places where the wild frontier diminished and the fledgling civilization began to take hold.

"On the surface Abilene was corruption personified," wrote historian Walter Prescott Webb. "Life was hectic, raw, lurid and awful.... But if Abilene excelled all later cow towns in wickedness, it also excelled them in service—the service of bartering beef of the South for the money of the North."

And the cow towns served the cowboys as well—offering them a brief escape from the bleary isolation of the trail. The towns were lifelines to a world the cowboys implicitly rejected in their daily lives, yet one they impulsively dreamed about at night. Arrival at a stockyard town in Kansas, Nebraska, or Montana after enduring months of dust and stupid cattle meant finally getting clean and putting on new clothes; it meant wild comradeship, binge drinking, and as many dalliances with the rouge-cheeked professional women as a

"On the whole the settlers were a pretty good lot," wrote cowboy John Leakey. "But most of the boosters, speculators, and land agents who tolled them in were the lowest class of vermin that ever infected a good country." (Craig Pozzi)

cowboy's meager wages would allow. "When he feels well (and he always does when full of what he calls 'Kansas sheep-dip'), the average cowboy is a bad man to handle," noted a Wichita, Kansas, newspaper in 1882. "Armed to the teeth, well mounted, and full of their favorite beverage, the cowboys will dash through the principal streets of a town yelling like Comanches. This they call 'cleaning out a town.' " One Kansan apprehensively described the sound of an approaching cowboy this way: "His spurs jingled loudly, suggesting fatality like a rattlesnake's rattling."

But the cowboys were as often the victims of skulduggery as they were its instigators. They were young and naive—and they had just been paid. "The cattle season has not yet fully set in, but there is a rush of gamblers and harlots who are 'lying in wait' for the game which will soon begin to come up from the south," the *Wichita Eagle* reported in May 1874. "The purlieus of crime [here] are no more than in many eastern cities of boasted refinement and good order. But woe to the 'greeny' who falls into the hands of the dwellers therein, especially if he carries money."

The cow towns were first cut out of the prairie sod at the points where northbound cattle trails met the expanding east-west tracks of the railroads. Unlike the fictional towns that seldom seemed to have any reason for arising where they did, the real cattle camps were anchored by the brisk commerce of the rails.

But ironically the railroads and the rush of migration they induced led to the end of the drives and the reining-in of the cattle within the barbed-wire perimeters of ranches. Until the Pacific Railroad Act authorizing construction of a transcontinental railroad across the vast lands of the interior West was signed into law by Abraham Lincoln in 1862, the Mormons in Utah were virtually the only Anglo-Americans settled between the Missouri-Mississippi basin and the California coast. But as the heavy ties were laid out and the rails were spiked into them, a colonization suddenly commenced: In the twenty-seven years between the start of construction on the Union Pacific and the Central Pacific Railroads in 1862 and the Oklahoma land rush of 1889, far more territory was settled with people, farms, ranches, and roads than had been settled in the hemisphere since the first immigrants had landed at Jamestown in 1607. It was a frantic, obsessive rush to the West, spurred by the buoyant hopes of the homesteaders and merchants, by the grandiose and greedy schemes of the railroads themselves, the huge mining operations and land companies, the bankers, and more than a few con men. "On the whole the settlers were a pretty good lot," wrote cowboy John Leakey in his memoir, *The West That Was*. "But most of the boosters, speculators, and land agents who tolled them in were the lowest class of vermin that ever infected a good country."

But whatever their intentions and degrees of integrity, the people who poured into the prairies and piedmonts of the West had a profound effect on the cattle culture. The federal lands that the cattlemen had considered their own for so long, that no one else had wanted or cared about, were suddenly in demand. Land was needed for farming; the creeks and river valleys were needed to provide irrigation; the gaping open-pit mines needed land; and so did nascent towns for their hotels, stores, streets, houses, and cemeteries. Rough roads were built to link each new town to the next, and if a camp was lucky or crafty enough, it got a railroad line—and with the railroad came more commerce, more settlers, still more of the boisterous boom of free enterprise. It was a heady time, a time when it seemed that anyone who wanted to badly enough could become a millionaire, a time when there was a big, open land just lying there for the taking.

At first, the Texas cattlemen couldn't believe their good fortune when a railroad began to cut across Kansas, providing them with a means for shipping their meat to the beef markets in the East. Later, they shouted their objections to the railroads' alleged monopolistic price gouging, to the enormous land grants they were awarded by the government (normally twenty sections, 12,800 acres, were deeded to each railroad for each mile of track it laid), to the way the railroads blocked the northbound cattle trails, and to the number of Eastern homesteaders they brought with them who inevitably filled up the range land.

Farmers and cowmen have never been thought of as allies, of course. Sod-busters, "tomato-kissin', plow pushin' fools," according to Judge Roy Bean in William Wyler's 1940 film, *The Westerner*, were initially as unwelcome as wildfire on the open ranges. The farmers built their small houses and staked out their fields throughout the best lands of the country and, worst of all, during the mid-1870s they began using Illinois farmer Joseph Glidden's newfangled "barbed wire" to fence in their steads—vicious stuff that could cut up curious cattle and that to every grizzled cowman's surprise could actually keep them out of the crops. An old cowboy song declared the wire downright demonic:

They say that Heaven is a free range land
Good-by, Good-by, O fare you well;
But it's barbed wire fence for the Devil's hat band
And barbed wire blankets down in Hell!

Glidden's "Winner" wire was first strung by farmers anxious to keep cattle from destroying their fields, but soon even a few cattlemen were using it. On the huge Texas ranches where breeding programs were under way, it was essential to keep stray cattle away from purebred herds, and the barbed wire was equal to the task. Then as individual ranches began to be enclosed, as more and more farms and fence lines emerged, it finally became advantageous for virtually every stockman to enclose his holdings. During barbed wire's first year of commercial availability, 5 tons of it were manufactured and sold. Six years later in 1880, more than 40,000 tons were sold and strung across the pastures.

An old cowboy song called barbed wire "the devil's hatband." Its widespread use made the trailing of cattle almost impossible, and it symbolized the dividing up of the open range into private, impassable holdings. (Stephen Trimble)

When Texas entered the oil age, the West's economy began to undergo its most fundamental change since the introduction of cattle. In Thomas Hart Benton's Boomtown, the quiet prairies have given way to the entrepreneurial rush of the petroleum industry.

But not every stockman and wary cowboy took to barbed wire like a cat to cream. Its stringing changed the way in which cattle were husbanded so completely that the previously-nomadic horseback occupation became a sedentary one, and many sure senses of purpose collapsed. Most cowboys shrugged and got back on their horses inside the fences. But some old hands just quit cowboying, convinced that their way of life had tragically disappeared. "Now there is so much land taken up and fenced in that the trail for the most of the way is little better than a crooked lane," wrote a Texas trail driver in 1884. "These fellows from Ohio, Indiana, and other northern and western states— the 'bone and sinew of the country,' as the politicians call them—have made farms, enclosed pastures, and fenced in water-holes until you can't rest; and I say, Damn such bone and sinew! They are the ruin of the country, and have everlastingly, eternally, now and forever, destroyed the best grazing land in the world.... Fences, sir, are the curse of the country!"

Fences, railroads, sprawling farms, and too many towns to count! It may have been naive for the horseback boys to imagine that the West would always remain just as it was when they encountered it. But if so, it was a naiveté born of care for the look of the land and the strange, rough, romantic work they did on it. They couldn't help but mourn the changes when they began to feel that squeeze of civilization. By 1919, western writer and poet Badger Clark's voice could have been joined by thousands more when he chanted:

Today, oilfield pump jacks are scattered across the cow country, and oil and gas income is critical to many ranchers' economic survival. (Nicholas DeSciose/ The Stock Market)

> The trail's a lane, the trail's a lane
> Dead is the branding fire.
> The prairies wild are tame and mild
> All close corralled with wire.

"WHEN MY FATHER WAS TWELVE MY GRANDFATHER SENT HIM, ALONE, WITH A small herd of steers, to Graham, Texas, a town about forty miles from our ranch," wrote novelist Larry McMurtry in 1968 in his book of essays on Texas, *In a Narrow Grave.*

> At twelve I would have been hard put to drive a very docile herd of steers forty yards.... [But] even if I could have driven a herd of steers to Graham I should have had to cut a hundred fences to get there, or else open a hundred gates.
>
> In their youth, as I have said, my uncles sat on the barn and watched the last trail herds moving north—I sat on the self-same barn and saw only a few oil field pickups and a couple of dairy trucks go by.

Just as Texas was the place where the cowboy first took shape, where feral cattle were rounded up for the first time and driven north, so it was the first region in the West to enter the oil age. On the morning of January 10, 1901,

*"Fences are the ruin of the country,"
wrote a Texas trail driver in 1884.
"They have everlastingly, now and
forever, destroyed the best grazing land
in the world." (Bill Ellzey)*

an exploratory well drilled into a deep salt dome beneath Spindletop Hill out-side Beaumont, Texas, began to spew mud and broken pipe. A few hours later a 75-foot geyser of crude oil blew up through the well's wooden derrick and into the Lone Star sky. By the time the well was capped a few days later, it was producing 75,000 barrels of oil a day, and it had already begun transforming Texas from a backwater cattle kingdom into the largest producer of gas and oil in the nation. A rush to Texas quickly commenced, and ranchers, dumbstruck by the developments and all the attention they drew, sold drilling rights to every wildcatter who came their way. Before long, tall derricks covered the rangelands like forests; somnolent little cities awoke to the sounds of money changing hands; and they bulged and sprawled and their skyscrapers shot up into the sky.

The transformation was overwhelming. The commodities that lay be-neath the land quickly became far more valuable than anything that could be produced on its surface. Cattle still roamed, but the cattlemen didn't rule any-more. In only half a century, Texas's population shifted from 80 percent rural to 80 percent urban. It became the third-most populous state in the nation, its people far outnumbering its cows.

The cattle culture could bemoan the change, but it couldn't do anything about it. Cattlemen complained and cussed, yet they accepted their royalty checks readily enough. Cowboys made room for the oil-patch roughnecks—a brand-new breed of frontier laborer—in the boomtown bars. From time to time, some of them went bare knuckles with the intruders in vain attempts to protect the imagined purity of the West; others threw their saddles into pick-ups and drove away in disgust.

> I'm going to leave
> Old Texas now,
> They've got no use
> For the Longhorn cow
> They've plowed and fenced
> My cattle range,
> And the people there
> Are all so strange.

That song preceded the oil boom, but cowboys sang it long after the boom had taken hold, perhaps because they felt that oil's intrusion wasn't really much different from the intrusion of plows and barbed wire into the range cul-ture. The oil boom was just another blow to a way of life that depended on open spaces, to a spirited and romantic pastoral enterprise, a way of life that had too much meaning to let it disappear completely.

And it didn't disappear, of course—not completely. The influences of the industrial age spread throughout the West; quiet cow towns became burgeoning crude towns; shining refineries and pumping stations grew up out of the spare soil; and still more people came driving in. But there was no fine tradition in drilling, welding, or selling machinery parts, no haughty pride in roughnecking, no special connection with the land other than the necessary negotiating of potholes on the hard roads that wound to the well-sites. It was the idea of *cowboying* that remained captivating. The money in the oil patch may have been too good to give up, but working on horseback would have been the nobler, the *truer* thing to do. Nobody made movies or sang songs about the wildcatters, and everyone still wished he could be a cowboy.

Ironically, these days those who still do ride and rope for a living and the stockmen who pay their wages receive critical support from the same oil business they spurned not so long ago. Few are quick to credit their sources, but as the economics of ranching become bleaker, the ranchers' dependence on their oil income increases. "Oil and gas income is the dirty little secret of the modern cattle business," wrote John R. Erickson in *The Modern Cowboy*. "No one wants to talk about it, perhaps because ranchers prefer to think of themselves as self-made men and are uncomfortable with the knowledge that they managed to get something for nothing. . . . Everybody in the business knows about it, yet no one will come out and talk about it."

If the cowmen are embarrassed to acknowledge the oil companies' patronage, perhaps it is that to do so would be just one more declaration that ranching today is not what it used to be. The television movies and paperback novels still make the cowboy out to be brave and independent, resourceful and proud. It is an image that pleases ranchers and cowhands reading or watching TV on their sofas; it is a myth they believe in, whether or not it is true—one that can't be reconciled with receiving unearned oil money or trading cows for shares of Mobil Oil.

For a hundred years, cowboys have complained about the coming of fences and oil wells and the filling up of the West with cities and missile silos. But they have nonetheless adapted to each change, putting their own mark on it in the process. (Kent and Donna Dannen)

HOLLYWOOD FILMMAKERS FOUND THEIR MOST ENDURING AND MOST POPULAR SUB-ject matter in the development of the West—heroic cowboy figures packing the mail across the badlands, running a stagecoach free of an ambush, protecting gold trains from attack, making the towns safe for decent folk, then kissing the girl goodbye. But the heyday Westerns paid little attention to the development of the West's companion and persistent themes of exploitation, abandonment, sorrow, and loss.

In the 1930s, filmgoers with problems of their own had little interest in movies about some kind of moaning melancholy out in the western mountains; they wanted action and escape, and they wanted the good guys to triumph. During the 1940s and 1950s, Western writers and directors succeeded in producing many of the genre's most enduring films: *Shane, The Gunfighter, The Westerner, My Darling Clementine,* and *High Noon,* each film concerned with the hard conflicts imposed by the settlement of the West—ranchers battling farmers and civilized towns fighting anarchistic outlaws.

Shane, a vagabond gunslinger played by Alan Ladd, befriends home-steaders threatened by cattle barons who despise the plowing up of the range lands. When the stockmen hire a gunman to drive the homesteaders out, Shane confronts him and kills him in a blazing shootout, protecting the new agrarian civilization, one that ironically has no place for itinerant men like him.

In Fred Zinneman's renowned *High Noon*, Amy Cane, the marshal's wife (Grace Kelly), complains that Hadleyville is "just a dirty little village in the middle of nowhere. Nothing really important happens here." But then something important does happen. Retiring marshal Will Cane, played ever so stoically by Gary Cooper, stands up to a gang of outlaws who have returned to Hadleyville to kill him. Cane is deserted by the community, and against all odds goes it alone, fighting the gang less to save his own life than to assert that lawlessness can't be tolerated in a civilized town. The hero operates alone in many "settlement" Westerns, supported only by his own courage and fortitude; yet he fights for the community, fights to make the West safe not so much for lone riders as for shopkeepers and farmers, teachers and telegraph agents.

The filmmakers of the 1940s and 1950s viewed the settlement of the West as part of America's legacy of ever-expanding wealth and power, but they ignored the possibility that the conquest could lay destruction in its wake. It wasn't until the 1960s, when the first Westerns set in the twentieth century were produced, that filmmakers discovered that the settlement of the West and its subsequent urbanization and industrialization weren't necessarily splendid undertakings. They discovered that the figure of the cowboy, the lonesome rider who had already survived more movie struggles than would have been thought possible, could also poignantly represent a last remnant of the frontier West still struggling to stay alive, still connected to horses and sweeping land-scapes and the integrity of earning one's keep in a dialing-for-dollars world of freeways, franchises, and sadly perplexed people.

A group of Westerns, all produced early in the 1960s and set somewhere in the half century from 1900 to 1950, including *Ride the High Country, The Misfits, Lonely Are the Brave, Hud,* and *Monte Walsh,* tried to ex-plore the meaning of the closing of the frontier and to discover whether anything was left of the West after its conquest by civilization. Set at the turn of the century, Sam Peckinpah's *Ride the High Country* is the story of two aging outlaws, played by Joel McCrea and Randolph Scott, who don't seem to belong in the "modern" West. One decides to try to take an honest job; the other goes after a final haul so he can retire in comfort. But neither succeeds because too much has changed; each man's talents have become archaic, their bold visions spoiled by a spoiled world. In John Huston's *Misfits,* Clark Gable resigns himself to working in the glib and glittery environs of a Reno, Nevada, casino when he realizes that his lifelong work of catching mustangs has been

In a scene from Shane, *Alan Ladd teaches Brandon De Wilde about the violent reality of defending the West's new agrarian civilization. Like* Shane, *many Hollywood Westerns of the 1940s and 1950s were concerned with the conflicts imposed by settlement. By the 1960s, films like* Lonely Are the Brave *asserted that the cowboy is out of place in the modern, "civilized" West.*

KIRK DOUGLAS "Lonely are the Brave"

co-starring
GENA ROWLANDS
WALTER MATTHAU

MICHAEL KANE with

CARROLL O'CONNOR · WILLIAM SCHALLERT

Screenplay by DALTON TRUMBO · Directed by DAVID MILLER

Produced by EDWARD LEWIS · Based on the novel by EDWARD ABBEY

A Joel Production · A Universal-International Release

IN PANAVISION®

THE
GREATEST
STORY
OF THE
WEST EVER
FILMED!

SHANE

ALAN LADD · JEAN ARTHUR · VAN HEFLIN
IN GEORGE STEVENS'
PRODUCTION OF
SHANE
CO-STARRING BRANDON DE WILDE WITH JACK PALANCE
BEN JOHNSON · EDGAR BUCHANAN · PRODUCED AND DIRECTED BY GEORGE STEVENS · SCREENPLAY BY A. B. GUTHRIE, JR.
ADDITIONAL DIALOGUE BY JACK SHER · BASED ON THE NOVEL BY JACK SCHAEFER
TECHNICOLOR®

In Sam Peckinpah's Ride the High Country, *Joel McCrea and Randolph Scott portrayed two aging outlaws whose talents and pursuits have become archaic at the beginning of the twentieth century.*

defiled by horsemeat entrepreneurs in the pet-food market to whom he has sold his horses. As Jack Burns in *Lonely Are the Brave*—based on Edward Abbey's fine early novel *The Brave Cowboy*—Kirk Douglas is a cowboy awash in a world that doesn't want him, a world he in turn despises. Throughout the film, Burns's adherence to his personal cowboy code, to the verities of an earlier West, runs counter to the pave-and-plunder values of an urbanized terrain that advances steadily in every direction. In the final scene, Burns—who has been trying to escape from the law and the world into the Sandia Mountains, bound for Mexico, where he has hoped to find the frontier still alive—is smashed by a semi-trailer truck hauling plumbing fixtures.

The final message in the modern-day Westerns of the 1960s seemed to be that the cowboy simply couldn't survive. He belonged to the nineteenth century; he gave pioneer America something good and heroic, but now he was done. All he remained was a horseback memory, a ghost in boots and a wide-brimmed hat.

During the 1970s and 1980s, Westerns wandered again, in search of themes and settings that could effectively examine and explain the mechanized and modern West without resorting to clichés and soured stories. Relatively few Westerns have been made in the last fifteen years, and fewer have been successful in their attempts to explain the cowboy in the midst of his civilized world. In 1974, movie critic Pauline Kael declared that the "Western is dead"—but if there is any truth to what she said, it seems to be only that the Western that glorified the development of the West is dead. And ironically, if Western movies continue to cyclically wane and rise in popularity as they now do, we may periodically be tempted to join Kael in sounding the death knell for the genre, just as we have always been tempted to do for the West itself. Ultimately, perhaps what we mean when we say "the West is dead" or "the Western is dead" is just that it isn't the same anymore.

In the opening sequences of the 1980 movie *Urban Cowboy*, for instance—a movie without a single cow or horse or lonesome look across the sagebrush, but every bit a Western—Bud (John Travolta) cruises into Houston in his new pickup. The gleaming downtown towers form a stunning backdrop against which the lone cowpoke makes his way toward the action. The action, no longer out in the open as it was in the earlier films, is in the city, inside a converted warehouse-cum-nightclub called Gilley's, a gigantic place, "three and a half acres of God's prairie," where oil refinery workers, roughnecks, delivery-men, shoe salesmen, and car dealers meet to try to keep the West alive.

Based on Aaron Latham's 1978 *Esquire* article of the same title, *Urban Cowboy* possesses only the thinnest of plots, some awkward acting, and a few cardboard characters. But it is nonetheless an important film, one that attempts to uncover some truth about the essence of the cowboy image and why it so doggedly endures. "[Bud] is as uncertain about where his life is going as America is confused about where it wants to go," wrote Latham, a native Texan who also wrote the film's screenplay. "And when America is confused, it turns to its most durable myth: the cowboy."

Although not entirely successful, *Urban Cowboy* makes a real attempt to define the reality of the freeway West—city kids living in trailer parks, working at petrochemical plants and plumbing supply houses to earn money to get by, but acting out their more personally important dreams inside the foam-insulated walls of Gilley's. There they dance the civilized world away like the range cowboys did in the early sawdust saloons, and buck it out of their systems on the mechanical bull, pretending that their grim Houston suburb isn't just another of the nation's place-less places, but that it really is right smack in the romantic heart of the West.

Urban Cowboy is a movie about deliberately choosing the mythic life and in so doing being true to an old cowboy tradition. It's a tradition that includes crying a little over all that the West has come to—the devil's hatband of civilization spreading into every corner—then shrugging your shoulders, kicking the dirt, and getting back down to the business of building it even bigger.

The frontier was chewed up much the way a coyote takes a rabbit—suddenly, frantically, and then it was done. In the aftermath of the frontier's demise, there has been little left to do but wonder how it vanished so quickly, to wax nostalgic and remember what a fine thing it was, *or surely must have been*—to wish that we could have remained cowboys out in the open spaces. Yet a few still earnestly imagine that they *are* cowboys. They fill their lives with a kind of saddle-won self-assurance, convinced that civilization is just whatever you happen to be up against, certain that the heart matters more than horses.

Urban Cowboy, *starring John Travolta, examined the freeway West, and focused on what happens to the cowboy when he abandons the sagebrush for the city.*

5

When he had just reached twenty-one in the spring of 1867, armed with a heart full of pluck and a .50-caliber Springfield breech-loading rifle he called Lucretia Borgia, William Frederick Cody went to work for the Kansas Pacific Railroad, hunting buffalo. In the eighteen months that he was under contract to the railroad, "Buffalo Bill" killed 4,280 buffalo and oversaw the slaughter of thousands more. Sixteen years later, the once enormous herds had nearly vanished from the North American grasslands that they had inhabited for centuries, but "The Wild West, The Honorable W. F. Cody and Dr. W. F. Carver's Rocky Mountain and Prairie Exhibition," which had just opened in Omaha, Nebraska, featured a spirited reenactment of a daring buffalo hunt, as well as resplendent cowboys riding bucking buffalo bulls. Cody's few exhibition bison were among the very last of the species.

144

CHAPTER FIVE

HUNTING BUFFALO

As the great westward expansion was beginning in the first decades of the nineteenth century, 50 million American bison (some estimates put the number as high as 150 million) ranged the continent's treeless prairies from northern Alberta to the spare deserts of the Mexican interior. But by 1900 an official count set the number of live bison at 541, about half of them living in captivity. In an astonishingly short period of time, this majestic animal, more commonly known as the buffalo, was rendered all but extinct, a victim of the new nation's quest for land and its riches.

The grim saga of the buffalo is that of a creature that had adapted perfectly over the centuries to the windswept grasslands it inhabited but that could never adapt to the rush of westering America. The first Europeans who encountered the buffalo saw a strange and mysterious creature that embodied much of the New World's exotic character. But as the wagon parties, the roads and railroads and the herds of bawling cattle pushed westward and northward, the buffalo stood inexorably in the way. America's tribal cultures revered the buffalo and depended on it for survival, but to the new Americans the buffalo was an enormous menace. Then necessity gave way to greed, and the slaughter commenced—a meticulous and mean-spirited attempt at extermination that left the grasslands covered with bones and reduced the buffalo to little more than a symbol of the nation's past.

Today the continent's buffalo population has rebounded to more than sixty thousand head. Most buffalo are in private herds—some on large

Although only a few stalwart and steel-eyed buffalo survived the guns and rifles of western hunters in the last half of the nineteenth century, today more than sixty thousand head are managed and marketed like cattle. (Laurance Aiuppy; LEFT: Stephen Trimble)

151

The buffalo is the only wild animal in North America that is pastured as a food animal. Buffalo meat, which contains very little fat, is rapidly gaining consumer popularity. (Bill Ellzey)

ranches where they are managed like cattle, others in pathetic groups of two or three in pens behind gas stations and at roadside curio shops. Thousands of bison roam in preserves and national parks in the United States and Canada, but none wanders freely over its ancestral terrain. No Indians hunt the buffalo for food and clothing. No cowboys gallop deep into lumbering brown herds of buffalo to cut out their straying cattle.

IN 1521 HERNÁN CORTÉS AND HIS COMPANEROS WERE THE FIRST EUROpeans to see an American bison—a single bull held in zoolike captivity at the palace of Aztec ruler Montezuma. De Solis, a Spanish historian who accompanied Cortés, described that buffalo as "a wonderful composition of divers Animals. It has crooked Shoulders, with a Bunch on its Back like a Camel; its Flanks dry, its Tail large, and its Neck cover'd with Hair like a Lion."

By the time Thomas Jefferson dispatched Lewis and Clark toward the Pacific in 1804, the exotic buffalo was well known. But few suspected that its numbers and territory could be so vast. William Clark wrote in his meticulous journal on August 25 that the party "beheld a most butifull landscape; Numerous herds of buffalow were seen feeding in various directions." Farther west, he noted "an inclined Plain, in which there is great numbers of Buffalow, Elk & Goats in view feeding & scipping on those Plains. Grouse, Larks & the Prairie bird is Common in those Plains."

By the time of Lewis and Clark's return trip two years later, sightings of huge numbers of buffalo had become so commonplace that no mention was made of them unless the size of a herd was particularly stunning: "I ascended to the high Country," Clark wrote, "and from an eminance I had a view...of a greater number of buffalow than I had ever seen before at one time. I must have seen near 20,000 of those animals feeding on the plain."

Lewis and Clark's expedition opened the way for fur traders, prospectors, farmers, and cowboys to move into the wild terrain—people who not only observed the buffalo but lived among them, people for whom the great beast was soon to become as much an obstacle as the forbidding mountain passes and galloping prairie fires. But many painters who ventured into the West from the eastern seaboard produced curious, investigative portraits of the bizarre animal that appealed to eastern audiences who were still captivated by the exotic image of the continent's largest animal.

John James Audubon's 1845 *American Bison or Buffalo,* a colored lithograph, is as cool, detached, and precise as are his familiar renderings of turkeys, hawks, and songbirds. Albert Bierstadt turned away from his mystical landscapes long enough to do a series of paintings and engravings with buffalo as the subject. And perhaps the most haunting of the paintings that preceded the wholesale slaughter is William Jacob Hays's *Herd of Buffalo* (1862), in which an

Many ranchers now raise buffalo instead of cattle because they are hearty and disease-free—and their meat is worth more per pound than beef. (Jay Dusard)

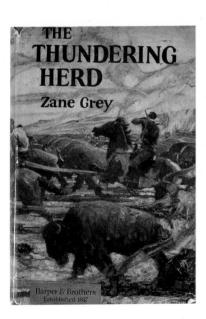

The buffalo's fate was sealed by the new nation's need for land. Even before the great herds were reduced to a few scrawny animals, they were hunted merely for sport. (Steve Collector)

ethereal yellow dust storm envelops a strange, bellowing bull, flanked by the ghostly images of other animals in the herd. Hays's buffalo are certainly odd and fearsome—haughty representations of those wild creatures that held back the advance of the burgeoning cowboy civilization.

While the bison still roamed the western plains in enormous numbers, they effectively prevented the establishment of cattle range and cultivated land and the construction of railroad and telegraph lines. Like the tribes of Indians that depended on them for sustenance, the buffalo were incompatible with the headstrong march of civilization. This left only one alternative: "Let [the buffalo hunters] kill, skin and sell until the buffaloes are exterminated," declared Army General Phil Sheridan. "Then your prairies can be covered with speckled cattle and the festive cowboy, who follows the hunter as the second forerunner of an advanced civilization."

Once railroad lines spanned the continent and brash towns began to fill the rangelands, the buffalo's fate was clear. The slaughter increased dramatically; buffalo robes were in great demand, and the meat sustained cattle rangers and construction crews, wagon trains and groups of hopeful plowmen that pushed into the opening West. After the plains had been bisected by the railroad tracks in the 1860s, portrayals of buffalo in paintings became markedly different from the earlier majestic buffalo images; in the later paintings and prints, the once proud buffalo are on the run or under attack. An anonymous wood engraving flippantly titled *A Lively Scene on an American Prairie—A Buffalo Hunt by Steam* (circa 1868) records hunters perched atop train cars and firing at buffalo that resemble huge rats. And Buffalo Bill assumes a heroic pose in the epic-style *Conquest of the Prairie,* painted in 1908 by Irving R. Bacon. The intrepid Colonel Cody seems to be herding a band of buffalo ahead of an advancing wagon train while Indian warriors stoically look on. The message is clear: The buffalo must go, and the Indian had better stay out of the way.

The Covered Wagon (1923), James Cruze's highly praised film, propounds the same theme in its opening titles: "The blood of America is the blood of the pioneers—the blood of lion-hearted men and women who carved a splendid civilization out of an uncharted wilderness." Set in 1848, the film chronicles a wagon journey from St. Louis, Missouri, to Oregon that is beset by every imaginable obstacle, including, of course, marauding buffalo. "Soon the cry of 'Buffalo!' rang throughout both trains," reads the title, "and every able man armed himself for the biggest hunt in human experience—the hunt for meat to fill hungry mouths." In the ensuing action, a trail hand gallops into the herd and downs a buffalo with a bow and arrow. Mountain man Jim Bridger, who has joined up with the wagon party, leaps from his horse, bulldogs a buffalo rodeo-style, and kills it with his handy knife.

Buffalo hunts and stampedes are action staples in many subsequent Western movies—thundering beasts charging across bleak landscapes, sending up storms of dust like dangerous funnel clouds. But the bison hordes are seldom, if ever, integral to a movie's plot. In later films, such as *Buffalo Bill on the U.P. Trail,* Walt Disney's *Davy Crockett: King of the Wild Frontier,* and the first Cinerama epic, *How the West Was Won,* the requisite herd is apparently introduced only to provide the threat of harm and a lot of noise and action.

Nearly every page of Zane Grey's 1925 Western thriller, *The Thundering Herd,* is filled with rampaging beasts and blazing Sharps buffalo rifles, but his cowboy hero, Tom Doan, falls under the enchanting influence of his sweetheart and eventually is repelled by the grim work of killing:

> Day by day Tom Doan killed fewer buffalo.... He wavered, he flinched, he shot poorly, thus crippling many buffalo. It made him sick. The cause was Milly. She dominated his thoughts. The truth was that Milly had awakened him to the cruelty and greed of this business and his conscience prevented him from becoming a good hunter.

Grey's perspective in *The Thundering Herd* is ultimately an equivocal one that acknowledges the brutality of the slaughter, yet seems to insist that it had to happen. He is at one moment entranced by the might and majesty of the bison, and at another convinced that their numbers had to be drastically reduced to allow the cattlemen to take hold of the land and make it theirs.

Relatively few Western movies or novels have dealt with the existence or issue of the buffalo at all. Part of the reason must be that by the time the novelists, screenwriters, and directors were at work early in the twentieth century, the buffalo had vanished; their numbers and their dominion were hard to imagine. But more important, the buffalo simply didn't make for much drama. They didn't fight back. They didn't lay in wait, ready to ambush wagon trains. And although wild and untamable, they couldn't be portrayed as savage and godless, as the Indians were usually portrayed. Their only crimes were their numbers and the fact that they were so utterly, impassively in the way.

"Let the buffalo hunters kill, skin and sell until the buffalos are exterminated," said General Phil Sheridan. *"Then your prairies can be covered with speckled cattle and the festive cowboy."*

AMERICA'S TRIBAL PEOPLES HAD HUNTED THE BUFFALO AND DEPENDED ON IT FOR survival for centuries. But from their perspective, the mammoth animal was never a menace; rather, it was a blessing, a gift. Listen to a Pawnee man, who was alive when the buffalo still roamed, tell how the world began:

> Once, long ago, all things were waiting in a deep place far underground. There were great herds of buffaloes and all the people, and the antelope too, and wolves, deer and rabbits—everything, even the little bird that sings the *tear-tear* song. Everything waited in sleep. Then the one called Buffalo Woman awoke, stretched her arms, rose and began to walk.... And now a young cow arose and followed the woman, and then another buffalo and another.... When the last of the buffaloes was up and moving, the people began to rise,

Artist George Catlin's many impressionistic paintings of buffalo, RIGHT, captured the animal's grandeur and alluded to its enormous might. (ABOVE: Harley Hettick)

one after another…out through the hole that was on Patuk, out upon the shining, warm and grassy place that was the earth.

The bison was central to the mythology and the earthbound existence of each of the tribal cultures of the plains. It provided food, clothing, shelter, and was accordingly revered. "What one of all animals is the most sacred?" the Blackfeet ritually asked. The reply, always firmly given, was: "The buffalo."

The lush, impressionistic paintings of George Catlin, the young Philadelphia artist who lived and painted among Western tribes for six years in the 1830s and 1840s, formed an entrancing record of the buffalo's grandeur, its reign over the plains, and its role in Indian life. Catlin's work reflects both a sensitivity toward and a fascination with the aboriginal worlds he visited—conjuring up images of a time when the new nation assumed that the West would always be wild, inhabited by only a few immigrant Americans, the province forever of the native tribes and those shaggy monarchs of the plains.

Pulitzer prize-winning novelist N. Scott Momaday in *The Way to Rainy Mountain*, a book about the history, legends, and mythology of his Kiowa ancestors, recounts the time—a century after Catlin—when he and his father encountered a tiny, remnant herd of buffalo:

> It was late in the spring, and many of the cows had newborn calves. Nearby a calf lay in the tall grass; it was red-orange in color, delicately beautiful with new life. We approached, but suddenly the cow was there in our way, her great dark head low and fearful-looking. Then she came at us, and we turned and ran as hard as we could. She gave up after a short run, and I think we had not been in any real danger. But the spring morning was deep and beautiful and our hearts were beating fast and we knew just then what it was to be alive.

Today, there are reminders of the buffalo throughout the West, but the sight of a living animal in the wild is still a rare occurrence. (Richard Ansaldi)

BUFFALO, FIRST HUNTED SPARINGLY TO SUPPLY MEAT TO THE TRIBES, TO FRONTIERS-men, and to parties of pioneers, were soon sought after for their hides. Sometimes just their delicious tongues were taken. And before the end, buffalo hunting had become a festive and obsessional sport. Writing in 1855, Rudolph Keim joyously recounted a buffalo hunt organized by the Kansas Pacific Railroad during which buffalo were gunned down from the train's rolling passenger cars:

> The barrage wounded two of the buffalo; the locomotive whistled "down brakes," and without waiting for the train to stop, every one, passengers, engineer, conductor, brakeman, jumped off the cars and gave chase…. A cheer wound up the railroad chase when the busy knives of "professionals" in hip-joint operations, soon had the "rumps" severed and after cutting out the tongues and a few strips of "hump" the rest of the two immense carcasses was left as a dainty and abundant repast for the wolf. The meat was put on the train, and again we continued our journey.

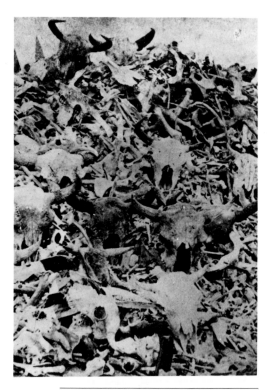

The aftermath of the slaughter left stacks of bleaching buffalo bones—some twelve feet high and wide and a half mile long.

Not every nineteenth-century cowpuncher was a buffalo hunter, but many had at least for a time worked in the slaughter trade. In fact, in the years immediately surrounding the Civil War, buffalo hunting was probably the easiest way to earn a living out in the open spaces. To get work cowboying, a man had to be hired on by an outfit—he had to appear decent and capable enough for a trail boss to take a chance on him. All a man had to do to pay his way with buffalo was to get hold of a powerful rifle—several made by the Sharps company were the preferred weapons—then head out in search of the herds.

Renowned Westerners of every calling could count stints as buffalo hunters. Showmen like Buffalo Bill Cody, cattlemen like Charles Goodnight, lawmen like Wyatt Earp, Bat Masterson, and Wild Bill Hickok had all hunted buffalo. But few boasted about their work, and once the slaughter was complete, men like Goodnight openly regretted it.

Following Cody's year and a half as a hunter, a popular jingle attested to his aim and agility.

Buffalo Bill, Buffalo Bill,
Never missed and never will;
Always aims and shoots to kill
And the company pays his buffalo bill.

Yet while Cody was proud of his nickname and understood its theatrical value, he was sensitive about being considered a major figure in the extermination. He reminded people that virtually all the buffalo he had ever killed were for meat. And Cody's biographer, Don Russell, claimed that The Wild West's show buffalo were, ironically, responsible for much of the burgeoning public sympathy early in the twentieth century that helped save the animal from complete extinction.

It's easy to understand why few people would willingly boast that they were responsible for the needless, nearly psychotic killing-off of a species. And perhaps the reason that so little folklore and celluloid myth-making surrounds the image of the buffalo is that the creature is bound up so hideously in the very worst aspect of America's entrepreneurial character.

The eerie aftermath of the slaughter left the sweeping plains littered with buffalo bones—white skulls, massive femurs, and the huge, high ribs that formed the hump, lying in macabre collections, souvenirs of the ruthless battles. Then the bones themselves became the wares of a brisk new trade, and by 1874 stacks of bones, some twelve feet high, as many feet wide, and half a mile long, waited for shipping beside the railroad tracks. Some wanderers went into the bone-gathering business, and many homesteaders helped pay their first years' way with the bones they picked up off their pastures and fields. The bone gatherers had a song about a man named Sed who was killed by his lust for bones:

Wagons pull in from the prairie dry,
To ricks of bleaching bones piled high.
Four dollars a ton—but not for Sed,
A rattler was watching that buffalo head.
One settler less to tear up sod
And pray for rain from a deaf old God.

Yes, even the buffalo's bones were preyed upon. Bones by the ton were freighted to carbon works in St. Louis. Fresh bones were used in sugar refining. Weather-beaten bones were ground into fertilizer. And a few perfect pieces from the frames of bulls were shipped to England where they were ground and molded and fired into delicate plates and saucers of fine bone china.

"THE HEROES OF THE FRONTIER MYTH WERE HISTORICAL CHARACTERS WHOSE REAL accomplishments formed the core around which folk legends and the more subtle fictions of historians and romance-writers grew," wrote literary historian Richard Slotkin. "Preeminent among them were the wilderness hunters…the often solitary plebeian adventurers who blazed the trails into the world of the Indian, the grizzly and the buffalo."

Daniel Boone, Davy Crockett, Jim Bridger, Kit Carson, Bill Cody—each of them once a flesh-and-blood being made forever larger than life—were the cowboy's real and symbolic forerunners. And in their roles as hunters—stalking, prowling their way into the West—they effectively bridged the nation's intellectual and emotional gap between the love of the wild and the desire for the tame. The country's hunters fulfilled a paradoxical role. They were at work—and, of course, most lustily full of life—in the free, natural, unfettered world of the wilderness. Yet their job was to kill off the wild things, to spread "progress" and civilization. Today's hunters, sedentary men who each autumn trudge into the high timberlands and cedar brakes, who wear day-glo orange cowboy hats and caps and pack rifles that are not much changed from the buffalo guns, embody that same strange paradox. They love, they say, "to get out into the country," to feel the rush of the wind and the thrill of the chase. Yet they explain their hunts as efforts to put meat on the table, to keep the deer and game-bird populations in check—in short, to provide sustenance and maintain order. Few will admit: "I hunt because I love hunting—tracking an animal, spotting it, sighting it in, dropping it." Western hunters who assume cowboy-style personas are attracted by the image of the hunter who can accomplish something, who is powerful enough and skillful enough to *provide,* to take care of himself. And that is the message implicit in the contemporary cowboy's rifle stretched across his pickup's gun rack—"I'm capable; I can get the job done."

Cowboy hunters hold to America's folkloric civic religion, and their patron saint of shooting is without a doubt Davy Crockett, that Kentucky fron-

Actor Fess Parker portrayed Davy Crockett in Walt Disney's popular series. Wilderness hunters like Crockett were symbolic forerunners of the cowboy.

A rancher proudly displays a basket of rattlesnake rattles. Poisonous snakes, along with the region's cougars, wolves, bears, and coyotes, have long been hunted as determinedly as were the buffalo. (Paul Chesley/Photographers Aspen)

tiersman who had the good sense to head to Texas once the wilderness west of the Appalachians began to wither. The real Crockett did once confess that he was downright "wrathy to kill a b'ar," perhaps one of the most succinct phrases ever uttered that expresses something of hunting's strange sexuality. The mythic Crockett, portrayed by Fess Parker in Walt Disney's immensely popular series, "Davy Crockett, King of the Wild Frontier," tries to "grin down a b'ar," to smile at him so long he just ups and dies. But a moment of danger ensues, and Davy has to pull out a knife and "do it the old-fashioned way."

The series also recounts Crockett's final hours inside the battered walls of the Alamo: Davy using his trusty rifle, "Betsy," to pick off Mexican soldiers even though he knows the battle is lost. Crockett's willingness to give his life to the Texan cause enshrined him in that Mexican territory-turned-nation-turned-state—and Texans, like all Westerners, have honored his memory over the years by packing guns and enthusiastically killing critters.

The buffalo along with the West's grizzly bears, elk, moose, antelope, mountain sheep, cougars, wolves, rattlesnakes, and coyotes had held command of a mighty, mystical region sorely coveted by the immigrants. And in order to take control of the land and fill it with people, seige had to be laid against the animals, and the consequences of the killing were of little concern. Notice the glib innocence in the lyrics of "Buffalo Hunters," an early pioneer ballad about the happy work of settlement:

> *Come all ye brisk young fellows*
> *Who want to ride the range*
> *Into some far-off country*
> *Your fortune for to change*
>
> *Oh, the cat will paw the monkey*
> *And the chick will roost and crow*
> *We'll ramble in the canebrake*
> *And we'll hunt the buffalo.*

Once the buffalo were gone, the obsession with the killing-off of the region's critters continued in other ways. Texans occasionally held "killing contests" for recreation—the men and women of one town vying against those of another for bragging rights as to which group best retained the frontier spirit. In one memorable one-day shoot-out in the 1860s, in which squirrels and rabbits killed counted for one point each, turkeys for five, and deer for ten, the two groups scored an incredible total of 3,470 points, just having a little fun.

As recounted in John G. Mitchell's book *The Hunt,* not long ago, according to Anderson County, Texas, constable Jerry Owens, "there was a hunter, shot a farmer's mule and insisted it was a deer. And he would have packed the carcass off over the farmer's protest but for the fact that the mule weighed a thousand pounds." Then Owens mused: "All those guys sitting in their offices

Coyotes are the archenemies of contemporary ranchers because they prey on lambs and calves when their natural food supply—rabbits, prairie dogs, and mice—is short. They are chased, hunted, and trapped relentlessly; yet their numbers are seldom successfully reduced. (Joe Van Wormer/Bruce Coleman, Inc.; LEFT: Bill Ellzey)

Although he was raised in the East, Theodore Roosevelt fancied himself both a wilderness hunter and a cowboy of considerable prowess after he had made a few visits to the West.

and factories wanting to get back to the way it used to be, to the way it *ought* to be.... They want to believe they still live on the wild frontier. I guess it helps to believe the hawks and coyotes are out to get you."

In southern Montana, elk hunters like to position themselves just outside the boundaries of Yellowstone National Park, where migrant animals who have never known the threat of humankind are easy prey. On private deer-hunting leases in the Texas hill country, some hunters build blinds that tower above the timber, then wait for deer to come to strategically placed feeders where they become quick victims of their own habits.

And in Arizona's Hat Rock Valley each year, hunters pay dearly for permits that allow them to take two shots at "surplus" buffalo, a controversial recreation that is the subject of Glendon Swarthout's book and Stanley Kramer's movie *Bless the Beasts and Children* (1971). The animals are culled from a herd of buffalo that once roamed the forests on the Grand Canyon's northern rim and whose numbers must be held in careful check to protect the fragile ecology of the valley preserve. During the hunt, three hunters at a time are allowed to enter a large ring where they wait for the buffalo to be driven toward them. Each fires his shots. If an animal is wounded but not killed, an Arizona Game and Fish Department officer finishes the job. The hunt is bleakly reminiscent of buffalo hunting on the frontier plains, except that no one skins the buffalo and pegs the hides out to dry, nor does anyone come along later to pick up the bleaching bones.

As early as 1873, buffalo hunting, previously considered no more than fortune-seeking in "some far-off country," began to be perceived as something a bit more complex. That was the year in which buffalo were obliterated from the southern plains, the year a man named Brewster Higley wrote a simple ballad that has become probably the most popular folk song of the Western frontier:

> *Oh, give me a home where the buffalo roam,*
> *Where the deer and the antelope play,*
> *Where seldom is heard a discouraging word,*
> *And the skies are not cloudy all day.*

Higley's "Home on the Range" may have been the first nostalgic assessment of the buffalo, certainly the first to place the menacing beast in the same company with the benign and playful deer and antelope. "Home on the Range" celebrates the West's clear skies, bright stars, rocks, sands, and wildflowers, but it laments the passing of the "red men" and the buffalo—a sentiment that was far from universally popular in the years of the huge push westward at the end of the Civil War. Yet there was always an awkward ambivalence toward the untamed country, the same ambivalence bound up in a hunter's *desire* for the prey he kills. There was tension in the wilderness, immediate danger in the secretive movements of the animals that inhabited it. But the wild animals were responsible for much of the West's exotic character, its sights and sounds and engaging mysteries. This is a stanza of "A Prairie Mother's Lullabye," an old bedtime song that is meant to lull a child to sleep with images of wolves and gliding snakes:

> Upon the mesa, bare and brown,
>   The slinking coyotes prowl,
> And, hark, upon the silent air,
> In ghostly cadence echoes there
>   Floats forth the gray wolf's mournful howl.
> The cowboy's song rings loud and clear,
>   As round the bedded cattle he rides,
> And from the stunted sagebrush near
>   The sluggish rattler smoothly glides.

Although they frighten many Americans, rattlesnakes pose only minimal danger to people and to cattle. Yet "rattlesnake roundups" remain a popular pastime in isolated parts of the West. (Bill Ellzey)

The romantic lullabies and ballads were really eulogies, however. By the turn of the century, much of western America's wildlife was in retreat; and the majority of the buffalo that remained were paraded in traveling circuses and Wild West shows, or were stuffed and mounted specimens hanging in railroad stations, restaurants, and saloons. Bison were still sought after, but not as hunting quarry: None of them roamed free for the hunt. The buffalo had vanished, and people sought souvenirs to remind them of a world that had existed only a few score years before. Douglas Branch, a historian of the buffalo slaughter, remembered the "huge and handsome buffalo bull who stood for so many years" in the foyer of the town auditorium in Houston, Texas, during his childhood. Branch wrote that regardless of the occasion and whatever the crowd, that stuffed bull "stared through them and past them all, through even the matty black frontlet that overhung his glassy eyes. There was a faint touch of regal contempt in that immobile stare; there was, it seemed to the youngster who saw him often, the self-pride that distinguishes a good loser."

The awesome and overwhelming herds of buffalo, moving like brown storms over the prairies, were first strange and exotic to the immigrants' eyes, then objects of fear and scorn to be rid of. But once the job was done, a little romance emerged, and some people even began to tell wistful stories about the time when buffalo had ruled the continent. The massive buffalo became a nostalgic symbol of an era whose duration was, to many, disappointingly short.

The venerable buffalo nickel was first minted in 1913, at exactly the time that the country's live buffalo population was at its lowest ebb, and at a time when the nation had finally begun to understand the poignancy of its loss. In the same peculiarly American way in which we have always honored our vanquished foes, we pressed the bison's image into the coin and stuck it inside every purse and pocket in the nation: The buffalo roamed the country again.

Beginning with the popular acts in Buffalo Bill's Wild West, and continuing in rodeos across the country, buffalo riding and trained buffalo acts have always been popular novelty events. (Craig Aurness/West Light; LEFT: Lewis Portnoy/Spectra-Action)

The first buffalo nickel was minted in 1913, at a time when the continent's buffalo population was at its lowest ebb.

FROM 1929 UNTIL LATE IN 1968, THE SEAL OF THE U.S. DEPARTMENT OF THE INTErior featured the image of a buffalo bull standing majestically on a grassy plain. Behind it were western foothills, beyond them the rays of the setting sun. There was always an uncomfortable irony in the fact that the Interior Department, which is charged with protecting natural resources, chose as its symbol an animal that had at one time been systematically exterminated. Perhaps partly for this reason, and surely in an effort to update its image, the Department of the Interior took the buffalo off the seal and replaced it with a picture of the Hoover Dam. Then soon after, in the midst of growing controversy over a seemingly endless series of government-funded dams and water reclamation projects, the buffalo was brought back and resumed its command of the seal.

In 1982, however, Interior Secretary James Watt, a man born on the Wyoming plains that were once the buffalo's domain—despised by environmentalists and adored by Western ranchers, miners, and timbermen—did a little personal redesigning of the seal. Bothered by the fact that the mascot buffalo faced left, Watt presented his top aides with little boxes containing a revised, unofficial seal in which the buffalo faced *to the right.* "Since 1849, the Interior buffalo has been moving to the left," the Secretary told his aides. "We are turning the buffalo around so that he will move in the right direction [and symbolize] the changes needed to RESTORE AMERICA'S GREATNESS." The aides cheered; the cattlemen doffed their hats; the buffalo, though spun around, remained impassive.

Many Western cattlemen, battered by a depressed beef market and high grain prices and interest rates, are paying even more attention to the buffalo than Secretary Watt did. The buffalo is the only wild animal in America that is pastured as a food animal, yet compared to the number of animals in the cattle industry, the buffalo business is miniature. But it's bullish. "They're easier to take care of [than cattle] if you're fenced and corral-equipped for them," says Colorado rancher Gene Linnebur. "In adverse weather they have the equipment. They can interbreed, you don't have to change bulls, and their meat is worth more . . . And the buffalo is almost disease free. . . . Buffalo live to 40. These heifers I bought will outlive me."

In grocery stores and restaurants throughout the West, buffalo meat is increasingly easy to obtain. And it is popular—even at prices that average 50 percent higher per pound than beef—partly because buffalo meat contains very little fat. Weight Watchers, Inc., has even recommended eating buffalo instead of beef as a means of trimming calories.

Although buffalo can be much more cantankerous than cattle, the financial rewards of raising them are growing, and according to many ranchers, something about the animals themselves holds special appeal.

Late in the nineteenth century, Charles Goodnight, the king of the cattlemen, also took a business interest in buffalo. He rounded up a few surviving animals, purchased others, and established one of the nation's largest private herds in Palo Duro Canyon, part of his huge ranch in the Texas panhandle.

Legends and stories abound about Goodnight, known affectionately as The Old Man by many, as Buenas Noches by the Comanches. One story holds that a haggard and hungry band of Comanches once rode all the way from their reservation in Oklahoma to visit Goodnight at his ranch house on the Quitaque River. They begged the rancher to give them a buffalo, but he refused. He later relented, offering them a scrawny and aging bull, assuming they would drive it back to the reservation to slaughter it.

Instead, the Comanches freed the buffalo while Goodnight watched. Then they whipped up their horses, cried out, and chased after it, quickly killing it with arrows and lances. Then they dismounted and stared silently at the carcass of the beast for a long time, as if that one animal embodied the whole strange and entrancing legacy of the buffalo. As he told and retold the story of the Comanche hunters, The Old Man must have understood that the Comanches recognized their own fate in the fate of that last dead buffalo, but that because the Comanches had always been hunters of buffalo, there was nothing else they could do but cut it down.

The buffalo on the U.S. Department of the Interior seal has always faced to the left. But Reagan administration Interior Secretary James Watt complained that it ought to face to the right to symbolize the administration's shift toward conservative Interior policies.

6

Horses were as central to Bill Cody's life as were the early exploits that gave him notoriety and the legends and shows that brought him fame. He held strong affection for fine horses, sat proudly astride those he fancied most, and showed great concern for their care. Occasionally, he gave a favorite mount away as a grand, sometimes grandiose, gesture of his friendship.

Cody's first horse was Prince, a sorrel stallion for which his father had traded with Indians in Kansas Territory. He later rode dozens of stout ponies during his months as a Pony Express rider, and then hunted buffalo from the back of Brigham, "the fleetest steed I ever owned." Then came Powder Face, Buckskin Joe, Tall Bull, Old Charlie, Knickerbocker, Lancer, Old Pap, Isham, a massive white gelding that he rode during his last years with The Wild West, and finally McKinley, who walked in Cody's funeral procession, elegantly bridled and saddled, the stirrups ceremonially turned backward.

The highly trained show horses of Cody's Wild West performed precision maneuvers, jumped through fire, and even danced. The legendary Sioux leader Sitting Bull, who traveled with The Wild West for a season, took a great liking to a particular gray dancing horse and Cody made him a present of it when he left the show. Four years later, Sitting Bull was killed in a skirmish with army cavalry at his home on the Standing Rock reservation. As the first shots were fired, the gray horse mistook them for his cue and began his dance routine. And who could blame him for confusing the reality of the moment with the mythic entertainments of Buffalo Bill's shows? Humans, too, had confused the reality and the myth many times.

CHAPTER SIX

HORSEBACK BOYS

WE CALL HIM A COWBOY—THIS MAN IN BATWING CHAPS AND A RED BANDANNA, riding in the western mountains, or frozen in time, galloping across Hollywood backlots, or trotting across the wide, night-lit billboards that hang above the freeways. But although the name conjures up a particular image to each person who hears it, it's a name that's exceedingly imprecise. The cowboy in all his guises is not so much a cowman as a horseman. Even among the ranch hands to whom the word most directly applies, *cowboy* isn't meant to describe solely a cattle herder or cattle tender. It is, instead, the definitive word for the western horseman in high-heeled boots on a big-horned saddle, an agile and adept rider who tends cattle because it's the only work he can get on horseback. The horse holds a cowboy's foremost fascination. It is his proudest possession, his closest companion, the equine heart of his western world.

The horse has fascinated humankind since the first attempts were made to domesticate it five thousand years ago. Something extraordinary happened when early man first straddled an apprehensive horse, drove it forward with a kick of his legs, and began to ride. He was transformed by the horse into something stronger and far fleeter than he could have been on foot. The horse became a kind of "God-slave, Faithful and True" (in the words of Peter Shaffer in his 1974 play, *Equus*)—a being far larger and stronger than man that was nevertheless willing to submit to him, do his bidding, and endure the pain he often induced.

The historic cowboy and his faithful horse were inseparable. The horse was the cowboy's means of transport, his principal tool in herding, cutting, or

Cowboys and their horses have long been inseparable. The horse is the cowboy's means of transport, his principal tool, and his constant companion. (BOTH: Nicholas de Vore III/Photographers Aspen)

Cowboys are often shamelessly sentimental about the proud and powerful horses who are willing to submit to them, to have iron shoes pounded onto their hoofs, and to carry their riders long past the point of exhaustion. (Scott Ransom; RIGHT: David Burnett/Contact)

catching cattle, his companion in the solitary open spaces. "The hoot of the owl and the howl of the coyote were music to my ears through the long night," recalled nineteenth-century cowboy Jim Christian about spending the winter alone at a remote line camp. "My comrade was my horse. A fellow could spend lots of time petting, currying and fooling with a horse."

It was no surprise when cowboys first began to be fictionalized that their horses were treated with respect and affection. Wild West show audiences were dazzled by the intricate tricks that horses could perform and by the precision roping and shooting that cowboys could accomplish on horseback. Early dime novelists put their heroes on steeds with unbelievable endurance and a devotion to their riders that rivaled that of the dearest mother. William S. Hart occasionally gave his faithful horse a hearty kiss in his silent films, and a few horses in later Westerns became as famous as the cowboys who rode them. Roy Rogers's Trigger and Gene Autry's Champion were all-American horses everyone loved, and the Lone Ranger's white stallion galloped away in every episode "with a streak of light, a cloud of dust and a hearty 'Hi-ho, Silver, away!'"

There is no denying that a strange and poignant bond often existed between a cowpuncher and his stout cayuse. The fictionalized portrayal of the cowboy only highlighted this connection and romanticized it a bit. And even in an age when there are more Oldsmobiles and eighteen-wheel tractor-trailers than there are genuine using horses, as cowboys sometimes call them, the horse curiously still holds its own. Quarter horses and their close cousins are still essential in working cattle; rodeo rough-stock riders get sentimental about the very broncs that might break their necks, admiring their high-kicking tenacity and grit. Jackpot roping contests are held weekly all over the West—cowboys haul their hot-blooded little mounts from contest to contest in trailers with bumper stickers that read "I'm A Ropaholic."

The Bureau of Land Management's "Adopt-A-Horse" program culls wild mustangs from overpopulated rangelands and sells them to folks with a spare acre of grass who aim to keep these stalwart feral animals away from the dog-food factories. Thousands of people buy a horse or two and corral them out behind their houses, with a bit of the same sense of self-importance the Spaniards must have felt riding those sure-footed stallions who arched their tails as they trotted across the deserts. But horses remain popular west of the Corn Belt heartland principally because they are forever associated with the horseback hands of the old days. And when someone takes title to a critter, tends its hoofs and curries it, worms it and feeds it through the winters, then rides it across the highway and out beyond the tract homes, he can call himself a cowboy without embarrassment, secure in the knowledge that the whole mythic experience doesn't have nearly as much to do with cattle as with straddling a good horse, then moving it on.

In Frederic Remington's His First Lesson, it is plainly the horse who is terrified. But in most cases, breaking a horse to ride is equally harrowing for the cowboy who mounts it and rides out its bucks and spins. (Kurt Markus)

Horses were introduced to the continent by Spanish explorer Hernán Cortés in 1519. Over the centuries, they have adapted so successfully to the western terrain that they now seem as native as scrub grass. (Jonathan Wright/Bruce Coleman, Inc.)

THE HORSES AND MARES WERE OUR SALVATION," HERNÁN CORTÉS reported to Spanish Emperor Carlos V from the New World following his conquest of the Aztec Empire in the Valley of Mexico. In 1519, Cortés and his *compañeros* had overcome the remarkable Aztec civilization with the aid of just sixteen horses —eleven stallions and five mares—brought with them from Spain. The Spaniards were significantly outnumbered, but the horses, strange and terrifying to the Aztecs, became a fortress for the Spaniards, "our only hope of survival," said Bernal Díaz, chronicler of the expedition. To the Aztecs, a horse and its rider appeared to be a "monster that could uncouple itself into two parts." When a group of Tlascalan warriors killed a horse in a fierce battle with the Spaniards, they severed its head from its body and sent the head from town to town to show that the monster was indeed mortal. But although it was mortal, it was becoming ever more plentiful.

Horses multiplied quickly in the New World, and additional stock was continually brought to the continent from Spain and the Spanish-held island of Hispaniola. Only twenty years after Cortés had landed at Vera Cruz, explorer Francisco de Coronado was able to assemble 1,500 horses for his march northward into the region that is now New Mexico. Many tribal people encountered by Coronado were so entranced by his "Big Dogs" that they smeared themselves with the horses' sweat in the hope of transferring some of the horses' power and magic to themselves.

The early Spaniards rode stallions almost exclusively. They admired their fiery virility and seldom gelded *potros,* colts, that were to become saddle horses. Mares, on the other hand, were considered merely breeding stock, and anyone who rode a mare was thought to be something less than a true horseman.

The Spaniards so completely sought self-esteem in horsemanship that the Spanish word for horseman, *caballero,* became the same word for "gentleman." Conversely, the word *peon,* which means "pedestrian," came to denote a peasant or serf—one who had to resort to walking.

Few Spanish noblemen ever walked any distance. But they believed that tending their valuable cattle—work that could best be accomplished on horseback—was beneath their dignity, so they eventually taught their servants to ride, and the horse became accessible to every class. Horses were prized, yet very plentiful. They were bred for desirable characteristics on the large *ranchos;* they were bartered and used in place of currency, stolen constantly, and sometimes butchered for meat.

But not every New World horse spent its life in servitude under the saddle. Hundreds stole away into open territory and quckly recovered much of the social and territorial behavior of their wild ancestors. Feral herds divided themselves into numerous bands, each one composed of a single dominant stal-

Cowboys prepare to brand and castrate a horse—to claim it as private property and to begin the process of making it a dependable and dedicated servant. (Jay Dusard)

181

Although mustangs are sought after by dog-food manufacturers and ranchers who believe they deplete range grasses that should properly feed cattle, a few tenacious bands of wild horses still survive in remote pockets of the West. (Paul Chesley/Photographers Aspen; LEFT: Ernst Haas)

lion and a harem of mares and their foals. Each stallion defended himself, his band, and the band's home range from predators and from the advances of unattached stallions who roamed in bands of their own and who were quick to take control of the harem of any stallion who began to grow old or weak. Such protective behavior ensured the survival of the wild horses. They grazed virgin grass, took cover amid the rocks and timber, and their safety was threatened only by the cougar and the mounted *vaqueros* with long horsehair ropes.

The Spaniards called the feral horses *caballos cimarrones,* runaway slave horses, as well as *salvajes* and *silvestres,* savage and wild horses; but the most common term was *mesteño,* a word that denoted the feral horse's lack of ownership, its availability to anyone who could rope it and settle it back to the saddle.

By the beginning of the nineteenth century, only three hundred years after the horse had been reintroduced on the continent, the number of North America's mustangs, the English corruption of *mesteño,* was estimated at two million head. They had become as numerous as their kindred domestic horses that still submitted to the bit. Frontiersman Josiah Gregg, who traveled throughout the Southwest in 1841, was fascinated by the mustangs, which had gained reputations as horses of superior spirit and strength. "The wild horses are generally well formed," he wrote in his journal, "with trim and clean limbs; still, their elegance has been much exaggerated by travellers, because they have seen them at large, abandoned to their wild and natural gaiety; but when caught and tamed, they generally dwindle down to ordinary ponies."

But Gregg noted that the reverse process could also occur, that "the gentlest wagon horse (even though quite fagged with travel), once among a drove of mustangs [would] often acquire in a few hours all the intractable wildness of his untamed companions." The God-slave could shed its slavery and quickly become a mysterious equine deity—its body lithe and powerful, its demeanor valiant and haughty as it galloped across the grassland.

THE EARLY COWBOYS WERE NOT JUST CATTLE HERDERS; THEY WERE MOUNTED herdsmen, and that distinction was of profound importance to them and to the development of the personal characteristics that began to shape the cowboy mystique. Shy, self-conscious young men suddenly gained poise and confidence in the saddle. Work that if done on foot would have been considered banal by most—and downright demeaning by many—became a proud occupation when carried out on horseback.

In traveling long distances and in chasing after maverick cattle, cowboy and horse operated much like a centaur, combining the lad's dexterity with a rawhide rope with the strength and speed of the quadruped. And if horse and man were partners, cattle were decidedly the foe. They were the commodity on hoof, a cowboy's prime responsibility, and tending them allowed him to pick

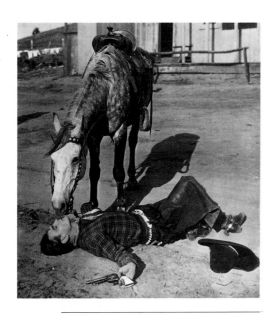

Matinee cowboy Buck Jones's horse, Silver, was so smart he could untie knots, bring Buck back to consciousness, and help him save the day.

up his wages. But more than that, cows were truly stupid animals, ones that made the horse appear all the more intelligent and capable in comparison. During the twenty-three years (1866–1889) of the Longhorn cattle drives that pushed north out of Texas, as many as a million horses—most of them captured mustangs—were also trailed out of Texas, destined to become plow and wagon horses in the midwestern farming regions. Yet the histories and folklore of that era all but completely ignore that herding and trailing of horses, perhaps because an image of horses as docile and dull-spirited enough to be herded like cattle, or like sheep, would have damaged the romantic notion of horses as super-animals, indispensable partners to the herders who rode them.

Range cowboys developed strong bonds with their best horses—those that could somehow always find camp on rainy and moonless nights, the mounts that would walk right up to be saddled every morning, the tenacious little ponies that would carry their cowboys long past the point of exhaustion. In *We Pointed Them North*, Teddy Blue Abbott remembered Billy, his "top horse for twenty-six years." Billy won Teddy Blue's heart simply by showing him some sass:

> The next day I caught [Billy] up to ride and he showed me a thing or two. He started to buck, and first my six-shooter went, then my Winchester went, then I went, and he finished up by bucking the saddle over his head. After that I would not have taken a million dollars for him. He was about ten years old when I got him, and was thirty-six years old when he died on this ranch of old age. He was a wonderful rope and cut horse, but I thought so much of him I never used him much, only to ride to town.

But Teddy Blue didn't go soft on every horse he encountered. He complained about occasionally having to work for an outfit that had nothing but a "string of damn bum horses. Anybody knows what that means who has ever tried to rope calves on a fool horse that doesn't know his business. It's enough to drive you crazy."

Yet most cowboys even found riding a bum horse preferable to being set afoot. On the ground, standing awkwardly in his high-heeled boots, the cowboy was literally shrunken in stature. His speed, power, and sturdy masculinity—all so much a part of him when he sat tall in the saddle—were gone. "Horse and man seemed one when the general vaulted into the saddle," wrote Elizabeth Bacon Custer in *Boots and Saddles,* a biography of her husband, General George Armstrong Custer. And although Custer was certainly no cowboy, he was indeed a horseman, and his wife viewed his relation to his horse in a context that was implicitly sexual: "His body was so lightly poised and so full of swinging, undulating motion, it almost seemed that the wind moved him as it blew over the plain. Yet every nerve was alert like finely tempered steel, for the muscles and sinews that seemed so pliable were equal to the curbing of the most fiery animal."

If there was sometimes a strange sexuality associated with horses, there was always mystery as well. The tendency of even the most dependable horse to occasionally shy at a jackrabbit, or at the sudden flash of a bandanna pulled out of a back pocket, kept even the most savvy cowboys alert. And virtually every decent using horse could be counted on to blow up, inexplicably, every now and again, to become terrorized by the routine slap of a saddle blanket, to decide, however irrationally, that the slipping of a rein around its neck was cause for all hell to break loose.

Cowboys were often superstitious about their mounts. Some refused to ride mares. Others were convinced that albinos or zebra duns or star-faced ponies would bring bad luck. Many considered bays to be the most even-tempered and dependable among the spectrum of colors of horses. And range hands often swore that horsehair ropes laid out around a camp or a bedroll would keep the snakes away.

Although few cowboy camp songs were serenades to specific horses, horses did figure prominently in them, especially when the songs dealt with death. Dying cowboys in the range songs invariably worried about what would happen to their horses when they were gone. Some wished that they could take them with them. Others specified the role their horses should play in their burials. In his own song about a dying cowpuncher, Teddy Blue wrote:

> There was one request he did crave, It's when he died he wanted to
>   ride Old Muggins to his grave.
> Oh lay my spurs upon my breast, my rope and old saddle tree,
> And while the boys were lowering me to rest, go turn my horses free.

In the familiar ballad, "Good-bye, Old Paint," the old wrangler had a different plan for his beloved cayuse:

> Oh, when I die take my saddle from the wall,
> Put it on my pony, lead him from the stall,
> Tie my bones to his back, turn our faces to the West,
> And we'll ride the prairie that we love the best.

It's doubtful that any cowboy ever really had such a send-off to the great beyond, but the boys liked to imagine it: partners in life's work, still partners in the rest that came with death.

"TO-MORROW—TO-MORROW I START FOR 'MY PEOPLE,'" ARTIST FREDERIC REMington wrote from London in 1892. "I go to the simple men with the bark on—the big mountains—the great deserts and the scrawny ponies." Remington, already renowned for his paintings and illustrations of the frontier West, had not been happy painting European scenes, and he had desperately missed the rich subject matter that western horses provided. Although a native of

Tom Mix's stocking-legged bay, Tony, was such a crowd pleaser that his name appeared on theater marquees alongside his famous master's name.

Trigger was the noblest of all of Hollywood's horses. Roy Rogers and Dale Evans were so devoted to him that when Trigger died they had the horse stuffed and placed on display in their Apple Valley, California, museum. (Larry Dale Gordon)

Gene Autry specialized in bounding up over Champion's hind quarters and landing in the saddle just as the horse galloped off to chase after outlaws.

New York state, Remington considered the West his spiritual province, and he endeavored to recreate it vividly and accurately in his work. Yet if most western horses were indeed "scrawny," he chose not to portray them that way. With the exception of a few drawings depicting haggard and half-starved old nags, Remington's horses were lithe, well-muscled, spirited creatures. He was proud of his horses and wanted to be remembered for them more than for any other subject he painted. One critic has even suggested that Remington became a painter of cowboys only because he was fascinated by the horses they rode.

Horses held no enormous fascination for the public at large at the turn of the century, however. They were still the principal means of conveyance throughout the nation, and nearly everyone had daily contact with them. Audiences did greatly appreciate the intricate tricks that horses performed in the Wild West shows, and elegantly outfitted horses were an essential component of the popular western pageants and parades. But it wasn't until horses began to disappear from daily life in much of America that they came to gain prominence in Western books and movies.

The first fictionalizers of the cowboy were interested much more in the man than the horse. The cowboys of the dime novels rode good horses that never gave up, steeds that could always be counted on; but the horses were seldom celebrated, and they never usurped the glory of the cowboys who rode them. Then a few writers began to give horses a bit of character in later stories, but they didn't always make them noble and invincible. In Clarence Mulford's original story of Hopalong Cassidy—a very different sort of horseman from the elegant, well-mannered Hopalong of the movies—Hopalong's horse, Red Eagle, was "an ugly old wart of a cayuse." And he screamed at the horse as it reared and bucked: "Don't you know I can lick four like you an' not touch leather! There, that's better. If you bite me again I'll kick yore corrugations in!"

Film directors discovered quickly that horses could provide important visual action. Ponies galloping across western horizons were endlessly exciting, and they could provide relatively logical transitions between the calmer scenes that had to carry the movie's plot. Cowboy stars like Tom Mix, Hoot Gibson, and Ken Maynard could be counted on for high-spirited, hoof-pounding action and some occasional trick riding. But quiet William S. Hart was the first movie cowboy to sentimentalize his horses, scratching their ears and hugging them with great affection, even bestowing on them an occasional well-earned kiss. Hart's own fine pinto pony, called Fritz, was Hollywood's first recognizable equine star. Posters for several movies proudly included his name with the names of the actors, and Hart made big public relations events out of Fritz's "retirement" and his few brief "comeback" appearances.

Many horses followed Fritz on the trail to movie stardom. Among them were Buck Jones's white horse, Silver; Ken Maynard's white horse, Tarzan; William Boyd's white horse, Topper; and Tex Ritter's white horse, White Flash

—the symbolism of their color all too obvious—Tom Mix's Tony, a stocking-legged bay whose name appeared on theater marquees; and Silver and Scout, a white stallion and a piebald pinto, who carried the Lone Ranger and his Indian companion, Tonto, through a thousand big adventures.

But perhaps noblest of all the Hollywood horses were Gene Autry's gentle sorrel, Champion, and Roy Rogers's palomino, Trigger, both sentient critters who could untie knots and drag rifles over to their captive masters if the need arose. Neither horse ever had to be tied or caught—Champion was always ready for Gene to bound up into the saddle over his hindquarters—and both were as well principled and mannerly as the young women with whom they vied for their cowboy's attention. Both horses were so popular that each was the subject of a comic-book series, and children throughout the world dreamed of the delight of riding them out in the fun-filled West. Rogers was so devoted to Trigger, and so appreciative of the horse's role in making him rich and famous, that when the horse died, he had him mounted (he resented the term "stuffed") and placed on display in his Apple Valley, California, museum. There Trigger stands saddled and bridled around the clock—as if waiting for the happy day when Roy will once again mount up and sit astride him.

When the age of television dawned, the Hollywood horses rode easily onto the small screen. A few, like Fury and Flicka, had series of their own, aimed at Saturday morning audiences. But most continued to serve their hero riders just as they had in the theaters—always at the ready, never eating or sleeping or defecating, never quite as smart as their cowboys, but smarter by far than the outlaws they helped to defeat.

Then as the television Western matured in the second half of the 1950s, a strange and unsettling thing happened: The horse became anonymous again. The horsemen in long-running series like "Bonanza," "Rawhide," "Gunsmoke," and "The Big Valley" rode horses without names. Television Westerns put more emphasis on human relationships than they did on action, and all the time cowboys spent talking and arguing and fighting with each other left little time for attention to their horses. By the end of the Western heyday of the early 1960s, the fictional cowboy and his horse hardly ever encountered each other: Matt Dillon *walked* from place to place in Dodge City, something unthinkable a few years earlier, and Sky King flew an airplane over the deserts of Arizona.

ONE OF THE FEW CONSTANTS IN A WAY OF LIFE THAT HAS BORNE BOTH SUBTLE AND momentous changes in the century and a half since it began to take shape is the role of the horse in the moving of cattle. Breeds of cattle today are unlike the cattle that were once trailed out of Texas; thousands of fences stand where once there were none; few ranches exist where there used to be many; cattle are moved in trucks instead of in trail drives; and bankers—not cowhands—

William S. Hart was the first movie cowboy to show unabashed affection for his horse, Fritz—occasionally even bestowing him with a well-earned kiss.

192

Rodeo rough-stock horses are called broncs, from the Spanish word bronco, meaning "coarse" or "rude." Cowboys compete during eight-second rides in saddle-bronc, LEFT, and bareback competitions. (Bruce Benedict/The Stock Market; LEFT: Susan Felter)

are a rancher's essential allies. But the using horse—the compact critter that's as quick as a cat but as patient as Job himself—remains vital to the efficient operation of every ranch cattle business. Today's cowhand "doesn't spend all his waking hours a-horseback," John R. Erickson wrote in *The Modern Cowboy.* "Fifty years ago, he might have. Today he doesn't. But when he does climb into the saddle, he had better know how to handle a horse under all conditions, because the horse remains the most important tool on a cattle ranch."

Nine out of ten ranch horses are quarter horses—either registered animals whose breeding gives them value quite apart from the kind of work they can perform, or grade horses with no papers and sometimes without much in the way of looks but with lots of what ranchers call "cow savvy," that uncanny ability to know what a cow's going to do before the cow does.

The first breed established in the Americas, the quarter horse is bred for agility, balance, and quickness—all fine cattle-working characteristics. Some western horsemen pay great attention to breeding and spend armloads of money on colts and fillies that come out of the lines of renowned animals like Cutter Bill, Doc Bar, Mr. San Peppy, Especial, Poco Bueno, and many others. But decent ranch horses can be acquired for as little as $1,000, and the vast majority of the horses at work in the West belong on the low end of the price scale. They aren't always creatures of great beauty or the best of bloodlines, but like their upper-class counterparts, they possess that same mysterious mix of domestication and wild spirit that has always made horses so serviceable and dependable in the brute work of chasing cattle, yet also so unpredictable—possessed by rare moments of rage and by moments of inexplicable and infectious pleasure.

Rodeo rough-stock horses, called broncs—from the Spanish word *bronco,* meaning "rough, coarse, or rude"—possess little of that wild/tame amalgam. They represent in the ritual of saddle-bronc and bareback contests the feral horses that cowboys "broke" into saddle horses a hundred years ago. But modern broncs aren't wild horses. They are rodeo horses, critters that just somehow like to buck, who are good at it, who lead pampered lives in exchange for eight seconds' worth of work every few days. Rodeo stock contractors are always on the lookout for good bucking horses. When the rodeo's in town, a rancher will get word to a contractor that he has a big, barrel-chested buckskin gelding that he just can't settle down, but that can kick holes in the moon. If the contractor gets interested, he'll give the horse a tryout, watch its bucking rhythm, the heights of its kicks, and whether it drops its head. If the contractor likes what he sees, the rancher gets a nice check for a horse he can't use, the contractor gets a new employee, and the horse starts to travel from one rodeo to the next, always eating well in the company of other horses, then a couple of times a week trying for all it's worth to get some fool cowboy off its back.

Because of rodeo's growing popularity and the increased demand for

In the ritual of rodeo, broncs symbolize the mustangs that cowboys "broke" into saddle mounts in the early days. (Ray Rector)

good bucking stock, a few breeding programs are now under way whose aim is to produce quality rodeo stock by breeding champion bucking stallions with high-kicking, high-spirited mares. At the Calgary Stampede Ranch in Alberta, Canada, geneticists and veterinarians use embryo transplant procedures to produce the greatest possible number of offspring with bucking potential specifically to supply the famed Calgary rodeo. After centuries of attempts by humans to breed the buck *out* of horses, it is ironic that some are now trying to breed it back in.

Cowboys' attitudes toward broncs are far different from those toward horses used in calf-roping, steer-wrestling, and cutting events (contests in which horse and rider are judged on their abilities to cut a cow out of a herd). These horses, which belong to the men who ride them, are extensively trained and must cooperate closely with their riders if they are to be successful competitors. Broncs, on the other hand, belong to no one but the stock contractor. They are modern-day *mesteños*, captive yet uncontrollable. Cowboys respect their prowess as buckers, their strength and spirit, but there is no comradeship between bronc and rider. Rodeo men strike at the broncs with straps and ropes; they swear at them as they're being prepared for a ride; they toss dirt at them; and some spit on the horses when they are trapped in the tight chutes just before being released into the arena. The spitting is a strange, ritualistic act that probably isn't meant to degrade the horses, and it certainly doesn't enrage them. It only obliquely signifies that the horse is the wild creature, and the cowboy the man who is about to tame it.

But broncs are never permanently tamed, of course. If one cowboy makes an eight-second ride, the next one probably won't. And some bucking horses are so good, so unwilling to be ridden, that their madness becomes legendary and their fiery temperaments are revered as symbolic of the wild nobility of the species. One famed bucking horse, a brutish black mount named Midnight, was so tough and so highly respected throughout the rodeo circuit that when he died he was buried like a family pet—and cowboy Dick Griffin wrote this epitaph on his gravestone:

Under this sod lies a great bucking hoss
There never lived a cowboy he couldn't toss
His name was Midnight, his coat black as coal
If there is a hoss-heaven, please God, rest his soul.

A few true mustangs—horses as wild as the pronghorn antelope with whom they share their pristine forage lands—survive in remote pockets of Wyoming and Nevada. But their numbers are very small, and their free-roaming lives are ironically in conflict with the very ranchers who might have been their staunchest allies if the horses did not depend on the same forage as the ranchers' cattle. The stockmen claim that wild horses deplete the meager

Some bucking horses are so good, so unwilling to be ridden, that their madness becomes legendary. (John Addison Stryker)

195

Horseback work can plainly wear a fellow out, especially in a wild horse race, in which three-men teams attempt to saddle an unbroken horse and then ride it around a designated course. (Glenn Short/Bruce Coleman, Inc.; LEFT: Frank Grant/International Stock Photo)

Honda three-wheelers may get a fellow from place to place, but they can't match the majesty and mystery of a horse. (Jack Parsons/FotoWest)

grasses on the federal rangelands where they own permits to run their cattle. They argue for a methodical decrease in the horses' numbers, or for their complete eradication. Numerous private groups, however, claim that the mustangs should be protected like any other endangered species, that their survival is ultimately more important than the feeding of a few extra cattle.

In a controversial attempt to both placate ranchers and offer some protection to the wild horses, the government now classifies wild horses as a "National Heritage Species," the only one of its kind—a designation that permits management of wild horses in reduced numbers that are small enough to do little damage to range grasses, yet large enough to ensure their survival. For $200 per animal, the Bureau of Land Management's "Adopt-A-Horse" program offers captured mustangs to anyone who can provide homes for them. Some horses are reportedly quickly resold to slaughter houses. Some adapt to their new fence-bound lives very successfully and become calm and steady saddle mounts. But others always hold to the wild life, forever flailing away at the gates and corrals that hold them, as if the haughty, untamed spirits of their ancestors survive in them and hunger to be out beyond the fences in the open and unfettered country.

In the American Quarter Horse Association survey of its 120,000 members not long ago, 12 percent noted that having read *Black Beauty* as a child, the story later became one of their principal motivations in buying a horse or horses. Horses have always dwelt deep in the atavistic dreams of the people who care about them. They engender the same delight and compassion in most people that all animals do, yet they possess an independent spirit and a coy self-consciousness that somehow set them apart. Books like *Black Beauty* and the songs, stories, and films that tell of legendary horses sustain those dreams about horses that are *more* than just animals, and they make people feel that owning a horse might inject a bit of flare and fire into their lives.

There are an estimated 8 million horses in the United States today, owned by about 6 million people. The Quarter Horse Association reports that there are 1.7 million animals in its registry, among them 137,000 newborn foals. And although western pleasure and competitive riding don't account for all of the $15 billion spent annually on the U.S. horse industry, they do represent a principal share. Magazines like *Western Horseman* and *Horse and Rider* fuel the diehard dreams and material desires of thousands of ersatz cowpokes with articles on horse dentistry and acupuncture, how to choose a saddle or train spoiled horses or pack into the wilderness, when to wean colts and what to wear to a chuck-wagon barbecue. Advertisements offer everything from horse wormers and expensive custom barns to special seminars on how to turn horseflesh into an effective tax shelter.

Amid all the money and the sometimes tacky commercialism that surround the western horse scene are people drawn toward horses in the same sad way that they are drawn toward speedboats and video games, jazzercise, and anything else that offers a ready diversion from the trouble and turbulence of the times. But there are many people for whom horses simply offer a little steadiness, people who settle themselves down as much as they do their horses when they curry their necks and withers and brush out their knotted tails. And there are a few genuine horseback boys still around, men whom novelist and cutting-horse trainer Thomas McGuane has called "hard-bitten romantics with Red Man coming out of the corners of their mouths who want to be 'plumb mounted' on some shining pony that goes back to studs like Old Sorrel or Oklahoma Star or Joe Hancock or My Texas Dandy or Midnight or Zantanon ('the Mexican Man o' War'). The thing is to be mounted and that is not on a Honda or a Ski-doo."

There is something between old men and horses—some strange understanding or degree of commiseration, something that is lodged in the quiet comfort of memory. It has a lot to do with being certain that horses, at least, lent their lives an anchor. "After their knees begin to stiffen," wrote Texas historian J. Frank Dobie in *The Mustangs*, "most men realize that they have been disappointed in themselves, in other men, in achievement, in love, in whatever they expected out of life; but a man who has had a good horse in his life . . . will remember him as a certitude . . . amid all the flickering vanishments."

Perhaps describing horses as *certitudes* is among the best of the meager explanations offerable. At least it gets to the heart of the matter, which is that in spite of the mystery that horses carry with them like a scar beneath their shiny coats, apart from their talents and sagacious traits, their quirks and bursts of brilliance, they are at bottom simply brave and certain companions, willing to submit to their riders and to move in graceful tandem.

"I see my son, age five, riding a mechanical horse in front of the laundrymat on Sunday morning," wrote Larry McMurtry,

> and the sight calls up my Uncle Johnny, when *he* was age five, sitting on top of the McMurtry barn watching the last trail herd go by. It is indeed a complex distance from those traildrivers who made my father and my uncles determined to be cowboys to the mechanical horse that helps convince my son that he is a cowboy, as he takes a vertical ride in front of a laundrymat.

It is a complex distance, yet if it can still be covered, if a cowboy can mythically get from then to now, it is a distance that is probably best traveled on horseback, riding a strong pony full of spirit and sass, riding a horse he can count on.

Novelist Thomas McGuane puts his champion cutting horse, Lucky Bottom 79, to work on his Montana ranch. Much of the rider's work on a cutting horse is simply to stay in the saddle while the horse stalks its bovine prey with the sudden quickness of a cat. (Hans Teensma)

7

In the summer of 1877, Bill Cody joined Major Frank North in a ranching partnership on the South Fork of the Dismal River in Nebraska. The two men bought and branded a herd of Texas Longhorns that had been driven to North Platte, Nebraska, and then drove the animals another 65 miles north to the ranch. Under North's management—Cody was earning his living performing in stage melodramas at the time and could give only occasional attention to the ranch—the operation sustained 4,500 head of cattle, and it gave Cody his first taste of the rigors of ranch life.

"In this cattle driving business is exhibited some most magnificent horsemanship," Cody wrote in his early autobiography, "for the 'cow-boys,' as they are called, are invariably skillful and fearless horsemen." But Cody was happy that cowboying wasn't his only livelihood: "As there is nothing but hard work on these round-ups, having to be in the saddle all day, and standing guard over the cattle at night, rain or shine, I could not possibly find where the fun came in, that North had promised me."

But Cody made sure there was a little fun once in a while. When he visited the roundup on the nearby Olive ranch, he brought a wagonload of whiskey with him and soon had the hands running horse races and holding shooting contests. The boys were having such a good time, in fact, that Cody went to North Platte to get a second load of whiskey, and nobody herded a single cow for a week.

Buffalo Bill had discovered something that would always remain essential to the cowboy legends he later helped invent: If you wanted to make cowboy life seem exciting and full of fun, you had to get rid of those bawling cows.

200

CHAPTER SEVEN

TAKING STOCK

IT HAS BEEN NEARLY FIVE HUNDRED YEARS SINCE THE FIRST SPANISH CATTLE WERE shipped to the New World, and during all these centuries there have been precious few *vaqueros* or cowboys who have professed affection for the cattle they have tended. Many, of course, have acknowledged the cuteness and playfulness of newborn calves; sturdy and dependable mother cows who cause little commotion and produce strong and shapely offspring year after year often earn a cowboy's quiet respect. And that same cowhand will occasionally express a grudging envy of the lives led by the purebred bulls whose huge scrotums hang down almost to the grass—lives filled with few demands, a steady supply of food, and all the amorous activity anyone could wish for. But real *affection* for cattle has been mighty rare, unlike the steadfast devotion cowboys have always held for their horses. Cattle have been, and remain, merely "stocks" and "beeves"—in the lingo of the trail cowboys—animals to be bought or bred, and sold. They have supplied humans with food, clothing, and tools for centuries; people have made killing profits from them, and sometimes have gone flat broke trying. They formed the hairy-hided foundation of a range industry that supported nascent societies, economies, and ways of life that spread over half the North American continent, an industry that, although battered and bruised, still survives today.

Cattle have always been associated with money. The Greeks stamped the image of an ox on the world's first coins; the Latin word for money, *pecunia,* comes from *pecus,* meaning "cattle." In many societies, including that of the

From the days when the first drovers cut Longhorn cattle out of feral herds—as shown in N. C. Wyeth's painting, Trouble with the Longhorns, LEFT *—to the present, cowboys have professed little affection for cows. They have viewed them as little more than cantankerous commodities to be herded, roped, branded, and ultimately sold for a profit. (Kurt Markus)*

207

Frederic Remington's engraving, In a Stampede, *shows something of the terror and danger of a cattle stampede at night. Trail hands so dreaded stampedes that they sang to their cattle through the night in hopes of keeping them quiet and settled.*

early West, being impecunious often literally meant having no cattle; and *chattel,* a word that is synonymous with *property, equipment,* or *stock,* comes from the Middle English and Old French word *chatel,* which again means "cattle."

Nineteenth-century Texans were so certain of their Longhorns' economic importance that an image of a cowboy chasing a steer was pressed onto the Republic of Texas's $2 note. A hundred and fifty years later, most beef cattle should probably be branded with an image of a cowboy trying to rope a $2 bill, because making money in the cattle business has become almost that difficult. But thousands of people continue to try. Ranchers whose daddies and granddaddies ran cattle on the same land where their animals now graze have to sweet-talk the bankers to keep them in business; but doctors and lawyers and the titans of industry can invest huge sums in purebred breeding operations and in the process provide themselves with attractive tax advantages and an illusory connection to the romance of the range, regardless of whether they make a profit.

Cowboys—the fellows who do the work—don't figure very prominently in the modern cattle trade. The moviemakers and the book writers never could get interested in cows, and no mystique has ever been built around the dull business of looking after them. Huge numbers of cows are fed from mechanical conveyors in enormous feedlots these days, instead of from cowboys' weathered pitchforks. And those few ranchers who still do mount up and work their cattle the old-time way complain that they can't find good hands anymore. Inside the honky-tonks and country discos and out at the rodeo arenas, everyone's a sure-fire cowboy, but out on the windswept ranches few of them are actually punching cows.

THE SPANIARDS BROUGHT THREE TYPES OF CATTLE WITH THEM TO THE New World: the *Berrenda,* with its white body and black markings around the neck and ears; a reddish cow called a *Retinto;* and the ancient black *Ganado Prieto,* the Andalusian fighting bull. *Ganado Prietos* were highly valued and bred carefully and guarded closely, so that few of them ever escaped into the wild. It was the *Berrenda* and *Retinto* cattle that, once abandoned to the rocky canyons of northern Mexico and the *brazada* (brush country) of south Texas, evolved into the mongrel creature that became known as the Longhorn—a breed characterized by a long, low-swinging head, a narrow body, spindly legs, a disagreeable temperament, and magnificent horns that could measure as much as eight feet from tip to tip. The horns appeared extremely cumbersome on the skinny-necked cows, but they were a valuable weapon against the attacks of wolves and cougars and the sometimes unwelcome advances of bulls. Although the long horns were of no practical value to anyone except the cows who wore them, people took great interest in their size and bulk, even in the earliest days of Anglo-American settlement in the Texas region. An old song claimed:

Old Joe Clark has got a cow—
    She was muley born,
It takes a jaybird forty-eight hours
    To fly from horn to horn.

Perhaps it was the nuisance of carrying those incredible horns that made the Longhorns so ill-tempered. They were free creatures, mean, and wild as the buffalo and almost as tough. But they did offer the promise of profit to anyone willing to charge into the brush to find them.

Charles Siringo's classic 1885 memoir of his early cowboying days, *A Texas Cow Boy, Or Fifteen Years on the Hurricane Deck of a Spanish Pony,* described his experience roping wild cattle for the renowned cattlemen "Shanghai" and Jonathan Pierce, who then sold the herd he had helped gather for $110,000. "That shows what could be done in those days," wrote Siringo, "with no capital, but lots of cheek and a branding iron. The two Pierces had come out there from Yankeedom a few years before poorer than skimmed milk."

With the building of stockyards and a railhead at Abilene and successive Kansas towns, the gathering of feral cattle in Texas became a huge business—Texas's main business. Cattle worth about five dollars a head in Texas could be trailed to Kansas at a cost of roughly one dollar a head, then sold for up to twelve dollars—a 100 percent profit. Prices did fluctuate wildly, and many stockmen went bankrupt in the cattle trade, but thousands were willing to take the gamble. In her poem "Cattle," Berta Hart Nance spelled out the certain source of the wealth:

Other states were carved or born;
Texas grew from hide and horn.

Other states are long and wide;
Texas is a shaggy hide.

Dripping blood and crumpled hair,
Some gory giant flung it there,

Laid the head where valleys drain;
Stretched its rump along the plain.

Other soil is full of stones;
Texans plow up cattle bones.

Stamped on Texan wall and roof
Gleams the sharp and crescent hoof.

Texas Longhorns are a mongrel breed of cattle that evolved from feral members of the Spanish Berrenda and Retinto breeds. Characterized by narrow bodies, spindley legs, and enormous horns, Longhorns can survive poor forage and harsh conditions that would decimate other breeds. (Nancy Wood)

A calf is herded into a mechanical "squeeze" where it is held tight for branding, innoculating, dehorning, and castrating before it returns, stunned, to the herd. (Michael S. Crummett)

*High above the hum and stir,
Jingle bridle-rein and spur.*

*Other states were made or born;
Texas grew from hide and horn.*

According to Siringo, the feral cattle became known as "mavericks" and the work of rounding them up as "mavericking" because of one Samuel Maverick, "a chicken-hearted old rooster [who] wouldn't brand or earmark any of his cattle." Maverick simply "went on claiming everything that wore slick ears.... At first people said, 'Yonder goes one of Mr. Maverick's animals.' Then, upon seeing any unbranded animal anywhere, they got to saying, 'Yonder goes a maverick.'" Texas historian J. Frank Dobie estimated that ten million maverick Longhorns were trailed out of Texas toward the northern plains and the Rockies during the big drives between 1866 and 1890.

Although those drives gave fledgling shape to the image of the cowboy as a loner and carefree roamer, and as a fine and faithful horseman, the drovers were just hired hands that were easy to come by. The cattle speculators were the principal actors in the trail dramas, and the cattle were the only things with any value placed on them. "Our comfort was nothing," wrote Andy Adams in his *Log of a Cowboy* (1903), "men were cheap, but cattle cost money." An anonymous cowpoke complained at the end of his trailing days: "I put in eighteen or twenty years on the trail, and all I had in the outcome was the high-heeled boots, the striped pants and about $4.80 of other clothes, so there you are."

The cowboys did learn expert horsemanship in their years on the trail. And those who stayed at it developed remarkable resiliency and stamina. They knew how to work hard and how to savor a rare good time. But they lived in dread of a stampede—the *estampida*—the terror-driven rush of animals that often killed men, horses, and cattle alike. Cowboys sang and played mouth harps and harmonicas at night in efforts to settle the cows. Night riders on the flanks of the herds sang constantly—if the singing stopped, their distant partners would know something was wrong.

Cowboys worried so much about stampedes that they sang about them often, and some drovers would recite this poem about how a stampede could turn a fellow downright religious:

*Lightnin' rolls in hoops and circles,
Rain in sheets is comin' down,
Thunder rattles through the gulches,
As the hoof-beats shake the ground.
Top hands ride like likkered Injuns,
Beggin' God for the break o' day.
A stampede beats the best camp meetin'
When it comes to gettin' men to pray.*

"Other states were made or born; Texas grew from hide and horn," wrote poet Berta Hart Nance. Cattle like Showboy II from Texas in Tom Palmore's painting were—and are—enormously important to the economies of Texas and the West.

A Colorado rancher cradles a Hereford calf. Although the beef industry has suffered greatly in recent years, cattlemen hang on, hoping for improved market economies that will allow them to remain in business. (Nancy Wood)

ALMOST AS DESPERATELY AS THE COWBOYS FEARED A STAMPEDE, THE STOCKMEN dreaded the day when the supply of Texas cattle would be exhausted and there would be no more Longhorns to send lumbering up the trails to the Kansas stockyards and to the burgeoning cattle spreads in the northern plains and the Rockies. A few grizzled cowmen like Richard King, John Chisum, and Charles Goodnight understood early on that there would not always be millions of maverick cattle to be trailed out of Texas. They began to breed their own cattle on huge ranches that they pieced together with profits from selling mavericks. During the last quarter of the nineteenth century, King owned nearly 1.3 million acres of south Texas rangeland; Goodnight controlled land he owned and land he leased that totaled 1.3 million acres in the Texas panhandle; and Chisum actually owned only a relatively small amount of land, but El Rancho Grande, Chisum's ranch in west Texas and southeastern New Mexico, was almost as big as all of New England—some of it leased, some of it simply lorded over with power, prestige, and high-caliber rifles. Cattle barons like John W. Iliff of Colorado, Moreton Frewen and Alexander Swan of Wyoming, and Granville Stuart of Montana similarly controlled enormous parcels of public domain land, grazed and overgrazed by Texas cattle and managed by poorly paid cowboys—men who had expert knowledge of cattle and horses, but who knew nothing of finance and even less about bargaining for better wages.

The wealthy stockmen had to contend with an oversupplied and fluctuating beef market, with an American populace increasingly resentful of the cattlemen's private profits derived from public land, and with the advancing farms, fences, railroads, and towns that made free-range ranching an ever more complicated enterprise. The cattle kings responded by fencing in their own properties, just as the farmers were fencing in theirs. Some even had to *buy* the land they had used free of charge for years in order to continue to graze it. With increased land costs, and less land to graze, the ranchers needed a more efficient meat-producing animal than the Longhorn had proven to be. Although that gangling critter was a marvel at sustaining itself on poor forage and could almost miraculously survive in the bitterest weather and during the longest droughts, its meat was often of poor quality. Furthermore, cattlemen could no longer afford to keep a slow-growing Longhorn cow or steer to maturity before marketing it and turning it into needed cash.

The cattlemen found the solution to the problem in the importation of British breeds—first Durham cattle, then Aberdeen Anguses, Devons, and Shorthorns were brought to the Western ranges and bred to Texas cattle. Then the Hereford breed gained great popularity—a stout red cow with a white-blazed face that mothered well and was meaty; the Hereford grew quickly and could winter adequately on a steady diet of the ranchers' hay. The introduction of British cattle was so successful that it wasn't long before the long-necked cows with horns like flying buttresses became scarce, even in Texas, and cowboys were tending strange exotic beeves they would have scoffed at a few years earlier. Many cattlemen were openly sorry to see the Longhorns go; they had admired their tenacity and longevity and, along with many drovers, they missed the nomadic freedom of the open range that tending the Longhorns permitted them. In *The Longhorns*, J. Frank Dobie described the melancholy demise of the critter whose ancestors belonged to Columbus, Cortés, and Coronado:

> Range men did not in their hearts choose to exchange free-running Longhorns capable of rustling their own living, for fine-haired stock requiring endless attention; did not gladly go from the self-sufficient breed to the care-requiring breed, turning from animals that existed for them to that form of slavery enforced by all dependent possessions.

By the end of the nineteenth century it seemed that the only place to find a scrappy Longhorn was in the maudlin songs of the cowboys:

> *The cowboys and the Longhorns*
> *Who pardnered in Eighty-four*
> *Have gone to their last roundup.*
> *Over on the other shore.*
>
> *They answered well their purpose,*
> *But their glory must fade and go,*
> *Because men say there's better things*
> *In the modern cattle show.*

Cattle auctions are a rancher's means of turning cows into money. The simple theory is that a cow should sell for more money than it cost to raise it, but theories are sometimes skewed in the modern cattle business. (James A. Cook/The Stock Market)

As early as 1888, young Theodore Roosevelt, always given to hyperbole when describing the wild West that so entranced him, lamented that "the best days of ranching are over. . . . The great free ranches, with their barbarous, picturesque and curiously fascinating surroundings . . . [had created what was] perhaps the pleasantest, healthiest and most exciting phase of American existence." Roosevelt did exaggerate, of course, yet he was far from alone in understanding the epic importance of the pushing of wide-horned, cantankerous cattle across the broad back of the American plains and in sensing that the disappearance of the Longhorn signaled the end of an era—an era that many men, themselves grown "from hide and horn," would consider the time when they had most fully lived.

THE CHANGES THAT THE EARLY BEEF INDUSTRY UNDERWENT WERE OFTEN INDUCED more directly by the demands of an urbanizing America than by economic imperatives out on the ranch lands. In 1881, Gustavus Swift invented a refrigerated train car that made possible the shipping of butchered beef to the East, thus eliminating the need to haul the weightier and costlier beef on the hoof. Suddenly, much more meat per carload could reach the expanding eastern beef

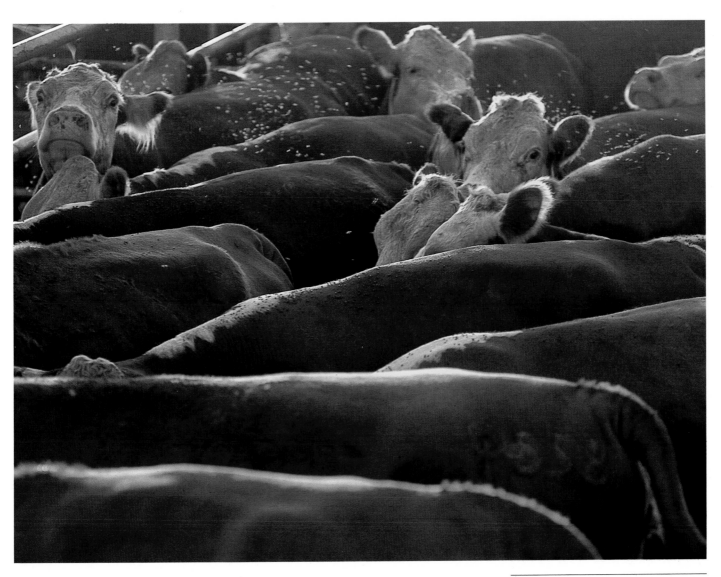

When stockmen encountered a need for
cattle that grew quicker and were more
meaty than the Longhorn, they began
importing "exotic" breeds from Europe,
Africa, and Asia like Brahmans, LEFT,
and Herefords, ABOVE. Today dozens
of breeds are raised throughout the
West. (Bill Ellzey; LEFT: Susan Felter)

Railroads have always played a critical role in the cattle business. Kansas railroads spurred the trail drives north out of Texas, and the invention of the refrigerated train car made it possible to send butchered beef to the East. And cities with giant stockyards beside the railroad tracks became the focal points of the industry. (Jonathan Blair/Woodfin Camp)

market. Then Swift developed a beef-slaughtering process carried out on what he called a "disassembly line" (like the "assembly lines" that followed it in other industries), which permitted dressed beef to be mass-produced. Cities like Chicago, Kansas City, Denver, and Forth Worth became the focal points of the cattle industry—an industry in which prices, production, and control of the distribution system were managed by urban interests. The cattlemen out in the back of beyond simply supplied the raw material.

Each stockman tried to produce as many market cows as possible in an effort to improve his profits—a situation that was encouraged by the railroads, stockyards, packing houses, and grocers, who were all happy to keep their prices low. But cattle began to dangerously overgraze the fragile rangelands—bluestem, grama, timothy, and buffalo grasses that had survived centuries of foraging buffalo were nearly destroyed by the hordes of cattle. Then in the summer of 1866 drought struck—baking the land and cracking it open—followed by a winter of fierce blizzards, whirling across the plains and leaving thousands of cattle carcasses in their wake.

Ranchers responded to the disastrous year by culling their herds even further, by increasing the importation and breeding of British cattle that could produce more meat per animal than the mongrel Longhorns could, and by raising giant hay crops to feed their animals through the long winters. The costs of hay ground and the farm machinery needed to cultivate it were huge, but those expenses were offset by the beefier cows that the hay produced and by the better prices that resulted from lower total cattle production.

During the next two decades, most ranchers fed each calf summer grass and winter hay for a cycle of about three and a half years before marketing a full-grown "fat steer." Then the depression at the end of World War I, which affected the whole agriculture industry, knocked the bottom out of cattle prices, and stockmen simply had to sell their animals sooner—before they reached maturity. But mountains of cheap grain were molding unused in the Midwest, and it eventually became a staple cattle fodder. The time it took to fatten calves from birth to market was reduced to less than two years. And the first commercial feedlots came into prominence—businesses that bought yearling calves from ranchers, then fattened them on grain for six months or so in huge factorylike feeding plants before selling them for slaughter. The feedlots added one more processing step in the chain between the raw material out on the ranch and the pot roast in the pan, but the system worked relatively well until grain prices shot skyward in the 1960s and 1970s. Expensive grain meant higher consumer beef prices—and ultimately a smaller demand for beef—but the yearling cattle brought no higher profits for the ranchers, who had to contend with ever greater fuel, machinery, feed, and land costs. Steaks, roasts, and hamburger meat grew steadily more expensive, but the prices for market cattle made merely breaking even an increasingly difficult task for most American ranchers.

Cattle still graze the barren lands of the West, but in the driest environments as many as fifty acres are required to sustain a single animal. (Scott Ransom)

The Kansas City stockyards covered more than a hundred acres in their heyday and handled a half million cattle a year. Today, with high beef prices and lowered consumer demand, cattle populations in stockyards and feedlots are dwindling.

High interest rates have recently posed still another obstacle for cow-men, according to Colorado feedlot operator Ken Monfort. "Our competition, poultry and pork and even fish now, are not nearly so dependent on the inter-est rates. They take less time to produce and therefore they're cheaper."

The beef industry has also had to contend with a growing public im-pression that other meats are more healthful and less expensive than beef. In 1982, the industry resorted to a $7.9 million television ad campaign designed to convince consumers that beef was a fine source of protein and that it was some-how *patriotic* to serve it regularly. Cattlemen were hopeful that the television commercials would make a difference, and some of them remained stubbornly optimistic in spite of the gloomy economic outlook. "Food is going to be the oil of the '80s," said Marshall Frasier, president of the Colorado Cattlemen's Asso-ciation. "We've got to bite the bullet for the time being, but I think this thing is going to turn around."

During the early 1980s, some of the stockmen who run large-scale cattle operations and who haven't had to bite the foreclosure bullet yet face a differ-ent and ironic problem: They can't find any cowboys. "It's just about as bad as it can get," said Dean Prosser, head of the Wyoming Stockgrowers Association. Prosser estimated that as many as two thousand jobs for working cowboys are currently going unfilled. There simply isn't enough money in it for the skinny-legged boys in boots and floppy-brimmed hats who stand on every street corner in every small town in the West, and few of them can throw a rope or pull a stuck calf out of its mother's womb, much less endure the isolation and the loneliness inherent in cattle ranching.

Yet there are thousands of so-called cattle ranches that wouldn't hire a cowboy or two even if the boys were standing in line waiting for jobs. These small operations—the sort that have "nineteen cows," in the words of a cynical Texas A&M agriculture professor—are one-person, part-time operations run by men and women who also work as school teachers and tax accountants, truck drivers and potato chip deliverers. Surprisingly, a Texas survey con-ducted during the 1970s showed that 18 percent of the state's five million cattle were owned by ranchers with herds containing fewer than fifty mother cows, and people with fewer than one hundred cows in their herds—still small by Texas standards—owned 38 percent of the total Texas beef population. "Peo-ple like you are just messing things up," a big-time rancher once scolded Texas writer and small-time cattleman John Graves. "You can't make a living out of a little herd like that, and nothing that you do with them is ever done quite right. But there are so damn many of you that you're interfering with the way things are supposed to be."

Graves guessed that despite the difficulty of making money off "nine-teen cows," he and the many other small-time stockmen continue to try because "we like the damned things, and our real motivation has little to do

Many contemporary stockmen complain that, at the wages they are able to pay, they cannot find cowboys willing to take on the grueling and incessant work. (Nancy Wood)

Cattle wait in a feedlot, RIGHT, before being slaughtered, processed, and placed on the table. The cowboy above prepares beef that was barbecued in an underground pit. (John Youngblut/The Stock Market; RIGHT: Jim Smith)

Some cowboys confess to actually liking cattle and to viewing their relationships to them a bit romantically. There is always a strong feeling of satisfaction in rescuing a helpless calf, RIGHT; and it is impossible to ignore the grim suddenness of death whenever a cow is slaughtered. (Timothy Eagan/Woodfin Camp; RIGHT: Bill Ellzey)

with money or labor but I suppose must be called romantic. Possibly the pull of the legendary Old West has something to do with it, for in the arteries of the purest romantics among us cowboy blood pumps hot and strong."

That may be the critical distinction between the true, old-time stockman and the part-time variety that's becoming ubiquitous in the West today. The old-time ranchers loved *ranching*, the whole complex, back-breaking mess of it, but they were ultimately indifferent to the animals that provided them with a livelihood. It was the open land and the joy of sitting proudly on horseback that obsessed them. An old joke tells of a long-time rancher who suddenly earned a million dollars from oil leases. When asked what he was going to do with his new wealth, he thought for a while, then said, "Well, I guess I'll just ranch 'til it's all used up, then look for another job."

Some of the small-scale cattlemen, on the other hand, contrary to a long legacy of cowboy contempt, do seem to possess real affection for their cows. They keep them because they like them, and for the first time in centuries, money seems to have little to do with it. On his ranch in southwestern Colorado not long ago, part-time cowman Archie Leigh found a heifer who was having trouble with her calf. Her stillborn calf had to be pulled, and her prolapsed uterus amputated once the vet arrived. Her hindquarters were paralyzed, but there was a chance, the vet said—a slim one—that the paralysis would be temporary. Archie buried the calf, fed and watered the cow, covered her with blankets, and for days looked after her like she was a child. He welded a frame to use to hoist her off the ground and fashioned a feed trough—elaborate arrangements for a single cow whose worth had been drastically diminished. But somehow he felt his attention, the time-consuming attempt that was ultimately futile, was far preferable to immediately taking his rifle out of the closet.

BUFFALO BILL'S WILD WEST AND THE NUMEROUS SHOWS THAT IMITATED IT NEVER paraded cows around their rings in the same way that they paraded horses and buffalos. Somehow, highlighting cattle would have seemed a little ridiculous. Calf roping was a regular feature of the spectacles, and cowboy performers rode, or tried to ride, bucking bulls in contests that were the forerunners of modern rodeo, but no cow was ever spotlighted because of its *cowness*.

The early writers quickly realized that a cowboy in the midst of his cows made for boring copy indeed—so they gave the lads blazing six-shooters, and plenty of opportunity to use them, to hold their readers' interest. Moviemakers barely even considered cows. Trail drives were tedious, and except for a stampede or two, and a wild time at the end of the line, little happened that was ever worth filming. Hollywood did produce one classic trail-driving film, Howard Hawks's *Red River* (1948), a popular and critical success. But it was admittedly just a remake of *Mutiny on the Bounty* in Western form, employing

Bull riding is unquestionably rodeo's most dangerous event. One rodeo veteran says bull riders must wear very small hats because they haven't got much sense. (Susan Felter)

A rodeo cowboy practices roping on a calf with plastic horns strapped to its head to simulate the horned calves in a rodeo. (Kathryn Nelson)

the same conflicts between two men and substituting cattle for breadfruit trees. The television series "Rawhide," which began a seven-year run in 1959, has been that medium's only treatment of cattle driving. And in 1972, two surprisingly good trail-driving Westerns appeared: Dick Richard's *The Culpepper Cattle Company* and Mark Rydell's *The Cowboys*. Both films treated the drives as elaborate rites of passage for the men and boys who undertook them, and although John Wayne had survived the mutiny in *Red River*, he became its victim in *The Cowboys*.

Cattle did not get prominent treatment, however, in any of those three films, or in the television series. When viewers did catch glimpses of cows, they often looked more like rotund Herefords than the raunchy Longhorns that were actually on the trails. For the most part, moviemakers dealt with the West's cows by ignoring them, turning cowboys into *gunboys*, throwing away their ropes, and filling their hands with iron.

Rodeo has succeeded in paying a bit of homage to cattle, albeit by choking them with nylon ropes, cranking their horns, and fastening uncomfortable flank straps on enormous bulls before spurring them out to buck. Rodeo cattle are the sport's primary link with *tradition*, and every rodeo announcer in the nation is always mindful of that fact, endlessly telling his audiences that rodeo's modern events have descended from the cattle contests that early cowboys held on holidays and during roundups. But the cattle also remind rodeo's observers that cowboying has always been a man-versus-animal affair, one that man ultimately wins, at least part of the time.

Cattle receive far rougher treatment in rodeo than do horses. Calves are normally running at about 25 miles an hour when the lassos settle around their necks and suddenly pull taught: Broken necks are not rare. Steers are thrown to the ground by wrenching their horns and heads. And the bulls used in bull-riding contests are "psyched up" with electric prods before being released into the arena. Rodeo hands swear that far more people get hurt in rodeo than do animals, and more than one rodeo cowboy has suggested that people who think rodeo is cruel to stock should ride a bull to see who it is that gets hurt.

Bull riders do get hurt with gruesome regularity, so often that one rodeo veteran assumes they "take a size 6½ hat. That's what they take because they haven't got much sense." Rodeo bulls are huge and unpredictable and mean. Unlike a horse, which almost never goes after a cowboy after kicking him off its back, a bull will "hook and hunt" its rider once it has thrown him to the ground. "When you saw a guy get stomped [by a horse]," observed rodeo writer Douglas Kent Hall, "you could not say the horse did it on purpose. But there was no question about a bull. A bull would go out of his way to find you, to butt and gore and kick the living piss right out of you."

Nonetheless, the cowboys admire the imposing bulls because they embody power, virility, and courage. Bulls are unquestionably *masculine*—the antithesis of the passive cows and steers that are simply herded and fattened and turned into hamburger. Rodeo cowboys make much of their own masculinity, and despite bull riding's dangers, it is seen by many as the best way for a real man to pit himself against the toughest male of them all.

But "then all of a sudden [the cowboy] is whipped down and finds himself looking at the bull's balls," Hall wrote about a cowboy who has just been bucked off a spinning bull,

> looking at the two bells hanging from his belly, watching the sharp hooves coming down.... The bells swing and clang, hitting him in the side of the head. The brindle bull ducks back, that crumpled horn hooking, hunting...[but] the announcer is saying, "It looks like this cowboy's okay." Which is exactly what every announcer will say if they see that you can even twitch.

Cattle receive far rougher treatment in rodeo than do horses. In steer wrestling, cowboys throw the animals to the ground by wrenching their horns and heads. (Douglas Kent Hall/FotoWest)

THE BREEDING THAT PRODUCES THE SIZE AND POWER AND CRIMINAL INTENT IN rodeo bulls is similar to the much heralded "hybrid vigor" breeding that produces quick weight gain and stout, disease-free bodies in today's beef cattle. By deliberately crossing breeds of cattle, breeders can produce animals with a variety of dominant desired characteristics—whether they are bulls with the strength to kick and spin till the lights go out, or cows with wide hindquarters that facilitate the birthing process.

Rodeo bulls normally possess a considerable amount of Brahman blood. The Brahman breed was established in India and first imported to semitropical areas of North America, where it was presumed it could withstand the heat. A Brahman is characterized by a massive hump on the back of its neck, by a gray, slick-haired hide, and by an altogether disagreeable temperament. But few rodeo bulls are purebred Brahmans. A little Angus or Shorthorn blood—for hybrid vigor—somehow makes them just that much meaner.

When it comes to breeding beef cattle these days, it is true that the stalwart British breeds have lost some of their luster in the eyes of the cattlemen whose annual income is determined by the weight of the cows they sell. For all their desirable characteristics, the Herefords and other British cattle just aren't as big as other "exotic" breeds. In the 1950s, cattlemen seeking weightier calves began importing European *Charolais, Simmental, Limousin, Maine-Anjou, Chianina,* and other breeds in efforts to "beef up" their herds. Then they became fascinated with the idea of crossbreeding, and after a few years they had created stabilized new breeds from their crosses. The first of the "American" breeds was the Santa Gertrudis, established on Texas's King Ranch even before the arrival of the European cows. The Santa Gertrudis is a cross between the Shorthorn and the Brahman that produces a massive sorrel cow suited to humid south Texas. The Brangus followed, a cross between Brah-

228

Cowboying has always been a man versus animal affair, a confrontation in which the man always wins—except on those occasions when rodeo bulls can extract a little revenge. (BOTH: Fred Baldwin and Wendy Watriss/Woodfin Camp)

The Longhorn, ironically, is now more than just a momento of the past. Because of its tenacity and its ability to thrive on little feed, it is making a comeback in lean economic times. (Jack Parsons/FotoWest)

man and Angus; then came the Beefmaster, a Brahman-Shorthorn-Hereford cross. Today, new breeds appear all the time, each supposedly the perfect cow, according to the geneticists responsible for it, each a guaranteed moneymaker, according to the breeders who supply the registered bulls and mother cows.

And there is no small irony in the fact that the lowly Longhorn is making a comeback. In the midst of lean economic times, a breed that can gain weight on marginal forage, that needs less winter feed than other breeds, that is disease-resistant, and that has an impressively high reproductive performance is bound to catch the cattlemen's attention. Purebred Longhorn breeders throughout the West are doing excellent business, and herds of fat British, European, and Brahman cattle are spotted more and more frequently these days with a few anachronistic creatures whose ribs poke through their hides and whose horns seem to span the pastures.

But ultimately, these animals are all just cows, humble members of the genus *Bos*—the rancher's means of making money, the very things he spends his money on. They are stupid and ornery; they are troublesome and mean; but they are the hide and horn, muscle and sinew that gave shape to the West, that made it a kind of pastoral paradise for some, regardless of its bleak economics—a place where cattle *belonged* on the land, and where long-suffering cowboys belonged among them.

Cowboys scatter as a bull breaks loose. Despite being troublesome and at times downright mean, cattle are the foundation for all that the cowboy has become. (Douglas Kent Hall/FotoWest)

8

A few days after General George Armstrong Custer and his troops were killed at the Battle of the Little Bighorn in Montana in the summer of 1876, William F. Cody, already a star of stage melodrama, joined the army's 5th cavalry as a scout in an attention-seeking effort to avenge Custer's death. During a skirmish at War Bonnet Creek, Nebraska, a fortnight after the Little Bighorn battle, Cody killed the Cheyenne leader Yellow Hand, then quickly scalped him, claiming "the first scalp for Custer!" Later that same year, Cody produced and starred in The Red Right Hand; or, Buffalo Bill's First Scalp for Custer, *a dramatized exaggeration of the events at War Bonnet Creek. Cody went so far as to display Yellow Hand's scalp outside the theaters where the melodrama was prested in a macabre attempt to attract audiences.*

Only a decade later, however, the renowned Sioux medicine man Sitting Bull began a yearlong tour with Cody's Wild West show, and numerous other Sioux had become regulars in the show—parading, performing tricks and feats of horsemanship, and taking part in mock battles between the "Indian warriors" and the "veterans of the United States Cavalry."

It is a testament to Cody's lifelong blending and blurring of reality and fiction that fully half of the Indian actors in his Wild West reenactments of the Battle of the Little Bighorn had participated in the actual battle. Cody ultimately avenged Custer's defeat only by hiring many of the men who had contributed to it to act out the grisly events of the battle in front of curious audiences throughout the United States and Europe.

232

CHAPTER EIGHT

COWBOYS & INDIANS

I WAS SURE STRUCK BY [THE INDIANS'] WAY OF LIVING," TEDDY BLUE ABBOTT wrote, reminiscing about his Nebraska boyhood, "and so one fall I made up my mind to run away and go on the buffalo hunt." But since he was only twelve years old, and Indian relations with settlers were tense in the fall of 1873, an elderly chief of the Pawnee hunters who had passed by Teddy Blue's home refused to let him join them, telling the boy: "Your father say we stole you, make plenty trouble for Indians."

When the Pawnees passed by Abbott's home again en route to their winter encampment, Teddy Blue went on,

> they had over a hundred horses packed with dried buffalo meat, dried tongues, and robes. I went down to their camp and had a feast, and when they pulled out, my heart went with them. I made up my mind that as soon as I got to be a man, I would join them. But they were moved down to Indian Territory and I never saw them any more. I did get to be a cowboy, though, and as Charlie Russell used to say, we were just white Indians anyway.

Although frontier cowpunchers like Teddy Blue understood the subtle similarities of cowboy and Indian life, the rest of America and the world has always considered them to be antithetical to each other. Cowboys and Indians became mythical foes—embodiments of the primeval West and of the West of burgeoning private enterprise. And in the dim collective national memory, cowboys and Indians are the only real images—however falsely envisioned—many

James Bama's painting, A Sioux Indian, LEFT, *reflects the pride and integrity of a contemporary Sioux; but to millions of Americans, indians remain wooden figures who are not quite real.* (ABOVE: *Jerry Downs*)

239

Anglo actors Jon Hall and Sherry Moreland starred in When the Redskins Rode. *Hollywood costume departments repeatedly used basic feathers-and-beads garb that seldom came close to authenticity.*

people retain of the American frontier. Indeed, there is probably nothing that is less descriptive of the reality of the West nor more readily identified with it than the phrase "cowboys and Indians."

Historical cowboys who rode the northbound trails had only casual contact with America's tribal peoples. They rounded up feral cattle that roamed on Indian lands; and the cattle trails were carved across those lands as well—sometimes with permission from the tribes in exchange for a modest fee, often with the brazen disregard for Indian rights that was characteristic of the attitudes of the majority of western immigrants. The cowboys often camped near bands of migrant Indians; they traded food and hides and horses with them; and, according to Teddy Blue, "the cowpunchers as a rule had some sympathy with the Indians. You would hear them say [that the Indians' treatment by the government] was a damn shame."

But the six-shooter cowboys created in books and movies became bitter enemies of the "redskins"—who were portrayed as vile, treacherous, and subhuman. The cowboys were the good guys; they were always right, and they always won. Many contemporary Indians have remarked that as children growing up under the influences of the Saturday afternoon serials and the blazing television Westerns, it was impossible for them not to cheer for the cowboys and the cavalry just like everyone else. They felt no identification with, nor support for, the Indians they saw on the screens. Those characters were too brutal, too inhuman, to reflect any truth about themselves, their families, or their aboriginal heritage.

The Pilgrims who established the Plymouth Colony were happy to accept the kindnesses and gifts of food and clothing provided by Pemaquid and Wampanoag Indians during their first harsh winter in America in 1620. Nonetheless, Pilgrim father William Bradford described the new land as an "unpeopled" country—"being devoyd of all civil inhabitants, where there are only savage and brutish men, which range up and downe, little otherwise than the wild beasts of the same."

That representation of the continent's native people as uncivilized heathens changed little during the succeeding two and a half centuries. It was an essential element of the systematic struggle to "subdue" the Indians: Only if they were perceived as far different from the rest of humankind could they be so wantonly hated, mistreated, and killed.

It wasn't until late in the nineteenth century, when America's "Indian problem" had been nearly solved by calculated annihilation, that the country as a whole developed a passive curiosity about its native inhabitants. Numerous Sioux tribesmen began tours with Buffalo Bill's Wild West that were to last many years, reenacting frontier battles, offering schoolchildren their first glimpses of "real Indians," whose exotic lives they had only read about. Chiefs in the resplendent battle dress of their tribes were featured in Theodore Roosevelt's inaugural parade in 1901; and the first experimental films produced a few years later were often about Indians who were much like other people, possessed of problems and emotions and pride.

But as the medium matured in the 1920s and the demand for on-screen action increased, directors simply focused on the simplistic and fictitious struggles of brave cowboys trying to win the West from the Indians—who were once again portrayed as conniving creatures who pillaged settlements, stole livestock, and subjected innocent women to fates worse than death.

During film's first fifty years far more Indians were killed in the movies than were actually gunned down on the western plains during the preceding hundred years. And when Hollywood finally created its first Indian heroes—Debra Paget in *Broken Arrow* (1950) and Burt Lancaster in *Apache* (1954)—it seemed perfectly reasonable for Anglo actors to be given the parts. Max Factor's "Indian Tan" makeup had been liberally applied in Hollywood for decades; it wasn't until Chief Dan George appeared as Old Lodge Skins in Arthur Penn's 1970 film, *Little Big Man*, that a real Indian portrayed a *reel* Indian in a central role.

Few Westerns are made these days and few general-subject films feature Indian characters or actors. When Indians are dealt with in film or fiction, they are most often treated as historical relics, as people who shot arrows and wielded Winchester carbines back in the wild West, but who are now merely curious anachronisms. The truth is, however, that Native Americans are still vitally connected to the western land and its towns and cities. Despite the loss of most of their ancestral lands, despite chronic unemployment and persistent social problems, their numbers and their economic and political power are growing, as is their pride in their *Indianness* and their ability to endure.

Yet it is wonderfully ironic that in many Indians' love of horses and rodeo and country music, their attachment to pickup trucks, wide-brimmed hats, and fancy boots, they have become the West's most vivid and natural cowboys. For a hundred years, virtually anyone—including generations of Indians—has been able to be a "cowboy." Surely that has been part of its special lure. But as Teddy Blue discovered and Hollywood seems finally to be learning, you have to have always been an Indian to be an Indian.

When the 1954 film Apache *featured Hollywood's first Indian protagonist, it wasn't surprising that the role went to Anglo actor Burt Lancaster. Indians, it was widely assumed, couldn't act.*

CHRISTOPHER COLUMBUS CALLED THE INHABITANTS OF THE NEW world onto whose shores his boats washed in 1492 *Indios*. Popular history holds that since Columbus had hoped to reach India, he called the inhabitants *Indians* because he assumed he had reached his destination, or at least a part of Asia. But some historians, American Indians among them, sharply disagree, claiming that Columbus was searching for a nation that was then called Hindustan, and that when he used

Trail cowboys had only occasional contact with tribal peoples. They often pushed cattle across Indian lands and sometimes asked for help in locating stray animals, as depicted in Frederic Remington's The Long Horn Cattle Sign.

Buffalo Bill Cody reinacted the taking of the "first scalp for Custer" in the 1913 film, The Indian Wars.

the Italian *Indio*, he meant "native"—a word derived from the Old Latin *indus*, meaning "in" or "of." The Indians were *of* the new land; they belonged to it, and they were "so tractable, so peaceable," Columbus wrote to the King and Queen of Spain about the Tainos on the Caribbean island of San Salvador, "there is not in the world a better nation. They love their neighbors as themselves, and their discourse is ever sweet and gentle, and accompanied with a smile, and though it is true that they are naked, yet their manners are decorous and praise-worthy." But the natives' fatal flaw was that they knew nothing of the Gospel; they were heathens. And Columbus quickly concluded that the *Indios* should be "made to work, sow and do all that is necessary and to adopt our ways."

For the next three hundred years, the Spanish and English and other European settlers of the continent dedicated themselves to that end—to converting the Indians, to altering their customs and lifestyles, to destroying their livelihoods, and when all else failed, to destroying *them* in the name of civilization. But through it all, there was occasional passive admiration for the Indians' "nobility," "simplicity," and "innocence." Early-nineteenth-century writers such as James Fenimore Cooper created images of faithful, subservient Indians like Chingachgook, Natty Bumppo's noble friend in *The Last of the Mohicans*. Yet the admiration was always restrained, and as the immigrants' demands for land increased, the image of the Indian diminished proportionally. In the 1840s, Cooper himself wrote in "Civilizing the Red Man" that "as a rule the red man disappears before the superior moral and physical influence of the white." That blunt suggestion that the Indians wouldn't so much adapt as *disappear* was preceded by the statement of the aptly named Nathan Slaughter, a character in Robert M. Bird's 1837 novel *Nick in the Woods; or, The Jibbenainosay*: "The only good Indian is a dead Indian." Possessed of a perverse staying power, that sentence was repeated in books and movies for the next hundred years.

A few years after Bird's novel appeared, journalist Horace Greeley said virtually the same thing in slightly dressed-up language in *An Overland Journey*: "These people must die out. There is no help for them.... Squalid and conceited, proud and worthless, lazy and lousy, they will strut out or drink out their miserable existence, and at length afford the world a sensible relief by dying out of it." Young men should go west, Greeley asserted, and if at all possible they should kill a few Indians along the way.

Thirty years later, in the 1870s, when immigrants outnumbered Indians two to one in the region between the Missouri River and the high wall of the Sierra Nevada, journalists were still calling for annihilation: "When next, if ever, the savages shout their battle cry," wrote John Finerty, "civilization must meet them with a stern front and crush them relentlessly."

By 1880 the crushing was nearly complete. Kit Carson had forced the Navajo to endure the Long Walk from their homeland in Arizona to an army garrison at Bosque Redondo, New Mexico. Four thousand of the fourteen thousand Cherokee that were marched from Georgia to Indian Territory in Oklahoma died along that Trail of Tears. Hundreds of defenseless Cheyenne—men, women, and children—had been murdered by psychotic Colonel John M. Chivington in the massacre at Sand Creek, Colorado. The valiant Apache bands led by Cochise and Geronimo still roamed southern Arizona and New Mexico, but the many Sioux tribes had been confined to reservations in Dakota Territory. With the help of the Northern Cheyenne, the Sioux had succeeded in defeating Custer, but that victory in 1876 was the beginning of the end of their freedom. In retaliation for Custer's death, the Oglala, Brulé, Blackfoot, Minneconjou and Hunkpapa Sioux, and the Northern Cheyenne who had fought at the Battle of the Little Bighorn were subjected to more than a decade of harassment, treaty manipulation, and killing, which finally ended with the Wounded Knee, South Dakota, massacre on December 29, 1890.

The genocide that was underway in the West was not universally approved of, but there were few loud voices speaking out against it, principally because even those who sympathized with the Indians' plight understood that virtually nothing could impede the march of settlement and the inevitable subjugation of the natives. When Helen Hunt Jackson wrote in *A Century of Dishonor* in 1881 that the "government's repeated violations of faith with the Indians …convicts us as a nation, not only of having outraged the principles of justice, but of having made ourselves liable to all punishments which follow upon such sins," a storm of discussion followed. Jackson's book was a careful documentation of the cheats, frauds, and broken promises that had characterized the nation's negotiations with the tribal peoples. But despite her hard evidence and the force of her presentation, Jackson's book was soon forgotten. She was considered naive. People said she must not have witnessed the Indians' brutality firsthand. An irate Teddy Roosevelt, who had not yet gone west to see for himself, was certain that Jackson was sorely mistaken—that the settlers had behaved far more ethically than the Indians had: "The most vicious cowboy has more moral principle than the average Indian," he retorted, using the cowboy for comparison because he was considered at the time to be the most unsavory of all the West's Anglo immigrants. Even the awful cowboy was better than the Indian, said the man who twenty years later would openly envy the life of the cowboy and pose with Indian leaders at his presidential inauguration.

"We are vanishing from the earth," said Geronimo after the Apache had been defeated, "yet I cannot think we are useless or [God] would not have created us."

ALTHOUGH MUCH OF BUFFALO BILL CODY'S NATIONAL REPUTATION HAD BEEN BUILT around the exaggerated telling and retelling of his having secured "the first scalp for Custer" at the Battle of War Bonnet Creek two weeks after Custer's death in 1876, Cody was never an ardent Indian hater in the mold of Custer and Chivington; and throughout his life he refused to answer when asked how many Indians he had killed, contending that he had never killed anyone who

Today many Americans enjoy the spectacle of "exotic" Indian costumes displayed in parades and circuses, but few have any real contact with the lives led by traditional tribal peoples. (*Bernard Plossu/FotoWest; LEFT: Dan Budnik/Woodfin Camp*)

Iron Tail, who traveled extensively with Cody's Wild West, was the model for the Indian profile on the buffalo nickel. Three contemporary Indian cowboys, seen in profile, RIGHT, intently watch the action at a rodeo. (RIGHT: James Balog)

wasn't trying to kill him. "The defeat of Custer was not a massacre," Cody said in retrospect, years after the Battle of the Little Bighorn. "The Indians were being pursued by skilled fighters with orders to kill. For centuries they had been hounded from the Atlantic to the Pacific and back again. They had their wives and little ones to protect and they were fighting for their existence."

It was a daring decision on Cody's part to hire Indians as melodrama actors in 1878, only two years after Custer's defeat and at a time when national anti-Indian fervor was at its highest. But audiences responded with curiosity rather than outrage, and the "real Indians" became major attractions.

When The Wild West gave its first performances in 1883, Indian riders in tribal dress were featured prominently, and they participated in reenactments of Indian and cavalry battles. Although Cody was often somewhat paternalistic toward the Indians who worked for him, he genuinely cared about their well-being. He knew how important they were to his show's success. When Luther Standing Bear, a Sioux who traveled with Cody for several seasons, complained that the show's cowboys always gave the Indians the roughest mounts to ride, he was astounded when the following day Cody quietly directed the cowboys to henceforth ride those same unruly horses. And Standing Bear recalled that when the show Indians were served cold, leftover pancakes in a hotel in England, Cody cornered the restaurant manager and said: "Look here, Sir, my Indians are the principal feature of this show and they are the one people I will not allow to be misused or neglected. Hereafter, see to it that they get just exactly what they want at meal time."

Cody achieved a real coup when he convinced the renowned Hunkpapa Sioux medicine man Sitting Bull to travel with The Wild West during the 1885 season. Sitting Bull had previously toured with another exhibition and had been very unhappy with his treatment. When he agreed to join Cody's troupe, he demanded $50 a month, a very good wage, plus all the money he could earn independently by having his picture taken.

Being displayed like exotic curiosities must have been degrading at times for the Sioux and other tribal peoples who traveled with Cody. Yet an implicit acknowledgment of their personal integrity nonetheless accompanied their wide celebrity. Cody went to special lengths to treat Sitting Bull with dignity. He never required him to participate in the mock battles; and during each performance Sitting Bull was announced with great fanfare, and then he would ride alone into the arena, where for a few moments he was spotlighted as the sole attraction. "It is almost impossible today to understand the courage of the old Sioux," wrote political scientist and historian Vine Deloria, himself a Sioux, "...aware, perhaps, that some disgruntled patron in the audience, seeking to avenge the popular general, might take a shot at him. That such an incident did not occur is, I believe, testimony to Buffalo Bill's genius in emphasizing Sitting Bull's stature and humanity."

Jeff Chandler portrayed Apache leader Cochise in Broken Arrow, *an extremely popular film that was praised for its sympathetic treatment of the Apache point of view.*

When Sitting Bull left The Wild West, Cody presented him with a gray dancing horse that Sitting Bull greatly admired and a size 8 white Stetson hat that became his most prized possession. When one of the medicine man's relatives dared to put the hat on years later, Sitting Bull angrily grabbed it back, saying: "My friend Longhair gave me this hat. I value it very highly, for the hand that placed it upon my head had a friendly feeling for me."

At the same time that Sitting Bull, Kicking Bear, Young-Man-Afraid-of-His-Horses, and other Sioux leaders were touring with Cody, they were still officially regarded as troublemakers by federal agents in charge of the huge Sioux reservations. Cody had long been designated a special agent by the Bureau of Indian Affairs and had been put under bond to return Indian performers to their reservations when their show contracts were concluded.

When tension flared on the Pine Ridge Indian reservation, South Dakota, in the fall of 1890, Cody was asked by General Nelson "Bear Coat" Miles to travel to the reservation to meet with Sitting Bull and to persuade him to go to Chicago to confer with Miles. The army planned to take Sitting Bull prisoner, believing him to be the principal force behind the pan-Indian fervor created by the ghost dance, a widely practiced ritual performed in anticipation of the coming of an Indian messiah, that the army strangely feared would lead to renewed Indian wars. But Cody never got to see Sitting Bull again. A local Indian agent who was afraid Cody would botch Sitting Bull's capture or tip him off to the army's intention to take him in, quickly convinced Washington authorities to rescind Cody's special-agent status, and the old showman left the reservation soon after he arrived. A few days later, Sitting Bull was shot through the head in a skirmish when army troops and Indian police surrounded his cabin to take him away to prison.

When the ghost dance violence came to an end and the Sioux formally surrendered on January 16, 1891, nineteen Indian prisoners were briefly sent to the army prison at Fort Sheridan, Illinois, then were sentenced for their crimes to travel to Europe with the Wild West show. It was a strange punishment, but in retrospect no stranger than most of the other government dealings with the Indians; and it was fitting that although Cody had been unable to save Sitting Bull's life, he was able to offer an alternative to prison or the squalor of reservation life to the medicine man's comrades. In March, Cody was once again granted Indian agent status, and a hundred Indians set sail on the steamer *Switzerland* and joined Buffalo Bill and the show in France.

BUFFALO BILL PLAYED A VITAL ROLE IN SETTLING THE ANTI-INDIAN HYSTERIA THAT had infected much of the nation during the final years of the Indian wars. With his special gifts for image-making and sensing what entertainments and characters would capture the public's imagination, he transformed the figure of the cowboy from ruffian to rangeland hero, and he convinced many Americans that the Indians, however different their lives and customs, were not the treacherous people they had long been imagined to be.

Although the cowboy that Cody created remained a heroic figure in the melodramas, stories, and movies that succeeded The Wild West, the images of proud, courageous, and dignified Indians who had been integral to the show disappeared with its last performances in 1917. The dime novelists had always needed action in their stories; they needed simple plots, heroes and villains that could be easily identified; and above all they needed the loud and steady crack of rifle fire. Dashing and daring cowboys became ideal hero material, and Indians—together with assorted Mexican bandits and gangs of cowboys-gone-wrong—made perfect villains.

With the enormous popularity of the dime novels, it was no surprise when Thomas Edison chose Western shoot-em-ups patterned after them as fitting subjects for his penny arcade peep shows that swept the nation in the mid-1890s. Edison's newfangled mutoscope machines showed short films like *Sioux Ghost Dance* and *Parade of Buffalo Bill's Wild West*; but unlike Cody, Edison's filmmakers presumed that any attempt at authenticity in the portrayals of the lives and customs of the Indians was a waste of time and money. *Parade* was a documentary of sorts: An immobile camera rolled as Cody's show parade passed by. But *Sioux Ghost Dance* was nothing but sensational fiction. The "Indians" it presented were just white actors jumping around, but the ghost-dance violence on the reservations was still alive in the memories of most Americans, and they flocked to the arcades to see what the dance had *really* been like.

When the first narrative films were made in the opening years of the twentieth century, brief attention was given to Indians as people. Films like *Ramona* (1910), *A Squaw's Love* (1911), *An Indian Wife's Devotion* (1911), and *Indian Massacre* (1912) attempted to present Indians as people rather than as a swarming faceless terror, although in *Indian Massacre* director Thomas Ince attempted to create "real" Indian characters only to heighten the drama that surrounded their slaughter.

As Western movies became one of the medium's principal forms in the 1920s, the individual images of the American Indians were quickly and completely homogenized. In just a few years, Hollywood succeeded in bringing about what hundreds of years of close contact between the tribes had not accomplished: the disappearance of cultural distinctions between the tribes. Indians in the movies were seldom Iroquois, Arapaho, or Creek; they were just Indians. Members of a tribe that supposedly dwelt on the Great Plains would sport Mohawk haircuts, sleep in Cheyenne teepees, and wrap themselves in Navajo blankets. What did it matter? The Indians were simply foils for the cowboys and cavalrymen. According to Phil Lucas, whose recent five-part public television series, "Images of Indians," documented Hollywood's treat-

A participant in a tribal ceremony beats a drum as he sings. Although many Indians now assume cowboy personas, traditional rituals and customs remain important. (Edward Klamm/ FotoWest)

A Navajo cowboy leaves his hogan and his mother behind and heads out to saddle his horse. The Navajo ride throughout the desert plateaus and canyons, herding their cattle and sheep. (Paul Chesley/Photographers Aspen; RIGHT: Michael Freeman/Bruce Coleman, Inc.)

Jay Silverheels, as Tonto, the faithful friend of the Lone Ranger, epitomized the token "good Indian" that was featured in many films.

ment of Native Americans, a film studio's wardrobe department had three basic Indian costumes: "the Sioux or plains kit, Apache garb and Other"—each readily adaptable to the visual whimsy of directors and cinematographers.

The hundreds of Westerns produced in the early twentieth century embedded strong stereotypes in the minds of moviegoers—movie stereotypes that became supposed fact by mere force of repetition. Miscegenation, a common concern, was treated with curious and quiet acceptance when Anglo frontiersmen married compliant Indian "squaws" but was treated with disgust in cases where savage Indian men were presumed to want to rape every Anglo woman they encountered. In William S. Hart's 1916 silent movie, *The Aryan,* one title reads: "Oft written in letters of blood, deep carved in the face of destiny, that all men may read, runs the code of the Aryan race: 'Our women must be guarded!' " By the end of the film, the Indians have gotten the message. In *Winchester '73* (1950), Shelley Winters contemplates the prospect of that fate worse than death when she and a cavalry patrol are surrounded by Indians. James Stewart hands her a pistol and tells her she has only a few bullets to use. She nods in stoic acceptance and says, "I understand about the last one."

Suicide bullets weren't always handy, of course, and movie plots often called for Indians to take Anglo women and children captive. The movie Indians never tried to ransom them, and it was never clear why they bothered taking them. Movies like *The Searchers* (1956) and *Two Rode Together* (1961) by John Ford contended that living with Indians somehow made the captives crazy. It was an interesting notion: The Indians themselves weren't considered crazy—just savage—but they induced mental disorders by holding Anglos captive in a world too much unlike their own.

Although Indians *en masse* were seldom portrayed sympathetically, individual Indians sometimes emerged as good and decent people, especially if their characters fit either the old chief or the faithful friend mold. The wise Indian shaman appeared hundreds of times—perhaps most memorably in Ford's cavalry film, *She Wore a Yellow Ribbon* (1949)—uttering earthborn truths about the need for love and understanding and living in peace with the "white brother." The faithful friend, the Indian scout who helped the cavalry or the rangers find the redskins, was epitomized, of course, by Jay Silverheels, who appeared as Tonto in the very popular television series "The Lone Ranger," which appeared from 1949 to 1956, and which was followed by a Lone Ranger film that was released as the series ended. The Lone Ranger is a Texas Ranger who has been left to die by merciless outlaws. Tonto nurses him back to health and then has nothing better to do than spend the rest of his life with the *Kemo Sabe,* ferreting out injustice. Tonto is faithful, all right, but other than that there isn't much to him.

Other Indian good guys who began to appear in the 1950s were more believable characters than Tonto was, but they were always played by Anglo actors. *Broken Arrow,* a 1950 film based on Elliott Arnold's novel *Blood Brother,* is often considered a "breakthrough" in the treatment of Indian issues. In it, Jeff Chandler plays the Chiricahua Apache leader Cochise; Debra Paget is his comely daughter; and James Stewart is the Indian agent who befriends the Apache and falls in love with and marries Cochise's daughter. She is soon killed, of course, because in 1950 an interracial marriage was still a touchy subject, but her death helps both the Indians and the Anglos learn to live in peace.

A spate of films that were at least marginally sympathetic to Indians followed *Broken Arrow's* huge commercial success, starring such unlikely "Indian" actors as Burt Lancaster, Audrey Hepburn, Rock Hudson, Elvis Presley, Cyd Charisse, Donna Reed, and Martin Landau. Ricardo Montalban and Sal Mineo had central roles in Ford's final film, *Cheyenne Autumn* (1964), based on Mari Sandoz's passionate book about the incredible 1,500-mile trek of the Northern Cheyenne in 1878 from an Oklahoma reservation back to their Yellowstone homeland. The film was poorly edited, then drastically cut just prior to release, but it was a historically careful and visually stunning portrayal of the Northern Cheyenne, as well as a sobering reversal of the stereotyping and anti-Indian sentiments that had so often been a part of Ford's earlier pictures. "They are a very dignified people—even when they are defeated," Ford said in a British interview during the making of the film. "Of course, it's not very popular in the United States. The audience likes to see Indians get killed. They don't consider them as human beings—with a great culture of their own."

At the beginning of the 1970s, while the Vietnam war still plagued the American consciousness, several revisionist Westerns appeared that were motivated by liberal guilt and that compared the atrocities on the western plains with the killing of innocent people in Southeast Asia. In Ralph Nelson's *Soldier Blue,* the My Lai massacre is retold in frontier American images, using the Sand Creek massacre as a brutal allegory. And Arthur Penn's *Little Big Man,* based on Thomas Berger's largely ignored novel of the same name, examines the Cheyenne and their treatment by the government through the eyes of the 121-year-old Jack Crabb, an Anglo who was raised as a Cheyenne—a "Human Being"—and who is continually shamed by the cruelties and atrocities inflicted by his own race. *Little Big Man* was filmed in 1970, three-quarters of a century after the first Western films were made, but it was the very first movie to give an Indian actor a protagonist's role. The Canadian actor Chief Dan George received an Academy Award for best supporting actor for his warm and humorous portrayal of the Cheyenne shaman Old Lodge Skins. Yet it was hard to know whether the award was made more to applaud George's screen performance or to tacitly acknowledge and apologize for the industry's seventy-five years of assuming that real Indians couldn't act. Moviemaker Ernest Alfred Dench had observed as early as 1915 that "to act Indian is the easiest thing possible, for the Redskin is practically motionless."

Chief Dan George won an Oscar for best supporting actor for his role in Arthur Penn's Little Big Man, *starring Dustin Hoffman. It was the first Hollywood movie to give an Indian actor a central role.*

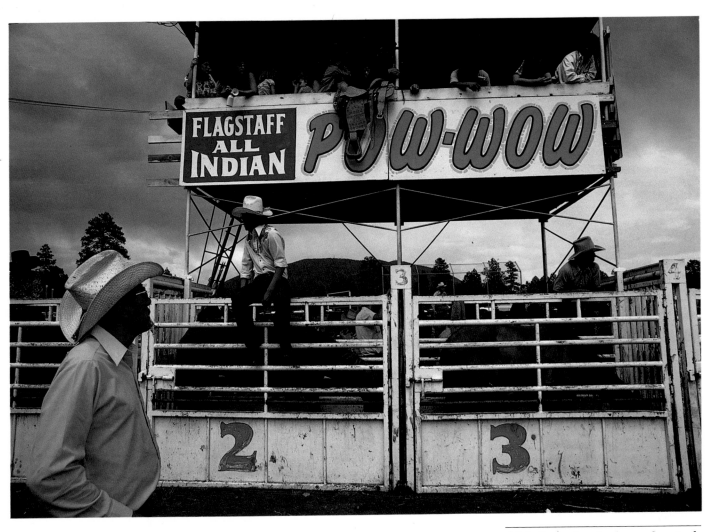

All-Indian rodeos have recently gained great popularity throughout the West. Indian cowboys compete for prize money and points during a long and grueling season which culminates at the National Indian Rodeo Finals in Albuquerque each November. (BOTH: John Running)

Evidently no one had reconsidered the question in the intervening years.

In 1976, Robert Altman directed an ambitious reexamination of the treatment of Indians and Indian images in *Buffalo Bill and the Indians, or Sitting Bull's History Lesson*. Altman effectively drew attention to the blurred lines between myth and reality in the life of Buffalo Bill, played by Paul Newman. But in his zeal to portray Sitting Bull and the show Indians as the West's true heroes, he created an often vile, egomaniacal, and misanthropic Buffalo Bill—a characterization that debunks the outlandish image of Cody as a frontier super-hero, but that replaces it with another image that is just as untrue. Like so many Westerns before it, Altman's treatment of the Indians is simple and naive. They are in this case quite remarkably good and wise, and that is that.

At a 1982 symposium entitled "American Indian Image on Film" at the University of New Mexico, a panel of filmmakers, actors, and activists was asked what films to date had been entirely successful in their portrayals of Indians. The panel members could not name a single one.

COWBOYS AND INDIANS ARE "AMERICA'S LONGEST SURVIVING SIAMESE TWINS," said literary historian Donald L. Kaufman, and his metaphor is an apt one. They have become strangely inseparable, joined at gut level by a populace that needed raw and blatant representations of victor and vanquished to explain the winning of the West, representations begotten not by history itself but by the creators of historical fiction. Of all the myths of the West that are less fact than fiction, the myth of the savage Indian pitted against the courageous cowboy is surely the most readily comprehended, as well as the most absurd. In simplified historical terms, the reality of the Indian in the West is the genocide of the tribal cultures, the stealing of lands, and the repeated disregard for individual rights and freedoms. That is a historical truth. But the celluloid images of marauding redmen who burned barns and farmhouses, ambushed wagon trains, raped and killed, and finally were wiped out by a cowboy culture that revered civilization and had the courage to protect its entrance into the West are also *mythically* true, simply because they have been accepted for so long.

Historical truths are facts, but mythical truths are explanations of what we have chosen to believe. "I don't feel we did wrong in taking this great country away from [the Indians]," said John Wayne, Hollywood's most renowned Indian fighter. "There were great numbers of people who needed new land, and the Indians were selfishly trying to keep it for themselves." Wayne's statement may not square with the facts of the broken treaties and the barren reservations, but it is the fiction we have chosen to protect us from the gruesome reality of the Indians in the West—a kind of "cowboy" truth that we have crafted out of the rich resources of the mythic process.

Real Indians, on the other hand, are invisible to most Americans today,

Joel McCrea played the title role in the 1944 film, Buffalo Bill, TOP LEFT. Although countless Hollywood films were about Indians, few showed any concern for accuracy or objectivity. Tables were turned in Robert Altman's film, Buffalo Bill and the Indians (1976), BOTTOM LEFT, in which Paul Newman portrayed a drunken and egomaniacal Buffalo Bill. The Indians in his employ were made out to be the West's true heroes.

Three Indian cowpokes are Street Strollin' *in this painting by Joe Jaqua. Many Indians present themselves as cowboys because the myth and its trappings appeal to them.*

although claiming a little "Indian blood" is curiously fashionable among certain Anglo sets. We have named towns and states, lakes, rivers, and mountains after the Indians, but the Indians themselves have disappeared from most regions. There are the Washington Redskins and the Cleveland Indians, but they are ball clubs, not cultures—and the owners of those teams see nothing shameful in designating a race as a mascot. The Washington White Boys or the Cleveland Caucasians will never take the field—that notion is obviously absurd—but Indians can be mascots because they still aren't quite real. They may make jewelry and rugs, sell margarine on television, and cause an occasional minor political fuss, but other than that they are simply historical relics that sometimes turn up like pottery shards in the dry desert ground.

But the popular image of the Indian as a relic cannot take hold in such states as South Dakota, Montana, Arizona, and New Mexico, because there the contemporary Indian presence is too strong. The Crow, Navajo, Hopi, Pueblo, and Sioux peoples still retain strong tribal identities; their religious rites and secular customs survive not as curiosities but as vital elements of their day-to-day lives. Moreover, among members of the tribes whose numbers are small and whose distinct tribal identities have nearly vanished, there is nonetheless a strong and strengthening pan-Indian identity, a realization among Blackfeet, Ute, Apache, and Cherokee that they share common interests and problems, a common history of defeat, but a longer history of endurance.

And they share the cultural effects of western myth-making. Just like everyone else in the West, the Indians have confronted the enticing images of Gary Cooper, John Wayne, and the Marlboro Man, and the romantic images of good lives nourished by good country. The mythic idea that cowboys are free and strong and connected to the land they live on is particularly vivid to many Indians, and it gives the cowboy mystique and its material accouterments a special lure. On every reservation in the West, sloe-eyed boys who have begun to wear their hair in traditional styles again nonetheless turn broad felt hats, pearl-snap shirts, and tight-legged Levi's with the imprint of a Skoal tin worn into the pocket into an obligatory uniform. They are proudly and vocally Indian—no more mute and *ugh*-ing imagery for them. But they are visual cowboys as well, not by way of affectation, but by way of casual cultural choice. The clothes they wear, the music they search for on the radio, the horses and trucks that grab their fancies, are the same as those that dazzle the young Anglo buckaroos. They are *Indians*—or Piute or Choctaw or Cheyenne—but they are western Americans as well, as captivated by the cowboy mystique as anyone else. Two lines from the song "Cherokee Fiddle," by singer and songwriter Michael Murphey, spell out the blurred images of our Siamese twins these days:

Oh, the Indians are dressing up like cowboys,
And the cowboys are puttin' feathers and turquoise on.

The ranks of the Professional Rodeo Cowboys Association include an increasing number of Indian rough-stock riders who are easily as foolhardy as their Anglo counterparts. (John Running)

Today the phrase "cowboys and Indians" still doesn't describe much about the West. The stereotypes simply aren't as static as they used to be. Like Teddy Blue and Charlie Russell before them, many Anglo cowpokes can still be considered "white Indians"—forever set slightly apart from the cultural mainstream. And many Indians are cattle ranchers and country musicians and rodeo stars—just as cowboy as anyone under a hat.

Eight all-Indian rodeo circuits travel to reservation arenas throughout the West during the summer, culminating in the Indian National Rodeo Finals in Albuquerque each fall; and the Professional Rodeo Cowboys Association's ranks include an increasing number of strapping Indian cowboys with astonishing talents for staying on sidewinding, psychotic horses. In Window Rock, Arizona, each September, the Navajo Nation Fair and Rodeo is a modern-day Wild West show, attracting as many as seventy thousand Indians from throughout the country. Sometimes a token Anglo country music star takes the role of Sitting Bull and is featured as an honored curiosity in the midst of the jubilant Indian entertainment.

The Navajo have even begun to finance the film projects of young Indian filmmakers, visionary men and women who spurn the Hollywood legacy and who want to make poignant and valuable statements about what it means to be Indian in the 1980s, who want to create a bonafide Indian film industry and vital roles for Indian actors. It's doubtful that Indians will be cast in Anglo roles in their films, however—even though acting like an Anglo is easy.

A Navajo horseman, LEFT, and a Navajo barrel racer pose for portraits. They are among the thousands of American Indians for whom cowboy and Indian lifestyles logically and comfortably converge. (BOTH: John Running)

9

Young Bill Cody hired on briefly in 1868 as a government detective—a job that involved searching for army deserters and chasing after thieves of government property. Occasionally he worked jointly with James B. Hickok, a deputy U.S. marshal whom Cody later convinced to appear with him on stage as "Wild Bill Hickok." Hickok had become a famous gunfighter and a lawman whose exploits perilously skirted both sides of the law, but he disliked performing and quickly gave it up and went back to work as a lawman.

Cody, on the other hand, loved to perform and was happiest when he was able to exhibit his astonishing shooting skills. The Wild West's printed program for 1886 carefully pointed out, however, that Cody was not a "fancy shot" but rather "a practical all-around shot," a man who could use his rifle to hit "objects thrown in the air while galloping at full speed," or presumably to bring down a dangerous outlaw if the need arose. Bat Masterson, gambler, buffalo hunter, sportswriter, and former marshal of Dodge City, Kansas, wrote that Buffalo Bill "could shoot a pistol with deadly accuracy," but he noted that Cody had never been involved in a gunfight duel, "perhaps due to the fact that he was never called upon for such a purpose," his skills being so renowned.

Cody understood that the threat of a gun could often accomplish more than the gun itself. During his stint as a justice of the peace in Nebraska, Cody once waived the need for the defendant in a burglary case to post a bond. He simply pointed his old buffalo rifle at the accused and got his point across.

CHAPTER NINE

THE LAW
OF THE GUN

THE EDITOR OF THE ABILENE, KANSAŚ, *CHRONICLE* DECLARED ON JUNE 8, 1871, that the time had come for civilized people to quit carrying guns. Law and order had come to Abilene in the form of Chief of Police James B. "Wild Bill" Hickok, who had declared that he would vigorously enforce the Kansas statute against carrying weapons inside towns and cities. The editor was pleased. "That's right," he wrote. "There's no bravery in carrying revolvers in a civilized community. Such a practice is well enough and perhaps necessary when among Indians or other barbarians, but among white people it ought to be discontinued."

Bona fide law enforcement and judicial agencies were not established until long after the first immigrants had made themselves at home in the West. In the early days, the citizenry had to become its own protector, forging flimsy rules maintaining basic order rather than establishing judicial principles. And in wild and chaotic cattle towns like Abilene, the gun was the only arbiter of order available. Samuel Colt's six-shot revolvers and a series of Winchester carbine rifles became the "peacemakers" only because they represented a life-threatening and often fatal alternative to peace. Hickok wanted to disarm Abilene's rowdy populace not to help make the people more "civilized," but in order to give *his* law—his guns—more force by lessening everyone else's firepower. Because institutional law remained scarce in the frontier West, guns were a ready substitute; they could coerce, and they could quickly punish.

Violence has always been basic to America's people, regardless of their degree of civility. The first immigrants to the continent waged war against

Early Texas Rangers, LEFT, and fictional lawmen like William S. Hart and comrades, administered a justice backed not by the tenets of law, but by the force of gunfire.

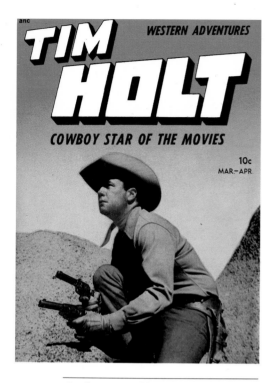

WESTERN ADVENTURES

TIM HOLT

COWBOY STAR OF THE MOVIES

10c
MAR.–APR.

Cowboy actors like Tim Holt used their six-guns to defend law and order and, more important, to provide plenty of action.

the indigenous peoples they encountered; the thirteen colonies revolted against the mother country and fought for their independence; the War of 1812 and the Mexican War were waged for land and to bolster national pride; in the Civil War the nation took up sides and fought itself. And in between the wars, individuals and vigilante groups fought and shot each other over disputed property and damaged honor, and out of a strange, obsessive need to affirm the power and inviolability of the American individual.

Westerners were no more inherently violent than other Americans, but their banditry and murder seemed more pronounced, more callous, and more colorful because it was played out in an anarchistic environment in which everyone looked out for himself, and in which "Judge Colt and his jury of six" handed down capital sentences and swiftly carried them out. Power rested in the hands of the wealthy, and the powerful used weapons to maintain their positions. The weak and disenfranchised peoples also used weapons—to protect themselves against wild animals, against the assaults of their neighbors, and against the capricious might of the powerful.

Trail cowboys were not powerful or prestigious figures. They were merely cattle drovers—horseback employees of the powerful cattle barons—and their six-shooters were simply tools for killing rattlesnakes, signaling to a partner, shooting a crippled horse, or stopping a stampede by firing into the herd. On rare occasions the drovers did turn their guns against rustlers or cow-town pimps or card sharks, momentarily becoming lawmen and dispensing an ill-defined personal justice etched with gunpowder. But the trail hands didn't see themselves as particularly good marksmen or their deeds as in any way heroic. To a cowboy, a good horse and a stout rope were far more important than a pistol, which was simply a useful and necessary tool.

Cowboys didn't emerge as expert marksmen or obsessive protectors of order and virtue until they were reinvented in the shows and novels and movies. Erastus Beadle created the first fictional cowboy gunfighter in an 1887 pulp magazine, and from that simple beginning, the cowboy, his guns, and the upholding of the law became inseparable, an imaginary convention that came to define the mythic cowboy more clearly and more emphatically than any connection to cows or horses or open spaces could. The popularized cowboy became an American knight in leather armor. From Owen Wister's Virginian to John Wayne, the cowboy heroes were men who knew right from wrong, by God, and who were always ready to shoot it out to prove it.

The mythical cowboy who lives by his guns is a far cry from the scrappy range hand who winced when he pulled the trigger, and it is the mythical cowboy whose image remains alive. The prosaic historical cowboy just couldn't compete with the bold and brave fictional marksman who became a symbol of the American culture's abiding conviction that it had to fight, and fight continually, to secure peace and justice. The firearms themselves, which

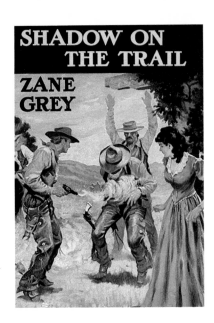

Guns blaze and a man falls in Charles M. Russell's Death of a Gambler. *The popularized cowboys of fiction and early illustration were American knights in leather armor who used six-shooters instead of swords.*

During the heyday of the B-Western, countless movies featured singing cowpokes like Roy Rogers who would capture the badmen, then croon a Western tune.

were originally used only for personal protection, came, strangely, to symbolize social order. Proponents of the proliferation of guns declared that gun ownership was directed not only at defending individuals but at protecting American ideals as well. And within the context of the cowboy myth, the man with the revolvers strapped to his hips became not only powerful but ethical, a compelling embodiment of all that was strong and all that was good.

G UNS WERE COMMONPLACE IN THE NINETEENTH-CENTURY WEST. Bankers and lawyers, shopkeepers and teamsters, farmers and bartenders and railroad men owned firearms and considered them essential. Although killing was a rare and grave offense, it was nonetheless a possibility that one had to defend against. Small settlements and towns often went for months or years unable to afford or to find a peace officer. And it was widely understood that the law-abiding marshal at work in a remote Dakota town might well be the same desperado who had escaped from a New Mexico jail a year earlier. So people simply sought to defend themselves. They tucked .45 caliber Colts in their trousers, put single-action Smith and Wesson pistols inside their coats, and kept Winchester '73 .44 caliber rifles tucked away in closets and in scabbards that hung from their saddles. Some women chose to carry the petite "Ladies' Friend," a tiny two-shot weapon with a razor-sharp dirk attached to the barrel, which was fastened on the inside of the wearer's thigh, nicely concealed but always handy.

When real danger presented itself in the form of a bank robber, or news was received that a gang of horse thieves was headed in their direction, the citizens often banded together to form vigilante committees—long on fervor but sometimes as lawless as the outlaws they confronted. Captured horse thieves were quickly hanged; captured known or suspected murderers seldom lived long enough to be hanged. Some vigilante posses—from the Latin *posse comitatus,* meaning the power of the county—became violent fraternal organizations —secret societies that offered only very cryptic explanations of how they administered their special brand of justice. Yet while some citizens' groups unquestionably made a mockery of justice, others made honest attempts to replace anarchy with order. A vigilante committee in Las Vegas, New Mexico, posted this notice of exasperation in 1880:

> To murderers, confidence men, thieves.
> The citizens of Las Vegas are tired of robbery, murder, and other crimes.... They have resolved to put a stop to crime even if in obtaining that end they have to forget [the] law and resort to a speedier justice than it will afford. All such characters are, therefore, notified that they must either leave this town or conform themselves to the requirements of law, or they will be summarily dealt with.

It is ironic that the objects of the early vigilante actions—the scoundrels who pillaged property and livestock and murdered innocent people—were often called cowboys, the name that would later become synonymous with the noblest ideals of western law enforcement. "Cowboys," explained U.S. Attorney E. B. Pomeroy in 1881, "is a generic designation…and in the local significance includes the lawless element that exists upon the border, who subsist by rapine, plunder and highway robbery, and whose amusements are drinking orgies and murder." That same year, an eastern journalist named John Bauman who traveled in the West discovered that the cowboy was "shockingly cruel, nasty in temper and unbridled in tongue…he is the perfect fiend." A Topeka, Kansas, newspaper advised its readers that a cowboy "generally wears a revolver on each side, which he will use with as little hesitation on a man as on a wild animal. Such a character is dangerous and desperate and each one generally has killed his man."

The only effective defense against the corrupt cowboys, people were warned, was a good weapon, one with enough firepower to efficiently protect them from the advancing menace. A Plattsmouth, Nebraska, newspaper advised against choosing small-bore pistols for protection: "Suppose you hit your man mortally? He may still run in on you and rip you up with a bowie knife before he falls dead." But a cowboy struck by a stout bullet from a good heavy gun "gets faintish and drops at once." If there was no legal system to protect the citizenry, then an individual simply had to do it alone, with the aid of an iron pistol and fast lead bullets.

Rowdy Texas was ironically the one region of the frontier West that developed a fearsome, efficient, and renowned law enforcement agency, one that sometimes was roundly criticized for its decided preference for sudden force over the slower considerations of guilt or innocence. The Texas Rangers were first organized in 1823, then formally commissioned in 1835—"twenty-five Rangers whose business shall be to guard the frontier between the Brazos and Trinity rivers." The Rangers had no uniforms, flags, or other official paraphernalia, and they each had to supply their own horses and make their own decisions about who constituted threats to public order and how to deal with the troublemakers. One Ranger boasted that "a Texas Ranger can ride like a Mexican, trail like an Indian, shoot like a Tennessean, and fight like the very devil." Armed with Colt revolvers and percussion rifles, the mounted Rangers far outmatched the Mexicans with their muskets and the Comanche, whose only weapons were bows and arrows. They fought border thieves and train and stage robbers and captured John Wesley Hardin, Sam Bass, and later, Clyde Barrow, all infamous Texas murderers. But one of their principal jobs was to protect branded Texas cattle, the state's essential natural resource, from "cowboy" raiders, who preferred taking the risks involved in stealing someone else's Longhorns to the grueling work of rounding up feral animals of their own.

Actor James Arness appeared for nineteen years as Marshall Matt Dillon on "Gunsmoke," television's longest-running prime-time series. His sidekick, Chester, was portrayed by Dennis Weaver.

"The desire to play cowboy is one of the principal inducements to buy guns," wrote cowboy historian William W. Savage, Jr. Pistol enthusiasts like those at right participate in quick-draw competitions throughout the West. And movie gunmen like the Cisco Kid can still relive their shoot-em-up roles. (BOTH: Bud Lee)

As early as 1835, the New York *Star* warned that Texan "cow-boys" were "mostly muscular, powerful men and great marksmen; and whether at a distance with the rifle, or in close combat they will be terrible." The term *cow-boy* referred only to the cattle raiders until the era of the Kansas trail drives was nearing completion; the Texas Rangers worked in alliance with men called "drovers"—not cowboys—in efforts to stem the thievery. But the drovers weren't necessarily the most righteous of men either. Most of them were the object of the Rangers' scorn at one time or another—but their cattle had to get to Kansas, and the thieving cow-boys posed an unacceptable impediment to free enterprise. Stealing cattle was plainly against the law, and the drovers, most of whom weren't particularly adept with rifles or pistols, forcefully attempted to uphold the law whenever the need arose. They were only moderately successful, however—occasionally wounding or killing a cattle thief, occasionally losing a finger or killing a cow in the process.

At the end of the trail, in the frowzy Kansas cattle towns that received the Longhorns and their tenders, the thousands of drovers were considered a far greater threat to "western civilization" than were the scattered cow-boy raiders. By the time they reached their destinations after months on the trail, the drovers were primed for a little revelry and excitement, and their festive high jinks were frequently interpreted as blatant criminal mischief by the prim entrepreneurs in the towns—who were nonetheless always willing to help relieve the drovers of their newly received wages.

Most marshals did at least attempt to maintain order by requiring the drovers to surrender their weapons when they entered the town, but guns were commonly concealed by drovers and townspeople alike. In any case, the lawmen in the Kansas cattle towns were usually far better armed than the rowdy trail boys they tried to keep in line. "The police wore their revolvers openly, as a symbol of authority and as a warning to troublemakers that, if need be, they would use them in their efforts to maintain or establish order," wrote Joseph G. Rosa in *The Gunfighter* (1969), a study of the frontier law of the gun. "It is not, therefore, particularly surprising that the cowtown police killed more people than did the bad men they were keeping in check." According to Rosa, between 1870 and 1885, only forty-five men were shot to death in the Kansas towns of Abilene, Ellsworth, Wichita, Dodge City, and Caldwell combined— less than one per year per town—nearly all of them cowhands, gamblers, and pimps gunned down by the supposedly peaceable lawmen.

When Buffalo Bill first produced The Wild West in 1883, he acquired an old stagecoach that had served Deadwood and other Dakota Territory towns, and he used the Deadwood stage in reenactments of horrible Indian ambushes. But tragedy had no place in Cody's entertainments, so the coach was always

As Sheriff John T. Chance in Rio Bravo, *LEFT, and as Marshal Rooster Cogburn in* True Grit, *John Wayne epitomized the fictional cowboy gun- fighter. He said his favorite roles were those in which he portrayed "the rough, lusty, wild guys who can change into heroes for the cause of liberty."*

The cowboy myth has succeeded in
equating violence in defense of law with
virtue. Sheriffs' posses and cowboy color
guards ride in rodeo parades throughout the West, proudly demonstrating
that the spirit of the cowboy lawman is
alive and well. (Fred Baldwin and
Wendy Watriss/Woodfin Camp; LEFT:
Lewis Portnoy/Spectra-Action)

Wild West star Johnnie Baker was billed as "The Marvellous Marksman." It was Cody's remarkable showmanship that began to change the image of the cowboy from ruffian to courageous hero.

rescued in the nick of time by riders in cavalry costumes, by the "Old Scout" himself, and even by "cowboys" who otherwise performed only in riding and roping acts.

It must have seemed strange at first when Cody trusted the daring "rescues" to ruffian cowboys whom his audiences associated with thievery, debauchery, and murder; no one else had yet begun to portray cattle drovers as heroic and moral men. But the crowds responded enthusiastically—they *liked* something about the cowboys—and before long Cody began to headline "Buck Taylor, the King of the Cowboys," a lanky Texas drover who had worked on Cody's Nebraska ranch. Taylor, Johnnie Baker, "the Cowboy Kid," and other cowboy stars whom Cody created were portrayed as fine, upstanding young men with indomitable spirits, great courage, energy, skills, and self-confidence. As Wild West audiences around the country clamored for more cowboy acts, Cody began to use the word *cowboy* prominently in Wild West publicity. The showman didn't have to apologize for his cowboys—no apologies were necessary. And soon there was little need to convince the public that the cowboys were good guys. That was simply understood. Cody's only real task was to supply enough cowboys to keep his audiences captivated. Many drovers were understandably appalled at the idea of giving up the open country for Cody's dirt arenas, but the showman enticed his cowboys with good wages and a chance to see the world.

It was Erastus Beadle, publisher of the Beadle Half-Dime Library series, however, who turned the cowboy hero into a gunfighter. Prentiss Ingraham, one of Beadle's most prolific staff writers, dashed off *Buck Taylor, King of the Cowboys; or, The Raiders and the Rangers* after seeing Taylor perform in The Wild West, and more fictional cowboy tales quickly followed. The figure of the cowboy proved to be perfectly suited to Beadle's highly successful series of adventure yarns that portrayed good winning out over evil, wrongdoers being justly punished, and heroes receiving the love that was their due reward. Gunplay was essential in the dime novels. It provided suspense, danger, and lots of action that enabled the cowboys to save the day and to dispatch the bank-robbing and woman-stealing villains to mortal judgment quickly and straightforwardly. The West of the dime novels was rough and savage, full of men who had no scruples, and guns were a cowboy's only protection. His two six-shooters symbolized power, efficiency, and the morality of killing when it was done to preserve order and ethical standards.

By the time "An Old Scout's" *Young Wild West's Whirlwind Riders* appeared in 1903, the pulp writers had even succeeded in making shooting *fun* without going so far as to openly endorse it:

> Look out, thar, ye pesky gimcracks! I'm goin' to begin shootin' right away! I'm a whistlin' streak when I git goin', an' I feel one of my spells comin' on now.... I'm Buster Bill, ther boss of Border Bend, an' when I git mad I spit out

red hot coals. Ther fun is goin' to begin! Here she goes! *Crack! Crack! Crack!*

Just then, however, Young Wild West, "a specimen of the true boy of the Wild West," steps in to put a stop to the festive firing—but he does so by shooting the guns out of Buster Bill's hands. The message was clear: The only way to put a stop to unwarranted shooting is to do some shooting of your own. It was a message that soon became a staple in Western fiction. "Gun-packin' in the west since the Civil War has growed into a kind of moral law," says Tom Lassiter in Zane Grey's *Riders of the Purple Sage* (1912). "An' out here on this border it's the difference between a man and somethin' not a man." Grey's gunfighters are always moral men: They only kill the bad guys who've got it coming to them; and their weapons are bold proof of their masculinity, proof that they are real men:

> [Lassiter] unbuckled the heavy cartridge belt, and laid it with the heavy, swinging gun-sheaths in [Jane's] lap.
>
> "Lassiter," Jane whispered, as she gazed from him to the black, cold guns. Without them he appeared shorn of strength, defenseless, a smaller man. Was she Delilah? Swiftly, conscious of only one motive—refusal to see this man craven by his enemies—she rose, and with blundering fingers buckled the belt round his waist where it belonged.

When cowboy gunfighters first appeared in film, their holsters and cartridge belts buckled tightly to their narrow hips, the pistol became an even more obvious phallic symbol. Cowboy heroes were emasculated without their guns; with them they were potent and brave, and they presented alluring images to the chaste women who sublimated their sexual desires by fawning over the cowboys' six-shooters and their prowess at using them.

Early William S. Hart films repeatedly featured "good badmen"— outlaws who were reformed by the persuasive influence of a pure and loving woman. "I reckon God ain't wantin' me much, Ma'am, but when I look at you I feel I've been ridin' the wrong trail," reads a title in *Hell's Hinges* (1916) when the hero discovers righteousness in the beautiful heroine's face. It was a common metaphoric treatment, one that was repeated in many subsequent Westerns: Guns were masculine and sexually powerful; correct behavior was equated with a woman's beauty. And when the good gunman and a pure woman fell in love, the mythic law of the gun—the protection of virtue and order by force—was made symbolically legitimate.

One of Hollywood's most enduring conventions was the rewarding of virtue and valiant gunslinging with the love of a good woman. Badmen always had their whores and dance-hall gals, but they never knew abiding love. Only the heroes deserved it and ever achieved it. Sometimes the conquering gunman, sad but stoic, simply moved on after he had saved the day, doomed like Shane to remain a proud loner forever. But in countless other Westerns, a woman's

Shooting acts and demonstrations by high-spirited, confident cowboys highlighted virtually all of the shows that imitated The Wild West.

As Marshall Will Cane in High Noon, *Gary Cooper portrayed an archetypal lawman who, against all odds, defends the townspeople and the principles of virtue.*

love was the reward for fighting for right, and it symbolized the peace that was an inherent companion of justice. In two of his most enduring Westerns, *The Westerner* and *High Noon,* Gary Cooper portrayed an archetypal cowboy hero, self-confident and soft-spoken, who fights alone to defeat the lawlessness of vigilante cattlemen and a vengeful outlaw gang. In both films, Cooper combined the steel nerves and stalwart determination of the gunslinger with a quiet and gentle civility that became his trademark, one that further entrenched the image of the noble yet violent cowboy in the public's imagination.

In the hundreds of inexpensively produced B-Westerns made from the 1920s to the 1950s, the happy ending for the law-protecting hero was absolutely assured. The audiences, both adults and children, who flocked to these movies wanted to see simple right-beats-might stories, and they saw them, filled with outlandish plot conventions that were repeated with amazing regularity: Villains died quick, unlingering and hygienic deaths; there was no blood, no muss or fuss. The lawman never lost his fine white hat; even in the midst of the roughest fights or the fastest gallops, it stayed properly on his head. The hero was unerringly accurate with his rifle and guns; he could shoot the gun out of an outlaw's hand without nipping so much as a finger, and he never missed and shot an outlaw's horse. The lawman could recover instantaneously from a fight with a dozen badmen, coming up clean and unrumpled, his teeth intact, a smile on his face. And, of course, the cowboy was always a handsome man, square-jawed and strapping, possessing superior social graces, a soothing voice, and a revolver that never had to be reloaded. The Bs created a West in which things were as they *ought* to be: Crime didn't pay; guns killed only those who deserved it; the cowboy hero got the prettiest gal; and the skies were not cloudy all day. And to top it off, most of the cowboys could sing. In their spare time—between fist fights, six-shooter duels, and thrilling rescues—they would strum their pearl-inlaid guitars and yodel a tune or two.

Looking back, it is surprising that audiences reacted so warmly for so long to the Pollyanna personas of the singing cowboys and to the outlandish ways in which they defended the frontier law. Yet until the mid-1950s, they offered steady assurance that America was a good and just place. The formula Westerns were a great escape from the war-weary and depression-ridden reality of America in the first half of the twentieth century, and it didn't matter that the cowboy characters and the badmen were nothing like the lads who had ridden the early ranges or the rustlers who had stolen their cattle. The fictional cowboy was vital because he was heroic, not because he was a reasonable facsimile of history. And his mythic heroism had far more cultural force than the *facts* surrounding the cowboys could ever have had.

When moviemaker Harry Sherman turned Clarence Mulford's Hopalong Cassidy into a film character in 1935, Hoppy underwent a profound transformation that was necessitated by the hero myth of the movies. Mulford's

A new sheriff rides into town in E. C. Wood's painting, Enter the Law. An image of quiet strength has always been essential to the lawman myth.

285

Brand inspectors like the men on these pages are charged with certifying that any cow or horse that is about to be sold really belongs to the seller. "There's no book that will ever teach you," says a Wyoming inspector. "Actually, we are a kind of detective." (ALL: Steve Collector)

Contemporary peace officers like Ed Bell, retired chief of police in Grants, New Mexico, and Charlie Sedillo, RIGHT, sheriff of Sierra County, New Mexico, dress like cowboys and emulate the law-men of the old days. (BOTH: Gregory Heisler)

Hopalong was a tough, crusty, alcohol-swilling, tobacco-spitting loudmouth who actually herded cows, and who "hopped along" because of an old bullet wound in his leg. Metamorphosed on screen, Hopalong, as portrayed by William Boyd, was a blond, black-clad super-hero who never smoked, drank, cheated, or thought unclean thoughts, and who walked without a trace of a limp. Boyd was so thoroughly identified with the movie character (whose strange name was never explained) that he never again played another role.

The enormously popular figure of the Lone Ranger introduced the element of mercy into the lawman myth. Created by George W. Trendle in 1932, the Lone Ranger is a brave Texas Ranger who is the only one of six lawmen to survive an outlaw ambush. After his gunshot wounds are nursed by Tonto, a friendly Indian who happens along, the Lone Ranger digs six graves (one to fool the outlaws) and then puts on a mask and vows to get revenge. But the silver-bullet–shooting Ranger aims his guns only to wound, never to kill, and he gets revenge in countless episodes by simply delivering the bad guys to the local authorities and then suddenly riding away, leaving the townspeople to ask admiringly, "Who *was* that masked man?"

The Lone Ranger and Tonto appeared over a span of more than two decades on radio and television, in comic strips, and finally in film—where Clayton Moore and Jay Silverheels roamed tirelessly across the silver screen defending purity and truth and battling injustice to the thrilling strains of the *William Tell* Overture, which all too obviously associated them with that daring, arrow-shooting hero of an earlier era.

The singing cowboys who rode the media trails at the same time—Roy Rogers, Tex Ritter, Gene Autry, and others—were all crack shots as well, of course, and they never ventured anywhere without their revolvers strapped to their sides. But their guitars were far more valuable to them than were their rifles, and they became the first of the heyday heroes who were guaranteed to save the day not because they were such expert marksmen, but simply because they were so unerringly *good*. They replaced the law of the gun with a code of correct behavior, implying to rapt young audiences that violence might not be necessary if everyone would just do as he or she should. Gene Autry even endorsed "The Ten Commandments of the Cowboy," a guide to proper living distributed to church groups and scout troops that dictated that:

1. A cowboy never takes unfair advantage—even of an enemy.
2. A cowboy never betrays a trust.
3. A cowboy always tells the truth.
4. A cowboy is kind to small children, to old folks, and to animals.
5. A cowboy is free from racial and religious prejudices.
6. A cowboy is helpful, and when anyone is in trouble, he lends a hand.
7. A cowboy is a good worker.
8. A cowboy is clean about his person and in thought, word, and deed.

As portrayed by William Boyd, Hopalong Cassidy was a super-hero who never drank, cheated, or thought unclean thoughts. Clayton Moore's Lone Ranger, LEFT, introduced the element of mercy into the lawman myth. He shot only to wound, never to kill.

Actor Clayton Moore became world-famous in his film and television role as "The Lone Ranger." Today he says that wherever he goes he still leaves a silver bullet as a souvenir. In The Naked Spur, *RIGHT, James Stewart portrayed a gunman anxious to get revenge. (ABOVE: Bud Lee)*

9. A cowboy respects womanhood, his parents, and the laws of his country.

10. A cowboy is a patriot.

They were ten admirable traits, of course, and young buckaroos who lived up to them would certainly grow up to be exemplary citizens. But it is interesting that the ten "commandments" described an ideal cowboy who barely resembled the historical trail hand that spawned the myth, and they completely ignored the fictional lawman who lived not by rules but by action. The guns that once symbolized the individual's power to protect himself were replaced by quasi-religious ethical standards to which every good "cowboy" was presumed to adhere. The society was coming of age, becoming more collective, less individualistic, and it appeared that the mythical gunman might just disappear if the cowboy became a saint who always played by the rules.

Yet there was one cowboy star who proved that the public would still respond to a cowboy hero who wasn't endlessly altruistic, but who was what he called "a more normal kind of fella." His name was Marion Morrison, but because the Hollywood studio bosses didn't believe a guy named "Marion" could ever have won the West, they dubbed him "John Wayne," and he became the greatest cowboy gunfighter of them all. His favorite Western characters were the "rough, lusty, wild guys who can change into heroes for the cause of liberty." And in four decades of films such as *Stagecoach, Fort Apache, Red River, She Wore a Yellow Ribbon, Rio Bravo, The Man Who Shot Liberty Valance,* and *The Sons of Katie Elder,* Wayne presented an enduring image of a "normal fella" who was nonetheless larger than life, who was—in the words of film critic Gene Siskel—capable of inspiring "grown men to curl up in his arms and ask about the Old West," as if they were reliving the cowboy dreams of their boyhoods. Wayne himself said, "I don't play heroes—good guys. I'm not what you'd call a villain, either. But one thing I make sure of—the guys I play are believable human beings.... Following my dad's advice, if a guy hits me with a vase, I'd hit him with a chair. That's the way we played it."

Wayne played it to self-parodied perfection in his Oscar-winning performance in *True Grit* (1969), but his legacy is more than his roles in over 140 films. John Wayne the actor, John Wayne the *cowboy,* will endure because his lifelong persona was that of a cowboy who lived not by rules but by instinct, who represented a vanishing era in which individuals were strong and had to depend only upon themselves. Wayne's cowboys were free, and their freedom was affirmed by their violence. Their guns were both proof of their freedom and their only means to defend it.

"You pit a big strong man against [the hero], Wayne said in reference to his Western films, "with both their lives at stake, and there's a simplicity of conflict you can't beat. Maybe we don't tell it with poetry like Homer did, but in one way we've even got him beat. We never let Hector turn tail and run from Achilles." Cowboys with true grit, of course, never run away from a fight.

USENSE ARMAS
WINCHESTER
PARA TODOS MODOS DE TIRAR Y CARTUCHOS
WINCHESTER PARA TODAS CLASES DE ARMAS

PIDASE LA MARCA

W

Buffalo Bill Historical Center, Cody, Wyoming.

Cowboy and western imagery is often used in ads by firearms manufacturers who want to connect their products to the lure of the legendary West.

IN THE SAME WAY THAT JOHN WAYNE WAS ATTRACTED BY THE "SIMPLICITY OF conflict" embodied by two men fighting to the death, Americans have always been lured by the imagined simplicity of resolution inherent in gunfire. From the time when Hispanic and British immigrants first explored the American continent, guns and rifles have offered comfort and protection from the unknown and the feared, from the hated and the mistrusted. Ennobled by the Second Amendment to the Constitution, guns embody the ideals of self-protection and individual freedom to millions of Americans. And the pervasive power of the cowboy myth has succeeded in equating weapons not only with liberty but with virtue. Outlaws have always turned their six-shooters against society, of course, but the western law of the gun has convinced us that firearms can only be fought with firearms. "If Guns Are Outlawed Only Outlaws Will Have Guns," read bumper stickers on pickups and Buicks throughout the West. It is a sentiment that to many minds is crystal clear: Guns are all the protection we've got, the only effective force separating us from the tyranny of lawlessness. Although violence and bloodshed are the bitter legacy of guns, the only alternatives to the proliferation of the guns of virtue are servitude and the loss of liberty. And besides, the gunfighter cowboys have proven that killing is quick and easy. Villains can be dispatched without pain or trauma, and the act of justified killing— what modern policemen refer to as a "righteous shoot"—insulates the cowboy killer from what otherwise would be the enduring anguish of having taken a life.

"The desire to play cowboy is one of the principal inducements to buy guns," wrote William W. Savage, Jr., in *The Cowboy Hero* (1979), his examination of the cowboy myth in popular culture. "[But] because the experience of having shot someone or of having been shot by someone is not shared by most people...the gun thus remains a toy, a loud and picturesque cinematic prop."

Yet the enticement to play is powerful. The National Rifle Association—the nation's strong anti-gun control lobby—advertises shooting as a fine family hobby in which participants can "relive American history with our authentic costumes and firearms." At a magazine shop in southwestern Colorado, eighteen different gun magazines are stocked for sale. They are filled with ads by Colt, Winchester, and other firearms manufacturers that claim that their weapons are "an American legend" and "The Gun That Won the West." Cowboy imagery abounds in the articles and advertisements, and the cowboy myth does double duty—selling the products and justifying the proliferation of guns as a means of keeping Western heritage alive. Small-town marshals and even some city policemen wear cowboy hats and boots and emulate the lawmen of the old days; pistol enthusiasts throughout the West hold "Fastest Gun Alive" competitions in which latter-day gunfighters square off against each other using slippery, hair-trigger six-shooters loaded with waxen bullets. And at Billy Bob's in Fort Worth, Texas, the world's largest country nightclub, an arcade game pits potential quick-draw artists against a ferocious gunfighter mannequin that shouts insults at passers-by until someone drops in a quarter. Then the electronic outlaw growls: "Okay. Step right up there, little shot. See if you can kill me. You'll know if I'm dead 'cause my face'll turn blank and my eyes'll roll back." Just like in the movies. Patrons who can't resist the bait line up for a chance to shut up the crude and ugly outlaw with one quick shot, for a chance at a two-bit connection to the legend of the gunfighter—proud patriots of the only nation in the world where gun ownership is enshrined as an inalienable right; defenders of the land where "taking the law into your own hands" is perceived as an expression of individual freedom; mythic descendants of the brave cowboys who packed iron to protect the righteous code of the West.

Reinacted gunfights, in which the outlaws are always felled by the lawmen's bullets, remain popular attractions in tourist towns and at amusement parks throughout the West. (Bud Lee)

IO

The 1906 dime novel Buffalo Bill and Billy the Kid; or, the Desperado of Apache Land *tells the fantastic story of the brave scout's hunt for the Kid throughout the desert Southwest, a hunt that culminates when Cody puts a bullet through the daring outlaw's heart.*

Actually, Cody never took a shot at Billy the Kid, nor did he ever even encounter him. But in 1863, while a member of the Red Legged Scouts, an informal Kansas militia, Cody was involved in "many a lively skirmish with the Younger brothers," an infamous outlaw gang. Buffalo Bill and the scouts never captured the Youngers, however. They continued to rob stages and trains and to murder with gruesome abandon until 1876, when they were captured during the robbery of the Northfield, Minnesota, bank. The Youngers' partners, Frank and Jesse James, escaped and continued the careers in crime that carried them throughout the West. Cole and Jim Younger went to prison.

Most Americans were genuinely repelled by the exploits of the western outlaws. Yet many of those same people were simultaneously entranced by the daring and adventure-filled lives of the badmen, many of whom knew periods of greater renown than even Cody, who represented the ideal of heroism and virtue.

When Cole Younger was released from prison in 1903, he and Frank James finally gave up their criminal ways and, aware of Cody's phenomenal success, opened the Cole Younger and Frank James Wild West Show in their home state of Missouri. When the improbable show began its brief tour, crowds attended to see in person the legendary outlaws whose lives had an aura of mystery and a strange anarchic nobility. They may once have committed heinous crimes, but in the spectators' minds they were captivating figures nonetheless. The men were outlaws, and therefore they were something special.

296

CHAPTER TEN

DARLIN' OUTLAWS

MORE THAN 270 DIME NOVELS WERE PUBLISHED IN THE LAST YEARS OF THE nineteenth century that recounted the exciting, *fictitious* exploits of outlaws Frank and Jesse James. Dozens of enduring folk songs extol the courage and compassion of infamous outlaws like John Wesley Hardin, Sam Bass, and Emmett Dalton. Butch Cassidy and the Sundance Kid are remembered as the nation's most handsome and fun-loving killers; and Billy the Kid, the most renowned badman of them all, "the fairy prince of the Old West," is mythically alive in books, movies, ballet, and songs. More than eight hundred books, articles, plays, and poems have been written about the Kid's short, strange life; and forty films portray him variously as a defender of the oppressed, a love-struck gunslinger, and a simple, hard-working cowpoke. The mythic Kid has had a much greater impact on American culture than the bona fide Kid did on Lincoln County, New Mexico, where he lived out his short, pathetic life. Just as we have done with countless western miscreants, we turned the Kid into a kind of protector of the common man, a gun-wielding hero who had the courage to do the things that we could never do.

Two months before his death the real Kid was asked by a Mesilla, New Mexico, reporter what he would like to say to all the people who were interested in him. He replied: "Advise persons never to engage in killing." But although his friends and those who followed his exploits knew this was probably good advice, they also knew that the Kid was somehow obsessed by his outlawry, that he *had* to be on the run, to live on the dangerous edge of death.

The Wild Bunch, an outlaw gang headed by Robert Leroy Parker, alias Butch Cassidy, became rich and infamous enough that it hired a full-time lawyer to manage its affairs. Fun-loving film outlaws portrayed by Paul Newman and Robert Redford, LEFT, have helped create an enduring outlaw figure who is a good-hearted underdog and a defender of the common man.

Country singer David Allan Coe once insisted that he had killed a man in prison—although he definitely had not—in an effort to boost his outlaw image and appeal. (Jodi Cobb/Woodfin Camp)

Merle Haggard, TOP, actually served time in prison, but it was Texas singers like Waylon Jennings, BOTTOM LEFT, and Willie Nelson, BOTTOM RIGHT, who succeeded in creating a popular brand of music called "red-neck rock" or "outlaw country." (TOP: Norman Seeff; BOTTOM TWO: J. Peter Mortimer)

That was what made him such a compelling character in their minds. If the rest of America knew it had to toil away at monotonous and grueling work, had to raise the children, pay the bills, and obey all the rules, at least a few men could live just as they chose to, defying conventions and regulations, unfettered and uncompromised, in some strange way embodying true freedom in their evil acts.

While the upholders of the law were always publicly revered and cheered—surely, a society had to maintain order to endure—secretly everyone knew the outlaws led more exciting lives; they represented the strength and determination of the individual and the American guarantee of freedom of choice: You could sure as hell choose to be an outlaw if you wanted to.

The factors that most likely led to widespread outlawry in the frontier West were severe unemployment and the legacy of violence left by the Civil War. When thousands of eastern immigrants reached the supposedly golden West, they were disappointed to discover that jobs were extremely scarce. Some found work on railroad crews or in the mines. Others began to ride the cattle trails. And some simply used their revolvers to earn their living, robbing any individual or institution that looked like an easy target. The young men who had fought the bloody battles of the Civil War had been taught that human life was cheap. In the hard times that followed the Civil War, it wasn't a long step from killing as a soldier to killing as a frontier bandit.

The outlaw killers were hideous men—vicious, unscrupulous, and without mercy. Fear of them was well justified. Unquestionably, they posed a serious threat to the prosperity and life of everyone they encountered. It wasn't surprising that, when the outlaws first began to be fictionalized in the 1880s, their crimes were roundly scorned, their characters were angrily denounced, and they were always brought to swift and brutal justice by brave and resourceful lawmen. But by the end of the 1920s, the fictionalized outlaws had become a better class of people. Some writers questioned whether anyone could be *all bad,* and others pointed out that many outlaws' acts were carried out in revenge for heinous wrongs that were done to them. Many writers began to assert that there were few absolutes of right and wrong, and their outlaws' motives were often outlined sympathetically.

During Prohibition (1920-1933) millions of Americans who surreptitiously drank alcohol began to understand that individual perceptions of correct behavior didn't always square with society's legal sanctions; and then, as government institutions collapsed, the economy was destroyed, and public corruption began to be exposed, many Americans began wondering who in fact upheld the law and who was a real threat to peace and security. In that context, the folkloric outlaws began to symbolize bold independence from institutions, and numerous legends assured people that individual frontier outlaws were noble men seeking to protect the oppressed common people. Western outlaws were increasingly portrayed as Robin Hood figures—jus-

tifiably stealing from the rich, the greedy, and the oppressive.

The romantic image of the outlaw has exhibited remarkable staying power, and it appears it will survive as long as it continues to appeal to an atavistic rebellious American spirit. The 1969 film *Butch Cassidy and the Sundance Kid*, a story of two carefree, wisecracking killers, was the most popular Western of the past two decades. Singer Bob Dylan eulogized John Wesley Hardin—a psychotic racist killer—as "a friend to the poor." And during the past ten years, "outlaw" country singers like Waylon Jennings, Merle Haggard, Willie Nelson, and David Allan Coe have had a major impact on the direction of country music. Some of them have actually served time in prison for assorted serious crimes, but their outlaw images principally have only had to do with their refusal to dress, sing, or perform according to the conventions of the Nashville music establishment. Waylon Jennings in his black clothes and hat, with his long dark hair and beard, and his songs asking "where has a slow movin', once-quick-draw outlaw got to go," is a contemporary outlaw symbol in the great Western tradition—the tough individual who's willing to fight it out alone, the cowboy who's gone wrong, as sentimental and alluring a figure as any good-hearted underdog.

> *We beat the drum slowly*
> *And shook the spurs lowly*
> *And bitterly wept*
> *As we bore him along;*
> *For we all loved our comrade,*
> *So brave, young, and handsome,*
> *We all loved the cowboy*
> *Although he'd done wrong . . .*

THE IMAGE OF THE WAYWARD COWBOY, THE GOOD BOY GONE BAD, IS one of the frontier's oldest myths. In numerous stories, and in songs such as "The Cowboy's Lament," good and decent cowboys make a fateful mistake that leads them to outlawry and, ultimately, to death. The stories and songs are important as fables, as morality tales, but they reflect little historical truth. Most real outlaws spent little or no time working as cowboys. And the cowboys themselves were considered anything but paragons of virtue. Many people warned, in fact, that working as a trail cowboy was simply the guaranteed first step to entering a life of crime.

Hundreds of young immigrants to the West at the end of the Civil War became cowhands nonetheless—when they could get the work. But jobs as drovers were not always plentiful, and many of the men who came west knew nothing about cows or horses. Some hunted buffalo for a time; others got jobs in the scattered towns as clerks and waiters and liverymen. But there had been a

Cattle Kate Watson operated a bordello in Sweetwater, Wyoming, where cattle were often the medium of exchange. After she and her partner Jim Averill branched out into cattle rustling, they were captured and hanged by irate ranchers.

promise of prosperity in the tales about the golden West—outlandish asser-
tions that every man could become a millionaire—and some of the new arrivals
refused to accept the region's stark and impoverished reality. The Civil War
had taught them the only trade they knew—shooting weapons, pointing them
at people—so they put their skills to work, turning robbery and gunplay into a
livelihood and a way of life. "I kill only those who get in my way," outlaw Harry
Tracy claimed—a perverse statement of his egomaniacal ruthlessness and
his sense of virtue that was sustained by the fact that at least he didn't kill
at random.

The legends and myths that surround the outlaws conceal their actual
depravity, their various dementias, and their proclivity for violence. They were
decidedly not nice men, and the fact that many of them later emerged in the
public's mind as champions of the poor and oppressed is one of the most intriguing examples of the ease with which the western myth has radically diverged
from historical accuracy. It is interesting to note, as well, that while the names
of many historical western outlaws are remembered in American folklore, the
only historical lawmen most people can readily identify are Wyatt Earp, Bat
Masterson, and Wild Bill Hickok—all of whom were memorable figures, in
part because of their penchant for operating on both sides of the law. The
outlaws are remembered as being somehow more vigorous and vibrant than the
lawmen they eluded. The peace officers, though sometimes heroic, are usually
portrayed as having simply been wage earners like everyone else, while the
outlaws are portrayed as the true adventurers.

Sam Bass was just such an "adventurer," an Indiana-born stage and train
robber who was tracked down by the Texas Rangers and mortally wounded
by them outside of Round Rock, Texas, in 1878, on his twenty-seventh birth-
day—his short life squandered on his lawless efforts to win fame and fortune.
Yet not long after his death, Bass did at least earn some fictitious praise: "The
Ballad of Sam Bass" affirmed that "a kinder-hearted fellow you'd scarcely ever
see," although the real Bass had succeeded in keeping any bona fide kindheart-
edness well concealed while he was alive.

John Wesley Hardin, the character in Bob Dylan's song, "was always
known to lend a helping hand." But the real John Wesley Hardin killed at least
twenty men, most of whom were ex-slaves whom Hardin believed had to be
wiped out. Hardin killed for racist and political reasons, becoming in the process
something of a hero in the eyes of anti-Reconstructionist Texans. Of one of his
coldblooded killings, Hardin later wrote in his autobiography: "Many of the
best citizens of Gonzales and DeWitt counties patted me on the back and told
me that was the best act of my life."

But no one in the folkloric annals of American outlawry did more in the
way of lending a helping hand than did that son of a Missouri minister, Jesse
James, brother of outlaw Frank James. Working alone and in cahoots with the

*"Cattle Annie" and "Little Britches"
were delinquent teenagers who rode
with the outlaw Doolin gang in Oklahoma Territory in 1894. Their outlaw
lives were colorful but brief. Annie got
married in 1895 and gave up her wild
ways to begin raising a family. Little
Britches died of consumption that
same year.*

Many contemporary country songs romanticize the drifters and the drinkers—lonely cowboys who pride themselves on being their own men. (Jonathan Blair/Woodfin Camp; LEFT: David Hiser/Photographers Aspen)

Life *magazine once called Billy the Kid America's best-loved badman. He was, without a doubt, the nation's most fictionalized and romanticized outlaw.*

outlaw Younger brothers, Jesse and Frank robbed banks, stages, and trains and killed bystanders whenever it suited their purposes. Although there is absolutely no evidence that Jesse James had been in any way philanthropic, "The Ballad of Jesse James" nonetheless contended that Jesse

> . . . *was a lad who killed many a man*
> *He robbed the Glendale train.*
> *He took from the rich and he gave to the poor.*
> *He'd a hand and a heart and a brain.*

Much of the populist mystique that surrounded the outlaws was shaped by the fact that their lives were so different from those led by the rest of the populace. Their exploits were shrouded in mystery—and it was that aura of mystery that captured the attention of the nation. The notorious Wild Bunch —an outlaw gang that included Kid Curry, Deaf Charley Hanks, Blackjack Ketchum, Harry Longbaugh, alias "the Sundance Kid," and that was headed by Robert Leroy Parker, better known as Butch Cassidy—eluded capture for five years in the rugged Hole-in-the-Wall country of northern Wyoming. The Wild Bunch audaciously and efficiently pulled off robberies throughout Colorado, Utah, Montana, Nevada, New Mexico, and Wyoming, becoming so rich and renowned in the process that the gang even hired a lawyer to look out for its collective interests.

Just before federal authorities closed in on the Wild Bunch in 1901, Cassidy and the Sundance Kid left the United States for Latin America, where they continued to ply their robbery trade until they were gunned down by Bolivian army troops in 1911 in the village of San Vicente. Or so the Bolivians contended. The families of both men claimed, and continue to claim today, that the outlaws escaped the army ambush and eventually reentered the United States. Cassidy, they say, lived quietly as William K. Phillips in Spokane, Washington, until his death in 1937; Sundance reportedly lived until 1957 in Casper, Wyoming. Both men may have actually remained alive for many years after the Bolivian shoot-out; the truth of the matter will probably never be known, and it doesn't really matter. The outlaws' enduring legends affirm, however, that they did indeed die on a South American mountainside—as daring desperadoes with their mysteries intact.

THE ENIGMATIC BUCK-TOOTHED BOY WHOM LIFE MAGAZINE (1941) CALLED "AMERica's best-loved badman" and whom others have called our "immortal legend" and "the cattle country's most romantic" figure is presumed to have been born as Henry McCarty in New York in 1859. By the time he was gunned down near Fort Sumner, New Mexico, by Sheriff Pat Garrett in 1881, "Billy the Kid," the fuzzy-cheeked misfit, had created trouble in three states, had killed four men, and had participated in the killing of five others. But death did not spell the end of Billy the Kid. His amazing legend was only being born as his small body was buried beneath the New Mexico plains. A hundred years after his shooting, the mythic Kid remains, in the words of Walter Noble Burns, one of his many biographers, "the boy who never grew old, [who] has become a sort of symbol of frontier knight-errantry, a figure of eternal youth riding forever through a purple glamour of romance."

The real events of Henry McCarty's life are not the stuff of legend, however. His childhood was spent in Indiana, Kansas, Colorado, and New Mexico. He was arrested at age fifteen for stealing clothes from a Chinese laundry; he killed an Arizona blacksmith during a fight three years later, then went to work as a hired hand for cattle barons John Chisum and John Tunstall in Lincoln County, New Mexico. He became embroiled in their feud with Lawrence G. Murphy, a rival cattleman—a feud that became known as the "Lincoln County War" and that festered for years, during which time the Kid killed three more men. He was mortally wounded by two bullets while standing in his stocking feet in a friend's darkened bedroom in the middle of the night on July 14, 1881.

The legend of Billy the Kid grew from the seeds of only those few facts. The first Billy the Kid dime novel appeared three weeks after his death and within a year was followed by six more. In 1882, Pat Garrett, the Kid's killer, wrote, with the help of a ghostwriter, *The Authentic Life of Billy the Kid, The Noted Desperado of the Southwest, Whose Deeds of Daring and Blood Made His Name a Terror in New Mexico, Arizona and Northern Mexico*—a book that Garrett claimed corrected fictitious statements about the Kid made in the dime novels but that actually only replaced them with different flights of fancy, ones preferred by Garrett because they portrayed the sheriff in a heroic light. But unlike the dime novels, which concentrated on the Kid's devilry and his "pure wanton love of carnage," Garrett prefaced his book by saying he intended to "give [the Kid] credit for all the virtues he possessed—and he was by no means devoid of virtue—but . . . not spare deserved opprobrium for his heinous offenses against humanity and the laws." Pat Garrett's book was not much of a success, however, perhaps because the fictional Billy the Kid it created was too much of a mortal man.

It was Charles Siringo's extremely popular *A Texas Cow Boy* (1885), which contained a chapter on Billy (whom Siringo defined as a "romantic fool"), that served to keep the Kid's memory alive and to spur on the storytellers. Billy became what literary historian Stephen Tatum called a "bandit samaritan," in his book *Inventing Billy the Kid* (1982), an insightful investigation into the folklore and mythology of the Kid. Tatum noted numerous early twentieth-century romanticizers of the Kid, among them Kansas poet G. G. Price, who created a noble Kid fighting "for the honor of his mother" and taking

The 1938 ballet Billy the Kid, *scored by Aaron Copland and choreographed by Eugene Loring, portrays the Kid as an American tragic hero who is out of step with the rest of society, and who is doomed by his life of violence. (Peter C. van Dyck)*

. . . the side of settlers,
And natives who were poor,
Against ruthless cattlemen
Who had left a trail of gore.

In his 1928 novel, *Nevada,* in which he lumped both lawman Garrett and outlaw Kid into the same group of "noted killers," Zane Grey, the great Western moralizer, explained that:

There are bad men and bad men. It is a distinction with a vast difference. I have met many of the noted killers. Wild Bill, Wess Hardin, Kingfisher, Billy the Kid, Pat Garrett an' a host of others. These men are not bloody murderers. . . . The West could never have been populated without them . . . . And such as we could not be pioneers, we could not progress without this violence.

And in his 1935 book, *Under Texas and Border Skies,* Roscoe Logue went so far as to claim that "the average outlaw was a monster in human form with a sole mania for bloodshed and plunder, but not so the Kid. . . . He was a mild-mannered youth, kind and companionable. Just such a type as any mother could have taken to her bosom, loved and cherished."

The first film based on the life of the Kid, King Vidor's *Billy the Kid* (1930), presented Henry McCarty, a.k.a. Billy Bonney, as a proper American hero, killing only to right grievous wrongs, upholding "the side of justice if not the law," in the words of Vidor. The Kid, played by a handsome young Johnny Mack Brown, is quiet and courteous, a man who "has made this town a decent place to live in," according to his sweetheart, Claire. But he is also a deadly accurate gunman who can say, "Killin' rats comes natural to me," when he shoots down two of a villainous cattleman's hired men.

In the depths of the Great Depression, when the film was released, the moviegoing public readily accepted the presentation of a heroic outlaw. The notion that institutions and legal systems were corrupt and had to be dealt with from outside the law was palatable and even attractive.

Eight years after the first Kid film, Roy Rogers starred as a singing Kid in *Billy the Kid Returns,* which was followed by seventeen Republic Pictures B-Westerns (produced between 1940 and 1943), starring Buster Crabbe or Bob Steele as the heroic desperado. In Howard Hughes's *The Outlaw* (1946), the Kid, played by Jack Beutel, is less concerned with righting wrongs than with winning the voluptuous Rio, played by Jane Russell. By 1949, in *Son of Billy the Kid,* Billy has married, settled down, and become a *banker,* of all things, helping his daring young son capture the real outlaws in between attending board meetings and receiving big deposits.

Movies, novels, and historical accounts of the supposed *true* life of Billy the Kid proliferated during the middle decades of the twentieth century. Eugene Loring and Aaron Copland's ballet *Billy the Kid,* which presents him as a tragic figure doomed to loneliness and death, emerged as one of the nation's

Contemporary outlaw Claude Dallas, a self-styled frontiersman, told authorities that he only wanted to be his own man. "Nobody else lives like I do," he said, claiming that he had shot two game wardens in self-defense. An Idaho jury, which convicted him of only voluntary manslaughter, believed his story. (William Albert Allard)

By the time the 1930 film Billy the Kid appeared, the Kid, as portrayed by cowboy actor Johnny Mack Brown, was gentle and courteous. The misanthropic outlaw had been transformed into a man who had "made this town a decent place to live in."

most important folkloric ballets. Historian J. Frank Dobie wrote that the Kid was "an uncommon killer, he was an uncommon thief. . . . He was indisputably brave and he was, in his own sphere, absolutely supreme." War hero Audie Murphy starred as *The Kid from Texas* (1950); a young Paul Newman was *The Left-Handed Gun* (1958), a Kid who became a martyred Christ-figure; Chuck Courtney played a ludicrous hero in *Billy the Kid Versus Dracula* (1966); and Kris Kristofferson portrayed a Kid out of step with a changing world in Sam Peckinpah's *Pat Garrett and Billy the Kid* (1973), the latest of the forty films supposedly about the short life of Henry McCarty. The Kid has had remarkable staying power; his mythic story seems capable of being endlessly retold.

McCarty the man is said to be buried at Fort Sumner, New Mexico. The grave is surrounded by a high wire fence to protect the tombstone from chiseling, souvenir-seeking tourists and from another theft like the one in 1981 when a truck driver stole the tombstone and headed with it to California, joining the hallowed ranks of fleeing desperadoes before he was captured and the stone recovered. But fittingly, Billy's bones may not, in fact, rest at Fort Sumner. Some say they have been pilfered or moved to another grave. Some persistent legends claim that Pat Garrett and Billy buried two sandbags in the wooden coffin, and Billy made off safely to Mexico. In 1950, a man named "Brushy Bill" Roberts claimed to actually be the ninety-one-year-old Kid and asked the governor of New Mexico for a pardon—which was denied. And Hispanic parents in New Mexico still sometimes scare their children into good behavior by threatening that the ghost of the legendary "Bilito" will haunt them if they are bad.

Henry McCarty lived for twenty-one years and died a pathetic, inconsequential death. But Billy, the uncommon killer, the fairy prince, has survived him by more than a hundred years. As the poet Kid wistfully declares in Michael Ondaatje's prose poem *The Collected Works of Billy the Kid* (1970), "I'll be with the world till she dies." Perhaps it is his combination of youth and ruthlessness that has made the fictional figure of the Kid so compelling. Perhaps it is the brevity of the boy's life and the lack of verifiable details about it that have over the years made him so susceptible to the myth-making process; storytellers, writers, and artists who have dealt with him have been unencumbered by the restraining weight of facts. Yet one also wonders whether Billy the Kid has become legend simply because his lawless life has appealed to everyone who has sometimes yearned to act impulsively, happily ignoring society's rules.

AMERICANS HAVE LONG PROFESSED TO LOVE LAW AND THE SECURITY OF ORDER, but our boldest mythic characters have been carved from the lives of western misfits who regarded the law with cavalier contempt and who shattered order with their brazen crimes. Writing from his prison cell in 1931, Emmett Dalton, the last surviving member of the infamous Dalton gang, speculated that the American outlaw has been strangely revered "because he symbolizes the undying anarchy in the heart of every man" and that he is inevitably fictionalized as "a hero of democracy" because of his individual strength and determination and his distrust of institutions.

But Dalton was a prisoner of the American society while he wrote. He, like virtually every other historical outlaw, had been hunted for his crimes, then captured and punished. Only after the outlaws have been defeated, only after order has triumphed, have Americans dared to grow sentimental about the badmen—convincing themselves that the outlaws fought oppression by the rich and powerful, supported the poor, and defended the cause of individual liberty. "The outlaw hero who endures in our culture," Tatum wrote, "endures as both the deliverer and the defeated: what we come to see is that the outlaw only succeeds as he fails." Historical outlaws or contemporary criminals have never been society's champions. They have become attractive only after they have been safely defeated and dressed in the costume of legend.

At the close of the nineteenth century, when outlaw gangs were still a real and present problem to the nascent frontier society, the outlaws were portrayed, almost without exception, as savage remnants of the wilderness who had to be defeated to allow civilization to take hold. Dime novels, newspapers, and a publication called the *National Police Gazette,* which specialized in sensational crime and outlaw stories, focused on the evil work of the western bandits, making them out to be even more vile than they probably actually were.

But that perspective changed radically early in the twentieth century. By the time the stock market crashed in 1929, the western outlaws had been replaced in the public's mind by urban gangsters as the outstanding bona fide threat to the nation's peace and security; Americans had seen ethical standards quickly erode in a brutal European war; liquor had been outlawed, but liquor was still everywhere; Warren G. Harding's administration was riddled with corruption; and the banks had fallen, taking the public's money with them. Faced with a world in which individuals seemed helpless against the mysterious machinations of government and economics, and recalling a supposedly simpler world that had only recently vanished in the West, the fictionalizers of the outlaw began to imagine that he surely was somehow fighting the battle of the common people against the tyranny of wealth and power.

Evidence to support the laudatory claims made about numerous outlaws was in very short supply—it was nonexistent, to be precise—but writers and moviemakers and their audiences were a lot more interested in adulating proud figures who defied authority than they were in accurately assessing the outlaws' lives. The hundreds of stories, the dozens of films, the songs and poems about "poor Jesse," his brother Frank, and their comrade outlaws—persecuted by the police and hounded by poker-faced Pinkerton

Sam Peckinpah's Pat Garret and Billy the Kid, *starring James Coburn and Kris Kristofferson, is the latest of dozens of films about the short but mythic life of Henry McCarty.*

315

In N. C. Wyeth's The Outlaw, *a man on the run looks out for the lawmen who chase him.*

agents—engaged the ready sympathies of thousands of Americans and reassured them that even though personal failure might be inevitable, there *were* heroes in the land who would fight for the common people.

In the late 1950s and the 1960s, a new perspective on the nature of the outlaw emerged that paralleled the growing cultural concern about the dehumanizing effects of modern American society, and that reflected the growing realization that the distinctions between right and wrong had been largely obscured by the perception of world-wide violence in the twentieth century. Instead of representing the rebellious spirit of the oppressed, the outlaw was envisioned as a deeply alienated individual, struggling not for societal goals but simply for personal survival.

Clint Eastwood's "Man With No Name" character in a series of "spaghetti Westerns"—*A Fistful of Dollars* (1967), *For a Few Dollars More* (1967), and *The Good, the Bad, and the Ugly* (1968)—by Italian director Sergio Leone, epitomized the new amoral outlaw who was more brutal than ever, but who fought only to protect his own interests—not to avenge previous wrongs nor to defend anyone else. Eastwood's outlaw never smiled, seldom spoke, and remained stoically separate from those he encountered. His survival was his only heroism, his refusal to become subservient to anyone else his only code.

Arthur Penn's 1967 film *Bonnie and Clyde,* generally considered one of the most important films of the 1960s, was not a traditional Western, of course. It was set in Depression-era Texas and Louisiana and pitted characters, based on the renowned outlaw lovers Bonnie Parker and Clyde Barrow (Faye Dunaway and Warren Beatty), who robbed and murdered throughout the Southwest against the determined might of the Texas Rangers, and who were killed by them in 1934 outside the town of Plain Dealing, Louisiana. Like Penn's *The Left-Handed Gun, Bonnie and Clyde* examined the psychological motivations behind the bandits' way of life, treating them with empathy and subjective attachment. Penn commented that both films force viewers to recognize that "we find ourselves confronted with the terrible irony that we root for somebody for a relatively good cause who, in the course of that good cause, is called upon to commit acts of violence which repel us." But that "good cause" is really nothing more than the cause of desperate freedom—a freedom that cannot last because it is achieved through flagrant lawlessness.

The handsome heroes in George Roy Hill's *Butch Cassidy and the Sundance Kid* (1969) must die in the end as well, but unlike Bonnie and Clyde, who are obsessed with their love and their struggle to elude the law, Butch and Sundance, played by Paul Newman and Robert Redford, are two amiable, picaresque cronies who laugh and joke their way from one bank job to the next. *Butch Cassidy and the Sundance Kid* is an enormously enjoyable film; Redford and Newman emerge as appealing outlaw-next-door types. Ultimately, however, the film has more to do with fraternal love than with the role of the outlaw—it affirms that friendship is the one thing worth counting on, implying that among life's career choices outlawry may be as good a choice as any.

As Butch Cassidy and the Sundance Kid, *Paul Newman and Robert Redford fictionalized two historical desperadoes. The 1969 George Roy Hill film was the most popular Western of the past two decades.*

OUTLAW FILMS HAVE LONG BEEN A STAPLE OF THE WESTERN GENRE, SO IT WAS fitting that Australian director Fred Schepisi's first American-made movie was a Western—an outlaw Western starring Willie Nelson as the mystical Barbarosa. *Barbarosa* (1982) attempted to "use one American legend (Willie Nelson) to create another," said Janet Maslin in the *New York Times,* and it succeeded in doing so. Nelson's Barbarosa is a sagacious outlaw in beard and braids who roams the Rio Grande country of south Texas helping his friend Karl (Gary Busey) out of one scrape after another, entrancing local inhabitants with his power and his spirit, and once even rising from his grave. Schepisi—a foreigner dealing with the most American of film genres—created a film that examines the nature of legend and of hero worship without resorting to heavy-handed statements. His outlaw is clearly meant to be viewed as a superior human being, slightly larger than life, endowed with mysterious qualities that somehow set him apart.

Willy Nelson is a Texas-born singer and songwriter who worked for years in almost total obscurity in Nashville's music industry before finally having his fill of the syrupy sentimentality that characterized the "Nashville sound" and heading home early in the 1970s. Once back deep in the heart of Texas, Nelson took to wearing jeans and bandanna headbands instead of sequined suits, grew a beard and long hair, and became the pivotal figure in the evolution of an Austin-based brand of music variously called "redneck rock," "progressive country," and "outlaw country." Fellow Texas singers like Waylon Jennings, Kris Kristofferson, and Kinky Friedman accepted the tag of "outlaw" not because any had ever robbed a 7-11 store or cheated on his taxes, but because they rejected Nashville's successful music formulas in favor of an experimental kind of country music that had broader appeal, was far less conservative, and was often more complex musically.

In songs like Nelson's "I Gotta Get Drunk," Kristofferson's "Sunday Morning Coming Down," Ed Bruce's "Mamas, Don't Let Your Babies Grow Up to Be Cowboys," and Sharon Vaughn's "My Heroes Have Always Been Cowboys," the "outlaws" sang about years spent on the road or in honky-tonks, about cowboys who are drifters and loners, whose empty, antisocial lives comprise their implied outlawry. But curiously, those same cowboys sounded somehow heroic in the songs, just because they endured the sleepless nights and faded love affairs. The cowboy the outlaw singers described is "his own man through all adversity, even to the often bitter end," wrote William W. Savage, Jr., in *The Cowboy Hero* (1979). "His trials and tribulations may be of a different sort, but his nobility is the same as it was on the silver screen . . . ." It is an in-

Barbarosa, *starring Willie Nelson, is the story of a mystical border outlaw who entrances the local populace and once even rises from his grave.*

triguing phenomenon: No matter how down and out they are, the contemporary cowboys in the songs can still be romanticized—just like the legendary outlaws who were made into heroes despite the gravity of their crimes.

As country music grew in widespread popularity during the 1970s, many more young musicians were sometimes classified as "outlaws"—singers like Merle Haggard, who had served time for burglary at San Quentin and sang haunting songs about prison life. For some reason David Allan Coe, also an ex-con, insisted that he had killed a man in prison, although he definitely had not; perhaps he wanted to be considered the outlaws' outlaw, the worst of the bad lot. Hard-living Hank Williams, Jr., lamented the fact that times had changed and that nowadays "nobody gets drunk and gets loud . . . and all my rowdy friends have settled down," and Johnny Paycheck declared in an enormously popular song that an imaginary boss could "take this job and shove it."

The outlaw phenomenon in country music had next to nothing to do with banditry or other means of breaking the law. But in its reinforcement of that persistent American spirit of rebelliousness, it shared the outlaw tradition with the maudlin ballads about Sam Bass and Jesse James that had been composed many decades earlier. And today, Willie Nelson has indeed emerged as something of a legend—not so much because of his innocuous outlaw image as because of the remarkable way in which his music appeals to many groups of Americans and because he has a screen presence that is genial, relaxed, and mysteriously engaging.

Yet Willie Nelson is a very different kind of singing cowboy from Gene Autry or Tex Ritter; and as an actor he has little in common with John Wayne, Gary Cooper, and Lash LaRue. If he is currently the closest thing we have to a media cowboy hero, he is far more closely allied with the romantic outlaw tradition than with the legacy of the white-hatted boys who were always scrupulously good. Willie Nelson represents to many the common man who is faulty and contradictory but who has a warm heart and a quick-draw smile.

America's historical outlaws were by all careful accounts vicious men who could only be hated and feared. They evolved into mythic figures with whom we could identify and even learn to love as we slowly learned as a nation and as a people that few things are fair and few of us are uniformly good. The cowboy lawman, the upholder of justice, has been mythically important because he represents a compelling ideal. But the lawmen have been overshadowed by the darlin' outlaws because they have more closely resembled the people we actually are. The image of the cowboy who went wrong is not only a sweetly sentimental one; it is also one that at least in symbol represents each of us at one time or another. And Willie Nelson, Butch and Sundance, and dear Billy, the boy who never grew old, are figures we can envision living among us—good and bad in varying measure, but vibrantly alive, with us till we die.

IN HIS OWN WAY HE IS, PERHAPS,
THE MOST DANGEROUS MAN WHO EVER LIVED!

A FISTFUL OF DOLLARS

II

As the Buffalo Bill Combination, William F. Cody's melodrama troupe, prepared to disband at the end of its 1877 tour, Cody spent one Sunday morning in an Omaha hotel room with the troupe's four actresses. "And we all had a glass of beer or two, … and we were talking of the past season, and we were a little jolly," Cody said. Mrs. Cody, however, sat alone in her room down the hall, fuming with anger. After Bill kissed each of the girls goodbye, he returned to his room and was genuinely shocked to learn that his wife didn't condone the morning's merriment.

When that incident—along with allegations that Queens Victoria and Alexandra had designs on Buffalo Bill—became an issue in the Codys' 1905 divorce trial, the showman still seemed surprised at his wife's annoyance: "I do not think that most wives would have felt a little angry to know and hear her husband in an adjoining room on Sunday morning, drinking beer and kissing the theatrical girls of his company. I think they would have been rather proud."

Cody, like so many other frontier men, had always idolized women but had never been able to understand them. When he had married Louisa Frederici in St. Louis in 1865, he had said, "I adored [her] above any young lady I had ever seen." But by the time he sued for divorce—and lost—he was convinced she was trying to destroy The Wild West, and that she had often tried to poison him.

Louisa did detest show business, but she disliked the rough-hewn character of the West itself even more. Neither Cody the frontiersman nor Cody the showman came to be an appealing sort of mate in her mind. Cody dealt with her indifference toward him, and his toward her, by staying away from home almost entirely during the fifty years of their marriage. He preferred, he said, the company of cowboys and entertainers and of the jolly showgirls who were so easy-going that they might as well have been boys themselves.

CHAPTER ELEVEN

COWGIRL COUNTRY

"RUM, CARDS AND WOMEN ARE THE EPITAPHS IN THE COWBOYS' GRAVEYARD," remarked nineteenth-century cowhand Julian Ralph. "Some bunches all three, and some cuts one out of the herd and rides after it till he drops." Women were just as surely a vice as alcohol and gambling in the old cowboy's mind, and although the women he was referring to were likely the "soiled doves" of bordellos and dance halls, historical cowboys did consider women of every class and condition to be a little dangerous, highly unpredictable, and downright bothersome to the supposedly manly business of winning the West. Early cowboys compared women with cattle, claiming both were stubborn, thick-headed, and mean. They compared women with horses as well, sighting their wild spirits, independence, and charms. Yet the comparisons were only weak attempts to define women, to understand them, to attach images of the masculine western world to an unalterably feminine, hence foreign, creature. As perplexed as poor Henry Higgins was, western men wondered for decades, why couldn't a woman be more like a cowboy?

The answer, of course, was that she *could* be a cowboy—she could ride and rope cattle like a man—and many frontierswomen worked daily out on the ranges and pastures. But the majority of women, trapped by social convention, the demands of children, and the essential work of gardening, butchering chickens and game, and cooking, lived homebound lives in near total isolation, separated from other women and from all other men but their husbands. Their roles were critical to the collective business of surviving, but because they

Cowboys have been both enthralled and frightened by women for more than a hundred years—in part because, contrary to the myth, women can work cattle as well as any man. (Michael Lichter/International Stock Photo; LEFT: Jay Dusard)

327

worked primarily apart from men it was almost impossible for them to become recognized as integral members of the forming cattle culture.

Women had been vital citizens of the West from the time the first wagons rolled across the prairie hardpan. Yet they were often ignored or excluded in everyday life, and their images quickly changed when writers began to describe the hard-scrabble civilization that was taking shape in the West. The refined and genteel eastern lady for whom everything about the frontier was supposedly grossly repellent was soon replaced by the image of the long-suffering prairie madonna whose sunbonnet was as symbolic as the cowboy's hat, a woman who endured incredible hardships and made the comforts of home and family a reality in the gaping and unsettled spaces.

Then a kind of fictional backwoods belle appeared, the sort of woman the dime novelists called a "sport" or a "pard," who was virtuous and very feminine, yet who had become one of the boys—riding, roping, and chasing after rustlers. Dale Evans was the epitome of the cowgirl pard of the movies; she was pretty, brave, and true—and as pure as the driven snow.

But if pards were pure, they could also be a bit boring, and the bad woman of the West—represented by numerous fictional Calamity Janes and by a few ruthless and conniving ranch matrons—balanced the scale and added some excitement. The bad women were often sexually scandalous, of course, and movie audiences made it plain that they liked the combination of saddles and sex. It wasn't long before the cowgirl as sex object became a vivid and entrenched element of the western myth.

But contemporary cowboys, who drive trucks with bumper stickers that read "Cowboys Stay On Longer" and "Cowgirls Got What Cowboys Want," still seem unsure about whether women are their partners or playmates, their equals or superiors, or simply their carnal companions. The cowboys do, of course, express a genuine, if sometimes patronizing admiration of the western women who run ranches and wrangle horses. But the power and longevity of the masculine myth have made it nearly as impossible for some rodeo and ranch men to truly understand women and to forge friendships with them as it was for the historical trail hands, for whom "decent" women were as exotic as princesses and as inaccessible as angels.

A cowgirl scans the selections on a jukebox in a western bar. (James Balog)

T HE HISPANIC AND ANGLO IMMIGRANTS WHO FIRST VENTURED INTO the empty West were men, and the frontier culture they shaped reflected their masculine concerns and habits. Although some trappers, hunters, and early cattlemen took Indian wives, most lived without women. But when the massive expansion began in the mid-1800s, women began to go west as well—as daughters and wives of men itching to see the open terrain, as school teachers summoned by burgeoning communities, occasionally as mail-order brides purchased by lonely men out in the hinterlands, and sometimes as "adventuresses"—intrepid women willing to go it alone who found work as clerks, laundresses, cooks, prostitutes, and farmers. Twenty percent of the people who took out claims and "proved up" parcels of western ground under the auspices of the 1862 Homestead Act were women. And although the frontier laid drudgery, pain, and fear in many women's paths, it also offered them some of the same independence and escape from social conventions that it afforded men.

Cowboys have sometimes been unable to decide whether women are their partners or playmates, their equals or superiors. (Susan Felter)

But while many women did find freedom in the anarchic environment of the early West, the majority were bound by the traditional roles ascribed to housewives and mothers. They endured the hardships of living far removed from social, spiritual, and medical comforts. They often raised whole broods of children in tiny dirt-floored shacks, slept on the ground, and cooked over open flames. It was a grueling, monotonous existence that was the absolute antithesis of the lively pursuits of plowing fields and herding cattle. Yet one old-time rancher was expressing genuine shock when he said: "I can't figure out why my wife went crazy. Why, she ain't been out of the kitchen in twenty years." And Joyce Gibson Roach recounted in *The Cowgirls* (1977) the story she had been told about the time in far west Texas when after more than a month of driving, dust-laden wind, "40 women took up hysteria as a group project and had to be removed from the premises." In her book *No Life for a Lady* (1941), Agnes Morley Cleaveland wrote that "it was this deadly staying at home month in and month out, keeping a place of refuge ready for their men… that called for the greater courage. Men walked in a sort of perpetual adventure, but women waited—until perhaps the lightning struck."

The only means for many women to ward off the lightning strike of hysteria was to take off their aprons and go outside and work as a man. Some husbands had always been perfectly willing for their wives to join them on horseback; others relented only when they had to have help; and hundreds of widows had no choice but to take up ranching when their men were suddenly felled by heart attacks or tuberculosis or bullets. The outdoor work posed its own heart- and back-breaking demands, but its connections to the land and the cycle of seasons captivated women in the same way they had always entranced men. Trailing, branding, and castrating cattle and wrangling horses had always been strictly identified as male work, but "once the cows and horses accepted [women], the men generally followed suit," Roach wrote. "I am inclined to attach some importance to a theory," she continued, "that the emancipation of women may have begun when they mounted a good cowhorse and realized how different and fine the view was."

And once the slightest hint of emancipation appeared in the decades following the Civil War, a sartorial change began to occur: Women not only began to do men's work—some of them began to look like men as well. Across

Cowboys have long "protected" women from the gritty work in order to bolster their own capable, masculine images. (Kathryn Nelson)

the face of the West, the "lady" was seen less often, and the forerunner of the cowgirl took shape. Cleaveland joined the changing scene:

> My own great concession to a new age was to abandon the side-saddle.... [then] I disregarded, or rather refused to adopt, the sunbonnet, conventional headgear of my female neighbors. When I went unashamedly about under a five-gallon Stetson, many an eyebrow was raised; then followed a double-breasted blue flannel shirt, with white pearl buttons, frankly unfeminine.... Decadence having set in, the descent from the existing standards of female modesty to purely human comfort and convenience was swift. A man's saddle and a divided skirt (awful monstrosity that it was) were inevitable.

But although acceptable open-range apparel grew slightly androgynous by the 1890's, the men and women who wore it decidedly did not. They remained separated by hundreds of years of societal strictures, by mores that demanded that men be boss, and by the men's own abiding certainty that women just couldn't match up. Relations between the sexes were often awkward, distant, and unrewarding. Many marriages were only skeletal relationships at best, each partner playing his or her role with cold indifference or contempt. And as Douglas Branch wrote in *The Cowboy and His Interpreters,* "love in the cow-country was a brusque thing, an incident and not the aim of life in this woman-starved country with its traditions of clanship between men." The aim of life was principally to survive, and whether frontierswomen lived out their lives in front of earthen hearths and under sunbonnets, hoeing the summer's vegetables, or mounted on ponies out among the cattle, they lived forever only on the female fringe of a pastoral western world that celebrated its masculinity.

THE TRAIL COWBOYS WHO RODE IN THE LAST QUARTER OF THE NINETEENTH CENTURY were secure and at ease in their womanless world. They forged strong bonds with their horses, with their gritty and tedious work, and, most important, with their fellow drovers who often served as a kind of surrogate family. The friendships were relaxed and lasting because they possessed little sexual or competitive tension. Although there certainly were homosexual trail hands, the cowboys were, for the most part, heterosexual men who relished the range life precisely because it offered an escape from tense and tenuous relations with women, whom they considered at once frightening and attractive. Teddy Blue Abbott wrote:

> I'd been traveling and moving around all the time, living with men, and I can't say I ever went out of my way to seek the company of respectable ladies. We didn't consider we were fit to associate with them on account of the company we kept. We didn't know how to talk to 'em anyhow. That was what I meant by saying that the cowpunchers was afraid of a decent woman. We were so

damned scared for fear that we would do or say something wrong—mention a leg or something like that that would send them up in the air.

But the drovers were at ease in the company of dance-hall girls and prostitutes, and they certainly sought out their company just as soon as they hit town at the end of a drive and had received their wages, bought new hats, boots, and clothes, bathed and shaved and liberally doused themselves with hair tonic and cheap cologne. Many prostitutes were old friends and acquaintances of the drovers, and while quick and very loveless alliances were commonplace, it wasn't unusual for a drover to "marry a girl for a week," according to Teddy Blue. And occasionally, a drover would officially marry a prostitute who was ready to end her working days.

Teddy Blue's warm and frank memoir of the trail-drive era, *We Pointed Them North* (1939), is one of the very few books that openly discusses the sexuality of the reticent range cowboy. Teddy Blue admitted he dreaded "nice ladies," but he willingly confessed his regard for women like Cowboy Annie, Lily Davis, Mag Burns, and Connie the Cowboy Queen—Miles City, Montana, prostitutes of whom he was a friend and client for many years. He recounted the time when a drover who had spent a week with Cowboy Annie rode away owing her seventy dollars. When news of this reached the drover's foreman, the foreman fired him on the spot, as did another foreman who got word about the varmint all the way down in Texas. Teddy concluded, "the N Bar fellows took up a collection and paid her what he owed, because they wouldn't have a thing like that standing against the name of the outfit." Despite the fact that the prostitutes definitely were not "decent women," the trail boys took a certain pride in treating them as if they were. "Well, they were women.... And any man that abused one of them was a son of a gun," Teddy Blue wrote.

But Teddy Blue admitted that in spite of his many dalliances, his friendships and affections for the ladies of the line, he "secretly had in my heart the hopes of meeting a nice girl. I always wanted a cow ranch and a wife." And he was far from alone in perceiving such a clear, primly Victorian distinction between kinds of women. The prostitutes were accessible; they were bawdy and jolly, always willing to drink like a man and cavort like one of the boys. They were outcasts just like the drovers themselves, and the two groups shared the proud alliance of the underclass. But the drovers were attracted by the women they couldn't have—women whose demeanor and standing made them as alluring as they were inaccessible. The sporting women, who were fleeting partners and playmates of the cowboys, fit easily into the manly milieu of the frontier. But refinement and respectability were *feminine* traits that, although madly enticing, remained outside the reach of the drovers' ropes.

Although many frontierswomen were trapped inside ranch-house kitchens, some did work alongside their men, as shown in W. H. Dunton's The Helping Hand.

Square dancers whirl across a dance-hall floor, the hooped skirts of the women spinning like gingham pinwheels. (Chuck O'Rear/West Light)

This 1903 calendar cowgirl looks like a cross between Calamity Jane and Clara Bow.

"WE HAD A SAYING," WROTE AGNES MORLEY CLEAVELAND, REMINISCING ABOUT the West of the last two decades of the nineteenth century: " 'A six-shooter makes all men equal.' I amended it to 'A six-shooter makes men and women equal.' " Guns unquestionably did help make women secure in the violent frontier, yet even more they made a celebrity out of diminutive Phoebe Ann Moses, an Ohioan who had never been west of Cincinnati, but who as "Annie Oakley, the Peerless Wing and Rifle Shot" became known as the greatest female sharpshooter the West had ever seen. Annie was eight when she took her first shots; at fifteen she defeated sharpshooter Frank Butler (the man who became her husband a year later) in a clay pigeon contest; and in 1885 she became the first Anglo woman to join Buffalo Bill's Wild West show.

Cody called her "Little Missie," and acknowledged that she was perhaps the greatest single asset to his show's success. Dexter Fellows, the Wild West's press agent, affirmed in his memoir, *This Way to the Big Show* (1936), that:

> Even before her name was on the lips of every man, woman and child in America, the sight of this frail girl among the rough plainsmen seldom failed to inspire enthusiastic plaudits.... Her first shots brought forth a few screams of fright from the women, but they were soon lost in round after round of applause. It was she who set the crowd at ease and prepared it for the continuous crack of firearms which followed.

Annie shot cigarettes from her husband's mouth and dimes from between his fingers, and she could slice a playing card in two with a single bullet. In a favorite trick, two clay pigeons were first released from a trap; then Annie would leap over a table, pick up her gun, and shatter both targets. Sitting Bull called her *Watanya cicilia,* "Little Sure Shot," and it was only with the promise that he would see her every day that the Sioux medicine man joined Cody's show for a season.

Annie Oakley toured with The Wild West for seventeen years, becoming the first "western" heroine of national renown. She had never seen the short-grass prairies, the towering Rockies, or the buttes of the desert Southwest; but to millions of Americans, Annie was a child of that mysterious region that lay west of the Missouri River. Her marksmanship and saucy, independent style were proof of her frontier roots, and she embodied an image of the new woman the West seemed to be creating—skillful, capable, and confident.

By 1887, a dozen women had joined The Wild West, including Lilian Smith, a trick shot and trick rider; "Ma" Whitaker, who portrayed the settler's wife in cabin attack scenes; Georgie Duffy, "Rough Rider of Wyoming"; and Emma Lake Hickok, stepdaughter of Wild Bill Hickok, who could make her horse dance to music and stand on his hind legs to bow. An event that featured "Races Between Prairie, Spanish, and Indian Girls" billed the girls as both lovely and accomplished. These were not burly Amazons, no sir; they were petite and charming girls of the West.

Pawnee Bill's Historical Wild West—one of the numerous imitations of Cody's show—advertised its female performers as "beauteous, dashing, daring and laughing Western girls who ride better than any other women in the world." As the Wild West shows proliferated, so did the number of western girls who performed in expositions, publicity events, and in the riding and roping contests that were the forerunners of organized rodeos.

At the Cheyenne Frontier Days celebration in 1901, young Prairie Rose Henderson tried to enter the bronc-riding contest, only to be told that women were not allowed. When she pointed out that the rules made no mention of women, she got her ride and "created such a sensation that many of the rodeos soon included as a feature event a cowgirls' bronc riding contest," according to rodeo historian Clifford P. Westermeier.

Fittingly, it was Theodore Roosevelt, the long-time champion of the cowboy, who brought the term *cowgirl* to national prominence as well when in 1900 he applied it to Oklahoman Lucille Mulhall, whom he watched ride bucking stock and rope calves at a "Cowboy Tournament" in Oklahoma City. And a cowgirl she was—working as a hand on her father's ranch at age ten, riding in the 1901 McKinley-Roosevelt inaugural parade at sixteen, and two years later becoming the first "professional" rodeo cowgirl when she won a thousand dollars in prize money, out-roping the men with whom she was competing in a Texas rodeo.

By 1910, it was difficult to distinguish a "roundup" (or "stampede" or "rodeo") from a Wild West show. Both types of entertainment increasingly emphasized cowboy skills and contests and deemphasized the western pageantry that had been a staple of Cody's original show. When The Miller Brothers' 101 Ranch Show toured Europe in 1914, it featured numerous rodeo events, as well as specialty acts performed by comely cowgirls. According to one account:

> Lucille Mann was the leading bronc rider. Florence LeDue of Bliss, Oklahoma, roped a steer from the back of a running horse. Alice Lee of Dallas, Texas, made a specialty of falling off her horse, catching one foot in the stirrup, and doing a frog-hop along the ground. Lottie Alridge of Greeley, Colorado, lay flat on her horse's back and fired a Winchester at hordes of imaginary Indians. Babe Willets of Chicksasha, Oklahoma, rode a horse and cut out a steer from a bunch of cattle.

Although the abundance of rodeos and shows was sharply curtailed during World War I, by 1920 rodeos were again playing prominently throughout the United States and Europe. The twenties were a kind of golden age of the show cowgirl, an innocent time during which western women in silk scarves and jodhpurs, fancily tooled knee-high boots, and outlandishly large felt

Phoebe Ann Moses—"Annie Oakley"— had never been west of the Missouri River before she joined The Wild West. But her marksmanship and verve made her the show's star attraction and eventually the first widely popular "western" heroine.

The hard work and occasional rewards
of life on a remote ranch hold the same
lure for contemporary cattlewomen that
they have always held for western men.
(TOP: Craig Aurness/Bruce Coleman,
Inc.; ABOVE: Paul Chesley/Photogra-
phers Aspen; RIGHT: Timothy Eagan/
Woodfin Camp)

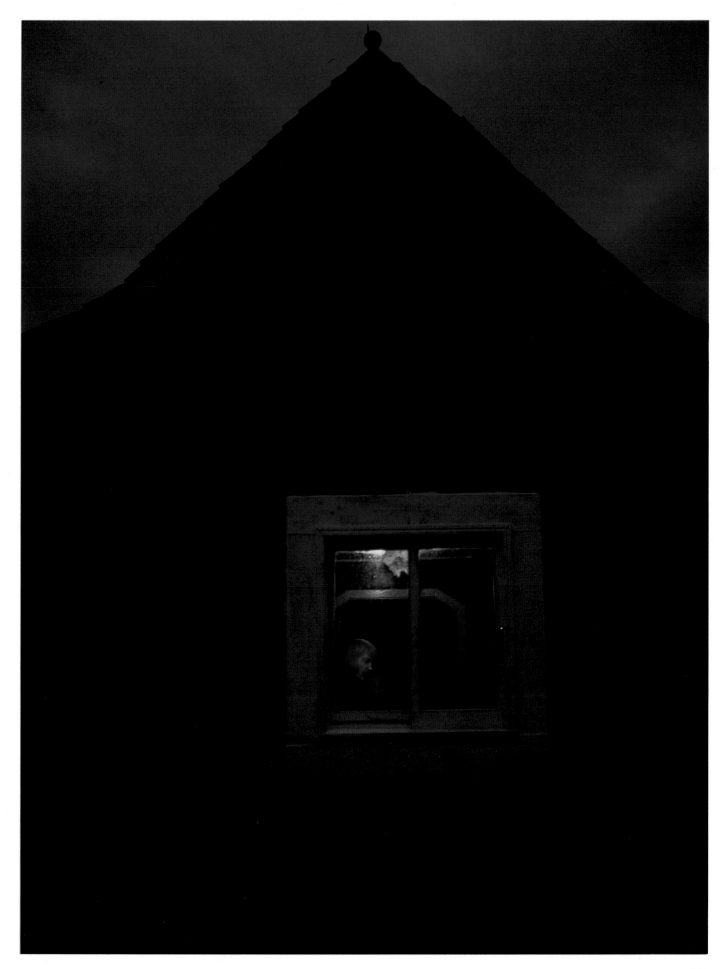

Rodeo star Mabel Strickland acknowledges the crowd after roping and tying a steer in the late 1920s. A decade later women began to be excluded from rodeo rough-stock events because the contests were considered—by men—to be too dangerous.

hats were portrayed as America's sweethearts. Renowned cowgirls like Mabel Strickland, Ruth Roach, Dorothy Morrell, Vera McGinnis, and Tad Lucas became national celebrities, appearing in rodeos, parades, and even movies. They were portrayed as pretty, jovial, and carefree cattle queens—but they were skilled horsewomen as well, earning their living riding high-kicking horses, and roping as well as any man.

But as the cowgirls' popularity grew, their supposedly glamorous lives were increasingly idealized, and their talents began to be ignored. Women's bronc- and bull-ringing contests were still featured in most rodeos, but many organizers felt that the women's rough-stock events detracted from the tough image of the men's, and they began to point out that the cowgirls rode special "safe" stock that supposedly only "bucked high and showed pretty." Others openly questioned whether fragile women should be allowed to court disaster in the arenas. The cowgirls had been dealing with potential disaster for decades, however, and they saw no reason to stop.

At the same time that their athletic abilities were being deemphasized, writers and press agents were gushing about the cowgirls' feminine charms and chuckling at their vanity. The Fort Worth *Star-Telegram,* seemingly uninterested in the dramatic business of risking one's neck on the back of a bucking horse, described how:

> This year's crop of rodeo cowgirls sets a new high standard of good looks and it takes more than an outlaw bronc to make one of the cuties forget her mascara.... The girls spend as much time on their makeup as any chorine in Rainbeau Garden.... No cowgirl would think of coming out in the arena without powder, rouge, lipstick, eyeshadow and mascara.

It was the era of Hollywood's romantic musical Westerns, and nobody seemed to mind if a rodeo cowgirl could actually ride or work cattle. It was her physical attributes that counted, and cowboys were coming to the conclusion that it just wasn't proper for women to ride bucking horses and maniacal, sidewinding bulls. The cowgirls continued to ride in bucking contests wherever they could find them, but in 1942, New York's Madison Square Garden Rodeo replaced female bronc riders with "sponsors" or "glamour girls" who represented the various western states like beauty contestants. The era of the celebrity cowgirls who had been reared on western ranches, and who proved that the old cowboy ways could be cow*people* ways as well, came to a sudden end.

AT THE SAME TIME that the images of the show and rodeo cowgirls were changing from curious novelties to skilled and popular performers to voluptuous glamour girls, similar changes were taking place in the portrayals of western women in books and movies. Neither medium ever made women stars in the way that shows and rodeos had done, however. And with the exception of a few dime novels and so-called ranch romances that highlighted their heroine's strength and courage or her curvaciousness, female characters remained of secondary importance to the brave and bold cowboys who protected them.

The fictional realm of the cowboy remained as indelibly masculine as an army post or a prison cell block. Yet women were always present. The West wasn't portrayed as a place where women were nonexistent, but rather as a place where they didn't matter much.

It has to be admitted that beginning around 1880 some dime novelists did make a concerted effort to transform their western heroines from the fragile and fainting variety that invariably got into some kind of trouble and that invariably got rescued by a daring hero, into hearty, often hefty, women who wielded rifles, axes, whips, or whatever was necessary to defend themselves, their clan, or even their heroes. Blowzy characters like Rowdy Kate, who boasted that she was "a regular old double-distilled typhoon, you bet," gained the attention of Erastus Beadle's writers. Hurricane Nell was the first dime-novel heroine to triumph over evil by disguising herself as a man—and a plethora of male-impersonator novels followed. Young Iola, heroine of *A Hard Crowd; or, Gentleman Sam's Sister* (1918) was "capable of shooting down instantly a man who accosted her in the street."

The dime novelists never called their frontierswomen "cowgirls," however. They generally referred to them as "sports" or "pards," and the distinction between the two was subtle but important. Sports were rather Amazonian; they were sometimes beautiful, but they dressed and comported themselves as men. They were as skillful as any man with any weapon; they could swear like men and often could drink their male counterparts under the table. Yet they never won the hearts of men, and they didn't much try. It wasn't that they were portrayed as being sexually attracted to other women— not in the 1880s and 1890s they weren't. It was just that they were far more interested in fighting than in falling in love. Pards also often dressed as men, and they could ride and shoot with the best of them—but they were *partners* of the cowboys as well, willing to share everything with them, and that occasionally meant a kiss or a sweet embrace.

The "ranch romances" that succeeded the dime novels early in the twentieth century (and that were published as hardcover books instead of cheap paperbacks on newsprint) transformed the basic character of the pard into a woman who was a bit more flirtatious and who dressed enough like a woman to make her femininity happily identifiable. According to Alan Bosworth, who surveyed early Western literature, the ranch romances followed the sexually suggestive "Sally's sweater" format: "The story, setting and characters are quickly introduced, and then back to Sally's sweater."

But the prurient concerns of the romances were pretty tame stuff, and

In the late 1930s, journalists and press agents chose to emphasize the cowgirls' vanity and charms. "No cowgirl would think of coming out in the arena without powder, rouge, lipstick, eyeshadow and mascara," said a Fort Worth, Texas, newspaper.

339

Sexual relations for the early trail cowboys were often drunken and decidedly unromantic affairs, as depicted in Charles M. Russell's watercolor, Just a Little Pleasure, ABOVE. *Intimate relationships between western men and women may have improved since Russell's time.* (LEFT: *Edward Klamm/ FotoWest*)

Actress Dale Evans epitomized the cowgirl "pard"—the fictional woman who was the pert, pretty, and courageous partner of the cowboy, able to help her man get out of trouble, and sometimes willing to give him a sweet embrace.

the readers of romances were primarily women who preferred them to the shoot-em-up stories because they spent less time killing off badmen and devoted more attention to their female characters. But the gun-blazing sagas of male-oriented writers like Zane Grey spent time on sexual titillation as well. In *Riders of the Purple Sage* (1912), Grey's heroine, Jane Withersteen, becomes fascinated by the hero's phallic pistols, and she insists on seductively buckling them around his hips. And in *30,000 on the Hoof* (1940), Grey spends almost two pages describing cattle baroness Lucinda Logan's new, tight-fitting jeans.

The first moviemakers must have felt that their new medium was simply too visually explicit to deal tastefully with intimate relations between the sexes. At the same time that the ranch romances were creating female characters who were both capable and coyly flirtatious, the earliest movies had heroines who most closely resembled the sometimes sweet, sometimes priggish, yet always proper young women of the Victorian era. By 1914—when in *The Hazards of Helen* a young telegrapher keeps the train moving in spite of fiendish obstacles—female characters could do a bit more than simply sit in the parlor and comment about how hot the weather had gotten. But there was still no hint of sexuality; and although some characters were said to be married to each other, nothing more suggestive than a demure smile ever passed between them.

But then only two years later, William S. Hart was bold enough to include the seduction of a minister by the town trollop as a peripheral plot in *Hell's Hinges*. It was romance not sex, however, that became a trademark of Hart's films. Always a supreme sentimentalist, Hart's female characters were either abidingly pure or unalterably evil—most often the former—and the good badman character that he portrayed time after time was invariably convinced to follow a virtuous path by the beauty and charm of a woman.

By the time Westerns were being churned out at a stampede pace in the late 1920s, few producers or directors would have considered casting a Western without a female heroine. They preferred young, unmarried, good-hearted female leads, of course—women whose fathers were harassed farmers or kindly storekeepers, but whose mothers were never to be found. The reason, according to film historian William K. Everson, was economic:

> A mother could never perform a useful function in a Western. Father could be robbed or cheated, used as a lever to force his daughter into marriage, or killed off, thus leaving the heroine dependent on the hero.... But the mother could perform no such useful function. She couldn't have babies, since pregnancies were unheard of.... Mothers couldn't be killed off, either, since that might be emotionally upsetting to the small fry. In other words, she was totally useless, eating up $200 of character actress money that could be better employed paying a stuntman for a horse fall.

It is not surprising that while many male actors—from William S. Hart to Roy Rogers, Gary Cooper, and John Wayne—became associated almost exclusively with their Western roles, there was only one actress who became known principally as a star of the horse operas. Countless actresses had appeared in the more than a thousand Westerns that had been made by 1940, but only Dale Evans—pretty, brave, and quick on the draw—had become exclusively a cowgirl heroine. Her marriage to Roy Rogers was a match made in heaven that was also roundly cheered in the Republic Pictures boardroom. Roy and Dale appeared together in dozens of feature films and serials—singing, riding together across the sands (with Dale's horse "Buttermilk" a fine match for Roy's "Trigger"), and saving the day in a variety of outlandish ways. In *The Cowgirls,* Joyce Gibson Roach parodied a typical film conversation:

> Dale speaks: "Roy, the rustlers are stealing all of my cattle. The well is dry. The creek is poisoned. Mama is dead and Papa is captured. Hadn't we better ride fast?" "Why yes, Dale. We sure ought to, but do you think we could sing just one more verse of 'My Adobe Hacienda' before we go?"

Dale was a wonderful cowgirl pard, helping Roy capture the mean hombres, cheering him on, and giving him a fond farewell kiss from time to time. And while the rest of Hollywood's Western stars were suffering through successions of bad marriages, Roy and Dale seemed gloriously happy on screen and off as they rode into retirement late in the 1950s.

During the robust and innocent years of the Rogers and Evans B-Westerns and subsequent television serials, something shocking was under way in the arena of "serious" Westerns. It had begun early in the 1930s when in *To the Last Man,* brave and unabashed Esther Ralston became the first actress in a Western to fight it out with a villain *and* to take her clothes off. Then in 1939, George Marshall's *Destry Rides Again* featured some rather tame sex between Marlene Dietrich and James Stewart and became a box-office smash. In 1943, billionaire Howard Hughes joined Howard Hawkes to co-direct *The Outlaw,* which was billed as containing "a sensation too startling to describe." Moviegoers discovered that the sensation was buxom Jane Russell appearing in various stages of undress before finally awaiting her fate as the prize in a high-stakes poker game. When King Vidor's *Duel in the Sun* followed in the mid-1940s with the story of the sexual adventures of three protagonists and audiences poured in to see it, sex as an element of the Western formula became firmly established.

For the next thirty years, virtually every Western featured some degree of intimacy, nudity, lovemaking, or suggestion of one or a combination of the three. But this recognition that women had appealing anatomies and legitimate sexual desires did little to help convince the moviemakers to portray them as vivid and complete human beings. Occasional female characters were presented as raunchy, funny, mean or wise—the sorts of women that had seldom been seen on screen before—but their roles remained supporting ones.

Howard Hughes financed and co-directed The Outlaw *in 1943, a film whose "sensation too startling to describe" turned out to be buxom Jane Russell appearing as alluring as the standards of the day would allow. Sex soon became an integral element of virtually every Western movie.*

"I've got 350 head of cattle and one son," said a Colorado ranchwoman, BOTTOM. "Don't know which was harder to raise." The only way for many women to escape the daily dreariness of a remote ranch house has been to go outside and take up the manly work of tending livestock. (TOP: Paul Chesley/Photographers Aspen; BOTTOM: Nancy Wood)

The Western remained a movie about men confronting men. And while cowboys fought cowboys to protect women or to win them, the girls stayed safely out of the way.

DURING THE TELEVISION ERA, THE IMAGES OF WESTERN WOMEN HAVE CONTINUED to multiply, but no single image, nor combination of images, has been able to meaningfully describe or explain the relation of women to the cowboy myth. The principal reason, of course, is that the myth's foundation and framework are formed by the generalized, and somewhat suspect, definition of American manhood—strength, courage, independence, and resourcefulness. The cowboy myth is masculine to its core, and women—who have been ignored, misunderstood, and stereotyped by the myth—have few ways in which to respond personally to it.

They can try to ignore it, letting the testosterone-crazed cowboys have their way, steering clear as best they can of its condescending conception of women. Or they can try to imitate the men by shunning the "feminine" attitudes of compassion, sharing, and expressed emotions in favor of a masculine veneer of toughness. A third option is simply to fawn over every stud who wears a hat and a pair of Levi's, to become the sort of woman who defines herself not by who she is, but by who she is attracted or attached to. There are other options as well, of course. There are thousands of women whose western lives have been shaped by their self-confidence, their relations to the land and to their loved ones, who are not much affected by the myth—women who may sell real estate or practice law or serve up peach pie in roadside cafes, but who live in the West because it somehow works for them.

But the cowboy image-makers—the books, movies, ad agencies, pageants, and modern rodeos—have never grown comfortable with women, and as portrayed by these media, western women remain as insubstantial as stereotyped politicians' wives, as merely picturesque as are models for shampoos or the current cars.

Television Westerns, which had their heyday in the ten years between 1955 and 1965, dealt with the problem of fitting women into the western myth by ignoring them altogether. "Bonanza," which began its fourteen-year run in 1959, was the story of a patriarchal rancher and his three sons, each born to a different wife. But their ranch was an enclave of men—even the cook was male—and women were seldom so much as mentioned. Miss Kitty, the saloon-keeper played by Amanda Blake in the "Gunsmoke" series, was an omnipresent character, but she seldom set foot outside the Longbranch, and her principal function was to slake thirsts, stop fights, and lend an ear and affectionate support to long-suffering Marshal Dillon. She was nonetheless television's foremost Western woman. Barbara Stanwick appeared briefly as a strong and domineer-

Three champion rodeo cowgirls model their trophy belt buckles on a diving board in Arizona. (Steve Smith)

ing ranch matron in "The Big Valley," but series like "Maverick," "Have Gun Will Travel," and "Rawhide" kept womenfolk well out of camera range.

In their comprehensive examination of Western films, *The Western: From Silents to the Seventies* (1973), George Fenin and William K. Everson maintain that Western films have continued the trend set earlier in the century by depicting women either as the "weak and defenseless female, without any personality of her own, essentially dependent on the hero," or as "the titillatingly sexual and aggressive heroine." A wide range of actresses have appeared rather unmemorably in the former roles, and the latter have gone to Raquel Welch, Brigitte Bardot, Ursula Andress, and others who have specialized in come-hither kinds of performances. It is ironic that one of the best-realized females in recent Westerns was a young girl—plucky Mattie Ross (played by Kim Darby)—in search of her father's killers in *True Grit* (1969). Allied with crusty and blustery Marshal Rooster Cogburn (John Wayne), Mattie is a girl pard *par excellence*, surviving even a pit of rattlesnakes as she helps Cogburn capture the killers. As portrayed by Darby, Mattie is neither weak, nor dependent, nor coy. She is a pain in the neck, to be sure, possessed of too much grit for her own good, but she is very nearly believable, and that mere believability sets her apart from hundreds of Western female characters.

Believability of a different sort altered women's roles in rodeo beginning in the 1940s when, despite nearly half a century of evidence to the contrary, rodeo men could no longer believe that women were capable of riding rough stock, or of roping or bulldogging cattle. Banished from the big arenas, the cowgirls responded by forming the Girls Rodeo Association in 1948, which in 1981 changed its name to the Women's Professional Rodeo Association. The WPRA sanctions less than two dozen rodeos annually, and the prize money the cowgirls compete for is pathetically small. But the WPRA offers the only organized forum for female competition in bronc or bull riding, calf roping, and team roping. Yet if the money is small, the knocks are as hard as they come. In a 1978 newsletter, the then-GRA director admonished girls who had been thrown from an animal to:

> if you are not at least dead, get out of the arena. Die behind the chutes. It looks bad to the crowd to lay out there, roll around, and then get up. It has been proven—crowds don't mind seeing hairy-legged boys get hurt, but they don't like to see women get hurt!

Women who aren't suicidal enough to join the WPRA circuit do have the option of barrel racing in men's amateur and professional rodeos. Barrel racing—a timed event in which a rider turns her agile little quarter horse in a clover-leaf pattern around three barrels placed in the arena dirt—is the only female contest allowed in Professional Rodeo Cowboys Association–sanctioned rodeos. Female riders often "post the colors"—carry the flags in the

Barrel racing is the only contest in which women can compete at Professional Rodeo Cowboys Association–sanctioned rodeos. Women do compete in rough-stock events in a few all-women rodeos held each summer. (Douglas Kent Hall/FotoWest)

No rodeo is complete without its queen and her attendants, and the resplendent riders who fill the arena during the grand entry. In his paintings, Wishing Well Bridge, *LEFT*, and Spring Doe, *ABOVE*, superrealist Richard McLean portrays the women whose chief rodeo function is to wave prettily at the crowds.

Keeping alive a tradition begun by Annie Oakley, rodeo trick riders and novelty act performers remain important parts of most modern rodeos. (Michael S. Crummett)

grand entry—at major events. And of course no rodeo worthy of the name is complete without a rodeo queen and her attendants—each decked out in matching aqua or lavender or gold polyester pants, jackets, and hats—whose jobs are to ride their horses at a fast gallop along the arena fence, waving at the crowd and hoping their hatpins hold.

Yet there are other rodeo-related women whose images are neither tough nor tinseled—the kind of compliant cowgirls who rodeo boys call "buckle bunnies" or "beeves," who supposedly are so attracted by the awesome virility of the cowboys that they can barely control themselves. The image of the cowboy stud who rides broncos all day and "fillies" all night is a carefully crafted hyperbole, however, as fictional as the glamour-girl images of the twenties and thirties or Jane Russell's sultry celluloid vixen who made certain that the cowboy had better things to kiss than his horse. Yet sexuality has become a vital element of the cowboy mystique. Cowboys no longer project images similar to the bashful, women-starved boys of the trail era. They make themselves out instead to be women-obsessed, constantly proving their manhood on the back of a bull, in the blanketed back of a pickup truck, or in a cold-water motel with a Bible on the bedside table. And they pretend that while men and horses represent the work that the West demands, women are simply convenient dalliances and quick diversions.

But the macho make-believe that inhabits rodeo arenas and honky-tonks bears little relation to the reality that women can work cattle—and even ride cattle—as well as men, that they can and do operate huge cow-calf operations alone or in conjunction with husbands or partners. They are women for whom the work and its occasional rewards hold the same lure that they have always held for western men, women who are *cowgirls* in the specific sense that they earn their livings from cattle, but for whom the mythical cowgirl trappings of deference to men, of cute affectation or a kind of sleazy sexuality have next to nothing to do with their land- and livestock-centered lives.

In the end it is really men who are more encumbered by the stifling mythic role of the western woman than are the women themselves. Women can play the parts of pards or princesses if they choose to. Or they can reject those false façades and demand that they be understood as individuals whose "western character," in whatever degree they possess it, stands quite apart from their womanhood.

Most modern cowboys remain as mystified by women as were the timid trail drovers, and as uncertain with them as were the B-movie boys who longed to steal a kiss. Except for those who see no reason not to treat men and women equally, most pretend to be veritable rodeo Romeos who can capture any woman they choose to with nothing more than alluring muscle, aloof attention, and maybe a little money. But secretly they fear that the country's cowgirls just might be able to live without them.

Many western women are cowgirls not because they wish they could be cowboys, but simply because they too are enthralled by the world of horses and saddles and rawhide ropes. (Kurt Markus)

12

After attending a performance of Buffalo Bill Cody's Wild West in the summer of 1886, Mark Twain commented in Harper's Weekly that the show "brought back to me the breezy, wild life of the Rocky Mountains, and stirred me like a war song. Down to its smallest details, the show is genuine—cowboys, vaqueros, Indians, stage coach, costumes and all.... It is often said on the other side of the water that none of the exhibitions we send to England are purely and distinctively American. If you will take the Wild West show over there you can remove that reproach."

The following year, The Wild West did indeed go to England as part of the American exposition at Queen Victoria's Jubilee. And the show proved wonderfully exportable: It toured Europe regularly for the next nineteen years. Cody's cowboys, Indians, and special brand of brash showmanship were distinctively American—in spirit, in style, and in monetary success. Cody had taken the brief, bold American experience of the frontier West and shaped it into a marketable product. He had, in the words of the Hartford Courant, "out-Barnumed Barnum."

And Teddy Blue affirmed that the cowboys who still rode the western ranges while Cody was traveling the world also admired the way in which the old showman had taken the obscure figure of the cowboy and sent him out into the world at large to win millions of admirers and commensurate profit. "We had to hand it to him because he was the only one that had brains enough to make that Wild West stuff pay money," Teddy said. He remembered the time in a saloon in North Platte, Nebraska, when Buffalo Bill had gathered his long, wavy hair that had always been his personal trademark and had pushed it under his hat to get it out of his way. "Say Bill," the bartender asked him, "why the hell don't you cut the damn stuff off?"

"If I did, I'd starve to death," Cody replied.

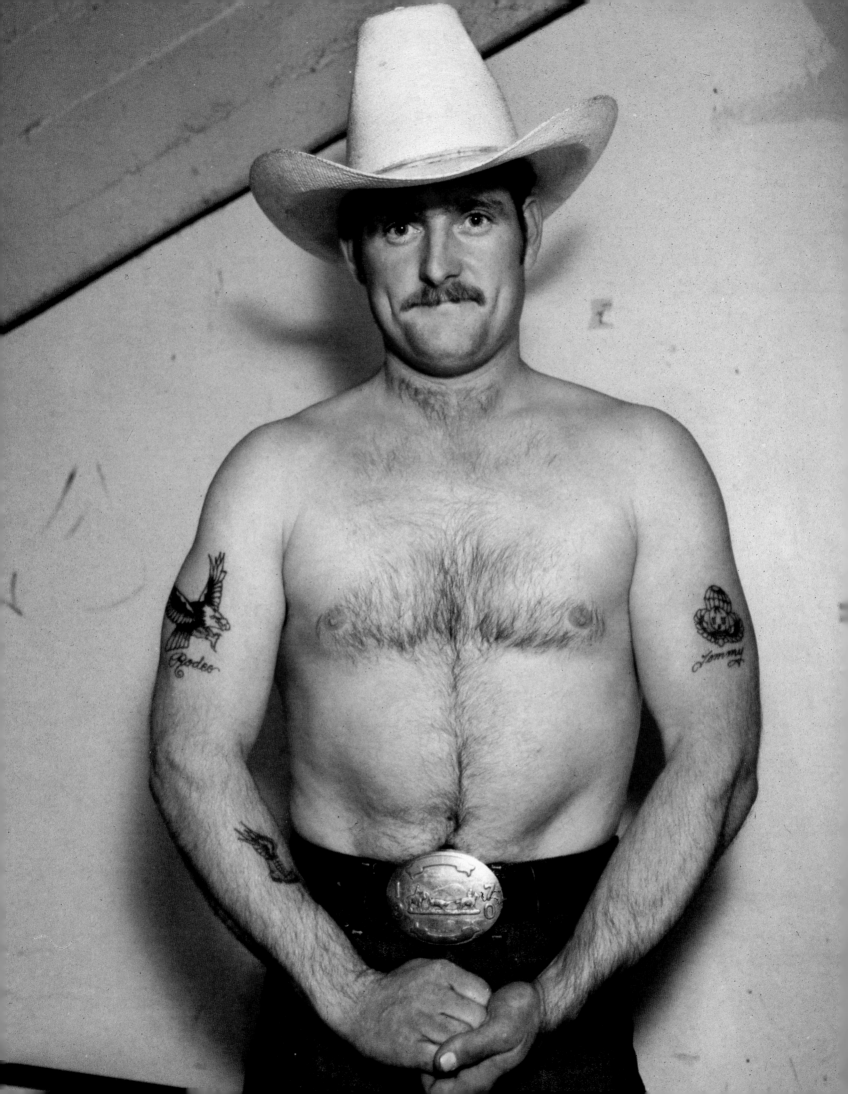

CHAPTER TWELVE

COWBOYS AT LARGE

THE COWBOY IS AT ONCE AMERICA'S MOST VERSATILE MYTHIC FIGURE AND ITS most elusive one. He has symbolized the settlement of the West and the taming of the wild. He has embodied a uniquely American wanderlust, the merging of violence and virtue, and the quiet courage that is often presumed to be an integral part of American manhood. Yet the mythic cowboy is shaped out of image, not out of substance. His wonderful adaptability is evidenced by his ability to represent many things to many people, to symbolize whatever our needs require. He can be an innocent vagabond, a wizened old laborer, a strapping and courageous protector of the community, a sad-eyed loner in search of solitude, or a dozen other figures that possess allegorical power and versatility. The mythic cowboy can symbolize caution or recklessness, stability or galloping abandon—because his image is a very pliable kind of cultural clay.

The scrappy boys who rode the dust-choked trails from Texas to Kansas, then on to the northern plains and the Rockies, and their professional descendants—the ranch hands who still work in the western cattle country—have been our only palpable, substantial cowboys. They are the raw material from which the myths emerged. Yet images have been of enormous importance even for them. It was their sense of the uniqueness of their occupation, their special skills and tools and attire, that gave the lowly cattle drovers a positive sense of identity. It was their *image* of themselves as being different, hence special, that gave them a measure of pride. And the fence-bound cowboys of the twentieth century have been carved by image as well. They have

Slim Pickens is perhaps the best and most widely recognized of a group of cowboy character actors. Western film star and gentleman rancher Ronald Reagan used his capable cowboy image to help him win the presidency. (John Annerino; LEFT: Dirck Halstead/ Gamma Liaison)

The Adolph Coors Company commissioned cowboy artist Gordon Snidow to paint a contemporary cowhand taking a quiet beer break.

consciously allied themselves with an image of cowboys other than themselves; yet, ironically, it is not the trail cowboys—the flesh-and-blood first of the breed—that they have emulated. For nearly a century they have focused on the fictional cowboy instead, and have copied much of his look and his style. "We may not have dressed like Tom Mix before we saw his pictures," remarked one worn-out old Texas hand, "but we sure as hell did afterwards." The early movie cowboys were proud and handsome, courageous and capable, and the ranch hands—who called themselves cowboys as well—imagined that they were cut out of the same hard piece of hide.

Yet the men who worked the ranches were obviously not alone when it came to fantasizing about the cowboy. They were joined by ad men and salesmen, politicians, artists and singers, preachers and teachers and athletes, by the writers of books and by the makers of movies—cowboy creators who shaped an enduring mythic image of the simple man of horses and the land and sent him out for duty in the non-cowboy world. They made him a kind of cowboy at large, an invention who worked with symbol instead of with horses and steers. "Americans have fantasized about the cowboy for a hundred years because in the general context of the West as a physical and psychological experience there has not been much else worth doing with him," wrote William W. Savage, Jr., in *The Cowboy Hero* (1979), an examination of the cowboy image in American culture. Savage, a professor at the University of Oklahoma—long the seat of "serious" cowboy studies—contended that it is pointless to talk about "real" cowboys, because any definition of who or what is real is only an isolated expression of imagination. And he agreed with Texas historian Walter Prescott Webb, who wrote in *Harper's* in 1955 that:

> Western history is brief and it is bizarre. It is brief because the time is so short and its material deficient.
>
> Western history is bizarre because of the nature of what it has got.... Westerners have developed a talent for taking something small and blowing it up giant size.

The western cowboy is the prime example of that talent for exaggeration. While it can be stated with certainty that young men, white, black, brown, and red, did push Longhorn cattle north out of Texas in the last quarter of the nineteenth century, and that men and women continue to work cattle in the West today, everything else that can be said about the cowboy, or the myriad cowboys of image, is couched in the rich cultural framework of fantasy. The mythic cowboys are the products of our imaginations, and as such they inevitably reflect less about who the "real" cowboys were and are than about who we imagine ourselves to be. Will Rogers, the cowboy humorist and raconteur, yodeling Roy Rogers, swaggering John Wayne, the silent Marlboro Man, and even the buckaroo businessmen whose Christian Dior trousers fall

The makers of Smirnoff vodka used actress Julie Newmar and the seductive image of a cowgirl gunslinger to sell their product in the 1960s.

over their high-topped Tony Lama boots are not real cowboys but cultural cowboys. They are just a few of the many vivid cowboy images that have supplanted the paltry *substance* of the cowboy in the American imagination, and they form much of what cynics say is more cowboy "fakelore" than "folklore." Yet it really doesn't matter whether our cowboys at large are selling Skoal or cigarettes or sour mash whiskey, running for president or crooning a country tune; they are indeed folkloric because they are born out of legend. And legends endure because they tell stories that people love to hear.

THE USES THE COWBOY HAS BEEN PUT TO IN THE MARKETPLACE IN THE twentieth century have been simple and straightforward. The engaging figure of the mythic cowboy has hawked everything from wristwatches to mobile homes, exhorting consumers to buy a bizarre range of products simply because cowboys are recommending them. And alternately, dozens of products, from cigarettes to diamond hatbands, have been sold with the promise that they could make the purchaser more like a cowboy, or at least induce a comfortable cowboy mood.

When William F. Cody first decided in 1884 to convince his Wild West audiences that lanky Buck Taylor was made of the stuff of legend, he couldn't have imagined that the public would respond to him so readily and so enthusiastically, or that the mythic cowboy who descended from Taylor would become one of America's most enduring and marketable commodities, as well as its ablest pitchman. "Cody, of course, never dreamed of the sales potential of the cowboy image," wrote Savage. "That discovery was made by entrepreneurs of a later day, and once it became known, the thread of cowboy imagery was woven inextricably into the fiber of American business, and near its most durable fiber, American advertising." The cowboy became a salesman of breakfast cereals and shock absorbers, however, long before the cowboy mystique itself was marketed in the form of jeans and after-shave lotion and a brand of cigarettes that created a mythic region called "Marlboro Country."

During the early decades of the twentieth century, while Zane Grey was prodigiously writing gallant horse operas and the Hollywood studios were releasing Westerns just as quickly as they could produce them, the image of the grand American cowboy was so pervasive that manufacturers felt little need to convince their customers to buy their products in order to keep the spirit of the West alive. That spirit seemed to be alive and thriving, and the strapping movie cowboys—heroes and heartthrobs of the nation—seemed to be ideal advertising spokesmen for an amazing assortment of products.

Beginning in the 1930s, several movie cowboys began to pitch clocks, of all things—wristwatches, pocket watches, and alarm clocks—and millions were sold in large part because Tom Mix, Gene Autry, Roy Rogers, and

Beer has been advertised for decades as the favorite beverage of the western man.

363

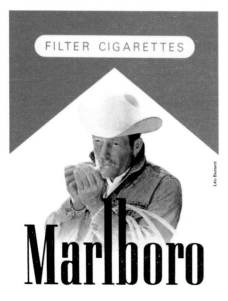

Cowboys have smoked cigarettes for as long as there have been cowboys, but it wasn't until Philip Morris, Inc. introduced the Marlboro Man in the 1960s that the cowboy image was used—and used with spectacular success—to sell a brand of cigarettes. (Bill Wunsch; LEFT: Don Hamerman)

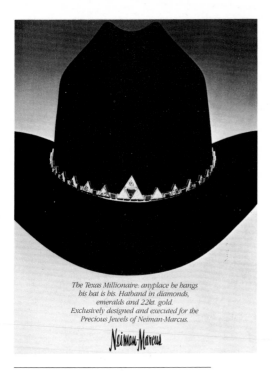

*The Texas Millionaire: anyplace he hangs
his hat is his. Hatband in diamonds,
emeralds and 22kt. gold.
Exclusively designed and executed for the
Precious Jewels of Neiman-Marcus.*

Neiman-Marcus

Ads directed at wealthy consumers
nonetheless utilize the common-man
image of the cowboy.

William Boyd (Hopalong Cassidy) swore they were a mighty good deal. The cowboy-clock connection continued, for reasons seemingly impossible to understand, for a couple of decades. When U.S. Time Corporation introduced a new model of its Hopalong Cassidy watch in 1950, ads claimed that it was "a means of bringing you great joy, happiness and success by keeping track of every minute of every hour."

The cowboys were remarkably successful in convincing people to purchase and to eat a variety of packaged foods as well, principally breads and cereals. On radio, Tom Mix sold Ralston Wheat Cereal; Roy Rogers pitched Quaker Oats; Buck Rogers, Grape Nuts Flakes; Sky King, Peter Pan peanut butter; Red Ryder, Langendorf Bread; and Hoppy represented the whole line of General Mills cereals.

Radio advertisers had to use well-known cowboys as their spokesmen; the only way listeners knew a cowboy was speaking to them was from the announcer's introduction, with lines like: "Just ask Tom Mix about Ralston Wheat Cereal; he'll tell you." Then Tom would start his spiel. But television, to its great advantage, could use anonymous cowboys—unfamous fellows who nonetheless looked like cowboys and whose opinions could therefore presumably be trusted. These generic cowboys have, since the beginning of the television age, hawked cough drops and barbecue-flavored potato chips, motor oil and bath soap, laundry detergent, flashlight batteries, and of course, beer, the preferred beverage of Western man. Television has become the cowboy's most comfortable selling ground, and a few famous cowboys occasionally still appear to pitch their wares.

Former Dallas Cowboy football player Walt Garrison, for example, whose drawl, rodeo background, and country attire certify his cowboy credentials, continues to do television commercials and print ads for Skoal, "the smokeless tobacco," which when placed between cheek and gum "feels real relaxin' in there." And even John Wayne broke a long-standing personal rule against doing commercials in 1975, when he appeared in cowboy duds to endorse United States savings bonds. Two years later, and again looking like he had just come in off a roundup, the Duke told people in no uncertain terms to take Datril 500 for their headaches, and it's hard to imagine how anyone could have disobeyed him.

But perhaps the most renowned advertising cowboy of all is one whose name nobody knows, and who was rather unceremoniously expelled from the television screen in 1970, yet who nonetheless remains America's most visible and arguably romantic cowboy. His handsome, wind- and sun-weathered, squint-eyed face appears on the pages of magazines throughout the world; he rides across thousands of billboards that hang above freeways and that are bolted to buses and high-rise buildings. His image is so clearly that of the proto-typical cowboy, tough and controlled and capable, that it's hard to believe that

Rodeo star Larry Mahan acts out a hard ride for the cameras. (Michael Lichter)

A cowboy and cowgirl of leisure take a break on a hot desert highway in Bill Schenck's painting, Flamingo Road.

The makers of Winston cigarettes help sponsor rodeos throughout the West, providing the prize money that rodeo cowboys compete for and touting rodeo as "America's #1 Sport." (Susan Felter)

In San Antonio, Texas, artist Roger Wade constructed a forty-foot high sculpture he straightforwardly called Boots.

he is, in fact, just a wage-earning cowboy on the down side of fifty named Darrell Winfield who hails from Riverton, Wyoming. Winfield was working on the Quarter Circle Five ranch near Pinedale, Wyoming, in the late 1960s when people from Chicago's Leo Burnett agency decided to use the ranch for shooting a commercial. Someone noticed Winfield, and the Marlboro Man was born.

It was certainly nothing new when Philip Morris Incorporated, the maker of Marlboro cigarettes, decided to use cowboy imagery to advertise its product; and the image of the rough cowboy was the perfect one to convince male smokers to try a cigarette that had originally been marketed for women. But since medical concerns about the effects of smoking had made it unadvisable to advertise that Marlboros were good for you, or even good tasting, all the manufacturer could advertise was an image, the image of a cowboy who was at once contemporary and traditional, a cowboy who never cajoled or coerced or even spoke, but whose commanding presence alone could entice smokers to "Come to Marlboro Country."

Marlboro cigarettes became so closely associated with Winfield's face that as a precaution, in the late 1970s, the Burnett agency began occasionally using photographs of other flesh-and-blood cowboys, just in case Winfield was ever thrown from his horse and stepped on, or otherwise rendered unphotogenic. But Philip Morris and Burnett would never have willingly surrendered Winfield or its basic cowboy campaign, neither of which has ever shown signs of losing appeal or effectiveness.

Philip Morris has been by no means the only American manufacturer selling the cowboy mystique. After being only regionally popular during the preceding half-century, western wear burst on the national fashion scene in the mid-1970s, drawing as much attention and excitement as if it had just been introduced in the Paris salons. *Gentlemen's Quarterly* magazine devoted its entire April 1975 issue to the chic new western look. Its editors affirmed that cowboy fashion was a "tradition: not a fossil, but a living, growing thing." Then they proceeded to wax nostalgic about that tradition:

> Some things never change. The rolling foothills of Arizona. The great Western sky. And the clothes. The faded blue denim. The soft checks of cowboy shirts. The mellowness of leather boots.

Mellow was an adjective that corral-bred cowboys would certainly never have used to describe their boots, but there was no denying that their home-spun look was finally catching the eyes of the arbiters of urban fashion. In 1978, designer Ralph Lauren introduced a cowboy-inspired collection of men's and women's clothing that he predicted would long remain popular because of its "integrity." Design competitor Oleg Cassini said his western clothing "helps us believe we are still free to roam the range."

As the Urban Cowboy craze took off in 1980—spurred by the popular film, the fashions, and the fact that no other fad came along to preempt it—sales of designer jeans, cowboy boots, and hats skyrocketed. More than ten million pairs of cowboy boots were sold in 1980 alone; the Western hat industry topped $500 million in annual sales for the first time in its history; men's colognes called "Chaps" and "Stetson" and "Colorado Sage" appeared and did land-office business. It seemed as though nothing imaginable could generate cash for merchandisers like the dream of being a cowboy.

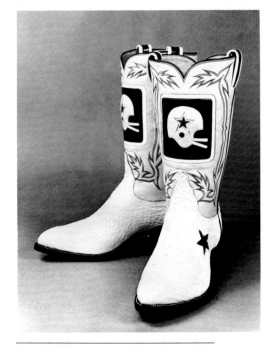

The Tony Lama Boot Company designed and crafted a pair of Dallas Cowboy cowboy boots for each member of that professional football team.

DURING THE LONG SUMMER AND FALL OF THE 1980 PRESIDENTIAL CAMPAIGN, posters and billboards appeared throughout the western half of the United States featuring a photograph of the Republican candidate wearing a cowboy hat and a work shirt, and grinning like a ranch hand who had just come in for supper. The poster bore a simple message: "This Is Reagan Country." And so it was.

During the many years that he campaigned for the White House, and then after he had finally moved in, Ronald Reagan never called himself a cowboy, but his image makers made sure that the public didn't forget the president's connection to the West's heritage of opportunity, self-reliance, and courage. Television cameras often caught glimpses of Reagan taking the afternoon off to ride the ranges on the banks of the Potomac River; his regular tours of the western states included the donning of a sleek rancher's Stetson at seemingly every public appearance; and during his many vacations spent at his Rancho del Cielo in California, reporters kept the nation informed that the president relaxed by repairing fences, chopping brush, and riding out to check on the cows.

Far from being alarming to the majority of Americans, the image of the president of the United States as a cowboy at heart who could still keep his cowboy persona intact despite the rigors and pressures of his office was somehow reassuring. This was a president who was one of the folks, an old but steady hand who talked straight, shot straight, and sat tall in the saddle.

Reagan, arguably the first president to truly understand how important image is to the office, rode into Washington during a flurry of faddish attention to the West, characterized by the popularization of western fashions, cowboy discos, and country music. But millions of Americans also associated the West with tradition, with stability, with *conservatism,* and that was the West with which the president allied himself. When he spoke about getting the government off the people's backs, about making America strong and self-sufficient and proud again, he was espousing the same mythic cowboy ideals that he had helped implant in the American consciousness with his roles in Hollywood Westerns. And it was his cowboy image—understated but ever present— that lent so many of his positions and policies an air of credibility. Would a cowboy back down to the Russians? Would a cowboy put up with OSHA regulations and burdensome unemployment insurance? Would a cowboy

Portraits of singing cowboy Gene Autry, ABOVE, and rodeo cowboy Larry Mahan, RIGHT, by Robert Rishell are permanently displayed at the National Cowboy Hall of Fame in Oklahoma City. The privately-funded museum is dedicated to the notion that the cowboy embodies the highest ideals of conservative Americanism.

Ronald Reagan was elected president during the height of faddish attention to the West. His cowboy image complemented his conservative politics. (Dirck Halstead/Gamma Liaison)

tolerate welfare cheats?

Although many Americans readily disagreed with his positions, Reagan long remained popular because his policies so perfectly matched his public image. He was a kind of cowboy, after all—polite but tough, engaging but independent—and a cowboy had to do what he had to do. The president reminded people, and seemed to remind himself, of the mythic golden era of the West when individuals were unencumbered by society, when actions undertaken boldly could surely succeed, and when right always won out. The cowpuncher president symbolized simplicity in an incredibly complex world, and his nostalgic image was an enormously appealing one.

Ronald Reagan was the third "gentleman rancher" president of the twentieth century, preceded by Lyndon Johnson and Theodore Roosevelt. Yet although Johnson's ranch associations were by far the most deeply rooted of the three, Johnson did the least to foster a personal cowboy image, in large part because his Great Society goals did not converge with the culture's mythic cowboy ideals. Unlike Reagan, who could readily employ the imagery of the cowboy in his presidency, Johnson's civil rights and social concerns had little in common with the self-reliant and stoic cowboy mystique.

Theodore Roosevelt, on the other hand, a native of New York State who as a young man had become immensely attracted to the image of the manly cowboy, portrayed himself throughout his political career as a public servant shaped by the dangers and delights of the western wilderness. During the Spanish-American war, Roosevelt deemed it appropriate to dub the First Volunteer Cavalry, in which he served, the "Rough Riders," a name already associated around the world with the horsemen in Buffalo Bill Cody's Wild West show. And once he became president, his jingoistic "big stick" foreign policy openly equated hostile foreign governments with America's Indians, and equated the United States with the cavalry and cowboys who had fought them in history and in legend.

Beginning with Roosevelt, and continuing throughout the twentieth century to Reagan, cowboy imagery has been much more readily employed by and aligned with the political right in America than with the left, certainly because notions of strength and individualism have traditionally had far more rhetorical appeal for the right. The mythic cowboy has from the beginning been imbued with steadfast common sense and has taken instructions from no one; he has offered assistance when it was needed, but has asked for nothing in return; and he has never endured insults or abuses—precisely the kind of figure who would spurn big government with its meddlesome interference in business and private lives and its unwillingness to let people help themselves.

When Gene Autry sang "Don't Bite the Hand That's Feeding You" as immigrants streamed into the United States at the end of World War II, he expressed the fears and prejudices of thousands of Americans who believed that the immigrants would destroy the country by begging instead of working. At the same time, Autry himself was billed on CBS Radio's "Gene Autry's Melody Ranch" as a "symbol of the clean-thinking, honesty and integrity of the American people." It was the foreigners who spelled danger, and the upstanding cowboys like Autry who sounded the alarm.

By 1955, cowboys and politics had become closely enough wedded that Swedish scholar Harry Schein could review Fred Zinneman's popular Western *High Noon* as a "convincing and...honest explanation of American foreign policy." Russian strategists read Schein's analysis of American Cold War policy with interest and some alarm because, in Schein's view, Gary Cooper represented America, and the town of Hadleyville represented the United Nations. The bad guys were Russia, China, and North Korea, and they were clearly in big trouble.

But Cooper's quiet, tough-guy image in *High Noon* (presumably presented with no political innuendo intended) was rather meek in comparison with the hard-line right-wing image of actor John Wayne. Wayne the actor had become so completely labeled a cowboy that when Wayne the individual spoke out in support of the Vietnam war, he was presumed to speak as a cowboy, and on behalf of his comrade cowboys. In 1968, when he briefly took off his cowboy hat and pistols for his role in the pro-Vietnam film *The Green Berets*, which he also directed, some critics insisted that Wayne—the nation's foremost cowboy hero—must have been secretly working for the Pentagon. Four years later, film critic Pauline Kael lambasted *The Cowboys*, directed by Mark Rydell and starring Wayne, because of its "simplistic right-wing ideology at a time when people may be ready to buy it." Kael didn't seem to believe that the movie was merely about a cattle drive, and that Wayne was only an actor in it—one who, in fact, was not triumphant, but who was murdered by his anarchistic cowboy laborers. Her reaction to the film attested to the degree with which conservative politics and presumed cowboy ideals had become synonymous: She could criticize Wayne's political views by criticizing the cowboy mentality that supposedly spawned them.

When former Nixon administration secretary of state Henry Kissinger spoke with Italian journalist Oriana Fallaci about his one-man diplomatic missions to the Paris peace talks and the Middle East in the 1970s, he said that his efforts had been supported by the American people because they had long been entranced by the image of the lone cowboy going up against great odds and finally saving the day. Henry Kissinger a cowboy? It seems that *he* perceived himself that way, or at least found the cowboy analogy an appropriate one to describe his diplomatic initiatives and his popularity. And President Nixon himself once described the United States's military retreat from Vietnam as "being like a cowboy with guns blazing backing out of a saloon."

The alliance between conservative politics and the image of the cowboy

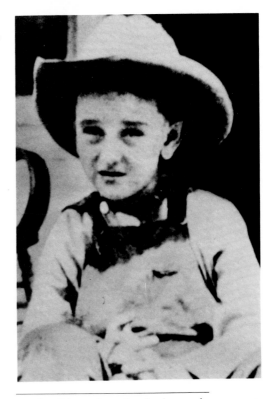

Lyndon Johnson's cowboy background was deeply rooted, but because his political concerns did not match the self-reliant and stoic mystique of the cowboy, he did little to foster a personal cowboy image.

The cowboy is perhaps America's most photographed figure, in part because in the modern West there are myriad kinds of cowpokes riding many intriguing kinds of mounts. (John Youngblut/The Stock Market; LEFT: Bruce Benedict/The Stock Market)

Olympic medal winner Billy Kidd was personally responsible for the burgeoning popularity of cowboy fashions on Colorado ski slopes during the 1970s.

continues to be protected at the National Cowboy Hall of Fame and Western Heritage Center in Oklahoma City—a museum and shrine of sorts that is "operated in full belief and faith in the free enterprise system." The privately-operated institution, which is visited by more than 300,000 people each year, contains art galleries, dioramas of early western scenes, the National Rodeo Hall of Fame, and even the hallowed graves of renowned rodeo broncs and bulls. The Cowboy Hall of Fame and its quarterly magazine *Persimmon Hill* are staunchly dedicated to the notion that the cowboy represents the highest ideals of Americanism, and they proudly counter what they call "liberal" subversion of cowboy heritage by proclaiming that "the American Cowboy is probably the greatest hero the world has ever known." The Roll of Honorees in the Hall of Fame of Great Westerners includes Abraham Lincoln, Theodore Roosevelt, and Dwight D. Eisenhower, as well as Will Rogers, Tom Mix, and Gary Cooper—good and brave men all. One of them, Rogers, actually was a cowboy in his youth, and the others were presumably heroic enough that they might as well have been.

THE COWBOY DREAM, THE DESIRE—WHETHER OPENLY ACKNOWLEDGED OR ONLY subconsciously experienced—to play cowboy, to escape into the cowboy's world, has had a pivotal role in the longevity of the cowboy myth. Millions of people have used the cowboy as a simple and sane escape from a world that lacks the cowboy's imagined heroism and resolve. Others have tried hard to emulate the mythic cowboy, fueling and perpetuating the myth in the process. Cowboys at large are singers, truck drivers, athletes, artists, Cowboys for Christ, and cowboys for Coors beer. Few of them have any connection to cows or the price of beef, yet because of the versatility of the myth, and its applicability to spheres well beyond the reach of a rancher's rope, they too are part of the culture's cowboy tradition, bound to it by their shared search for self-identity and a kind of fraternity symbolized by that ubiquitous wide-brimmed hat.

In the 1920s, for example, singers of what was then known as "hillbilly" music latched on to the image of the cowboy, and in so doing permanently altered the style of popular rural music. Hillbilly performers had appeared at dances and concerts up until that time dressed simply like the country folk they were—farmers and mountaineers from the hill country of Missouri, Kentucky, and Tennessee. Then an Oklahoma Ozark singer named Otto Gray began to bill himself as "The Singing Cowboy" and made an immediate mark on the world of hillbilly music. Dressed in a tailored shirt, bright western-cut suit, boots, and a ten-gallon hat, Gray cut a dashing figure; he appeared more sure of himself on stage than the other singers who had theretofore been content to project country-bumpkin images. By the early 1930s, virtually every hillbilly singer of note had undergone a sartorial transformation; a Texas-born brand of music called "western swing" was all the rage, singing cowboys were making movies, and the term *hillbilly music* had been all but abandoned in favor of the broader, cowboy-connected term *country and western*.

Country music and the image of the cowboy have remained closely wedded over the succeeding half century. Nashville, Tennessee, is as far removed from the native terrain of the cowboy as Cincinnati or Cedar Rapids, but the Grand Ole Opry, the city's guitar-picking cowboys, and its songs of faded love, faithful horses, and broken dreams mythically transport it into the sagebrush heart of the West. And throughout the nation, country and western music—running the gamut from Hank Snow to Asleep at the Wheel—continues to grow in popularity. In 1976, there were fewer than six hundred country and western–format radio stations, most of them scattered across the South and West. By 1981, nearly two thousand country stations were in operation, broadcasting in virtually every major city from coast to coast.

Although its popularity has yet to reach into every region of the nation as country music has done, a style of realist Western painting often called cowboy art is now undergoing a similar rise in public interest. Dozens of painters scattered from Texas to Montana produce carefully crafted paintings of cattle roundups and Indian camps in the Remington and Russell tradition that share an idyllic attitude toward the history of the cowboy and the West. Although shunned by the art establishment as nothing more than banal commercial illustration, paintings by the foremost cowboy artists can command staggering prices. In Phoenix in 1981 at the annual show of the Cowboy Artists Association, a prestigious group of twenty-three of the best-known painters of the genre, sales totaled $1,762,000 for ninety paintings and sculptures. And in 1982, at Houston's seventh annual Western Heritage Sale—an auction of cowboy art, prize quarter horses, and Santa Gertrudis cattle sponsored by former Texas governor and secretary of the treasury John Connally and two fellow businessmen-ranchers—sales of paintings and sculptures totaled $1,782,000, with the top-selling painting bringing in an astonishing $140,000, and that was less than half the final bid for the top-seller the year before.

The people who are anxious to purchase high-priced cowboy art are unashamed about its cost (the price itself is often a matter of prestige) and unconcerned about the fact that the pieces they proudly hang in their homes and offices aren't taken seriously by the majority of the nation's contemporary gallery operators and museum curators. The buyers respond to cowboy art because it is unabashedly sentimental, because it affirms the values of individualism and tenacity, and because as "art" it treats the image of the cowboy as being worthy of reflection and even adulation. Most cowboy paintings have a reverential tone, and their treatment of light, space, and action invariably conveys a sense of seriousness and transcendent importance. The cowboy is worthy of all the drama with which we can surround him, the painters seem to be

In cities throughout the West, businessmen in western wear cut dashing cowboy figures. (Bill Wunsch)

Since the 1920s, gaudy cowboy costumes have been essential apparel for Nashville greats like Hank Snow, ABOVE, and Porter Wagoner, RIGHT. Wagoner often appeared with Dolly Parton in the years before she became a nationally known country soloist and actress. (BOTH: Bud Lee)

Millions of Americans play out their cowboy fantasies inside country discos and honky-tonks instead of out in the open spaces. (Michael Murphy)

saying, and their patrons seem to heartily agree.

But if cowboy art is often reverential, cowboy religion goes one step further by combining the images and artifacts of historical and contemporary cowboys with fundamentalist Christian dogma. Ordained and unordained ministers who travel the rodeo circuit for the Cowboys for Christ organization tell rodeo performers and audiences that Jesus was the first cowboy. They remind listeners that Jesus was born in a stable, that he rode into Jerusalem on "an unbroken colt," and that he traveled constantly during his three-year ministry, just like rodeo cowboys do. And at least one observer has claimed that the coming of the western hero is a kind of Second Coming of Christ. In her book, *Rodeo: An Anthropologist Looks at the Wild and the Tame* (1982), Elizabeth Atwood Lawrence quoted a rodeo preacher who explains that:

> Jesus gave examples using the things rodeo people use in everyday life—livestock: sheep, cattle and horses.... Jesus spoke of "separating the sheep from the goats" and cowboys have worked this way in rodeo or on the ranch.... The Bible says Christ will be revealed to us sitting on a white horse—like a grand finale for a cowboy.... It is so much like rodeo it isn't funny.

Jesus Christ, John Travolta, Otto Gray, Abraham Lincoln, politicians, painters, Marlboro men, and the long-haul truckers in hats and snap-button shirts whose rigs have become their horses—all can become cowboys because they imagine they are, or because someone else so enshrines them. Unlike the scattered boys and buckaroos who still punch cattle, who still saddle ponies and ride out into the western space, the cowboys at large work at a mythic ranch, an amalgam of memories, identities, and dreams fenced in only by the limits of imagination. They possess little substance, but their myriad images have had amazing staying power. Their images explain the world in simple terms, spark the present with a sense of purpose, and trigger the reveries of those horseback halcyon days gone by.

Today Bantam Books offers its multivolume, hard-cover "Louis L'Amour Collection" to readers as a means of finding out:

> How [it would] feel to be stranded in the desert under a blazing noonday sun—with your canteen empty, your horse shot down at your feet, and your deadliest enemy lying in wait somewhere close at hand.... *You won't just read about the Old West; you'll live in it!*

A Colorado company offers "Rock-It," a $1,500 adult rocking horse for men who want to pretend to be boys pretending to be cowboys. A woman in a Wyoming bar tells Darrell Winfield that she recently had to drive to Baltimore, but it was almost as though she hadn't even left the West: "Saw you on a billboard about every three miles," she says, "and I wasn't homesick at all."

And at Gilley's, Houston's renowned country nightclub, amid the constant hawking of cowboy beach towels, Christmas records, T-shirts, bumper stickers, neckties and panties imprinted with the Gilley's logo, and souvenir photos of awkward out-of-towners perched on mechanical bulls, a grandmother in jeans and a gray sweatshirt cautiously hangs on to the boots of a four-year-old boy whom she has lifted onto the stage. The band plays "Whiskey River," oblivious of the little boy in a red rhinestone cowboy suit with the name "Travis" emblazoned on the back. But the grandmother hopes someone will notice and help make the boy a cowboy star just like so many others have become. She hands him a miniature guitar, and the boy begins to strum it. "Now sing, honey," she yells above the din of the band, the dancers, and the drinkers. "Sing proud just like a cowboy."

You're damn right cowboys are sloganeers. The cowboys at large proudly proclaim their connection to America's boldest myth even on the backs of Japanese pickup trucks. (Richard Ansaldi)

13

Although Buffalo Bill began a series of "farewell appearances" in 1910 as a means of bolstering attendance at The Wild West, six years passed before he finally took his last farewell bow.

At the end of his show's engagement at New York's Madison Square Garden in May 1910, Buffalo Bill Cody announced that he was about to go home for a well-earned rest. But although The Wild West had made Cody wealthy, a series of ill-conceived investments soon left him virtually penniless, and he was forced to go on working. He traveled and performed with a combined show called Buffalo Bill's Wild West and Pawnee Bill's Great Far East, with the Sells-Floto circus, and finally with the Miller Brothers and Arlington 101 Ranch Wild West, whose 1916 season ended on the evening of November 4. It was Cody's final public appearance.

It had been forty-seven years since Ned Buntline had published Buffalo Bill, King of the Border Men, *the first of more than 550 dime novels about Buffalo Bill; and thirty-two years had passed since Cody had first introduced Buck Taylor, "the King of the Cowboys," to his Wild West audiences. Theodore Roosevelt had published* Ranch Life and Hunting Trail *in 1888 and* The Rough Riders *in 1899, both of which heralded the cowboy's prowess and virtue.* The Virginian *had been published in 1902, and Cecil B. DeMille had directed its first film version in 1914. When Cody finally left the performing arena, he was old, tired, and ill. But his mythic West was still wondrously vital, and the zesty cowboys seemed certain to long endure. Despite early predictions that the image of the cowboy couldn't survive in the twentieth century, William S. Hart's popular film* Hell's Hinges *was playing in theaters all across the nation when Cody took his final bow, and Tom Mix made his Western film debut only weeks after Cody died in Denver on January 10, 1917.*

CHAPTER THIRTEEN

THE LAST ROUNDUP

"COWBOYS USED TO LOVE TO SING ABOUT PEOPLE DYING," SAID TEDDY BLUE Abbott. "I don't know why. I guess it was because they was so full of life themselves." And like the early trail hands, Americans have always seemed to enjoy speculating about the imminent death of the figure of the cowboy, about the certainty that he would soon disappear. The cowboy has always seemed so grounded in a specific terrain and time that it has seemed impossible that he could survive forever. As early as 1881, an old cowman and wagon freighter told artist Frederic Remington "there is no more of the West...and a poor man cannot make a living at all." Remington sadly agreed that the cowboy would soon disappear. He hoped his paintings could at least keep the memory of the cowboy alive.

But a century later the cowboy is still with us, and we are still saying goodbye to him, lamenting his passing and watching as the West continues to wither from view. In 1977, Jane Kramer, a frequent contributor to *The New Yorker*, wrote *The Last Cowboy*, a portentously titled account of the life of a Texas panhandle cowboy she called Henry Blanton, a man who mourns the collapse of his mythic West and whose own fears and failures are meant to symbolize the demise of the modern cowboy. And in 1982, two beautiful new books of photographs of contemporary working cowboys appeared—*Last of a Breed* and *Vanishing Breed*—as if, like Remington, they offered a final visual assessment of the cowboy before he rode across the dark horizon of oblivion.

Teddy Blue was right; the trail hands were very conscious of the

Observers have forecast the dreary and quiet demise of the cowboy for a hundred years, and continue to do so today. (Paul Dix; LEFT: John Running)

391

The mythic cowboy has always mourned not only the death of his comrades, but the loss of open land and a vibrant way of life. (Kevin Bubriski)

possibility of death, and they joked and sang about it as if it were their chief concern. It's doubtful that they were obsessed with death simply because they were full of life. But certainly, isolated on the open prairies, they had to wonder what would become of them and their motley kind. The fictional and folkloric cowboys who descended from the trail drovers had death on their minds as well, but more than fearing their own end, they feared the collective loss of the cowboy spirit and the demise of the western land that harbored symbols of independence and self-reliance. The creators of the heroic cowboy saw him as the final frontiersman, a figure who knew civilization was inevitable, but who nonetheless lamented the death of the wild West and the disappearance of the men and women who had known its grandeur and its adventure. Inevitably, nostalgia became an integral part of the cowboy myth: The cowboy was the last figure who had experienced the frontier and was therefore the last one who could openly pine for what he had known and lost.

But the nostalgia within the cowboy myth was for the myths themselves, not for the real West. Few of the fictional cowboys were nostalgic about the days and years of disease and deprivation, hunger and aching work that had been a part of the frontier. But most of the writers and filmmakers created cowboys who either blatantly or quietly longed for the days when men were freer, bold action was easier to undertake, and the grass was still growing in great abundance. "Out West America could still make in ringing tones her magnificent promises," wrote British literary and film historian Jenni Calder. It was those promises of independence, purpose, and plentiful land—promises that were never entirely fulfilled—about which the fictional cowboy could wax wistful and nostalgic. But once that theme of longing became an elemental part of the cowboy myth, a nagging question began to be asked: If nothing could ever be as fine and free as it once was, if the promises could not be kept, what would become of the figure of the cowboy himself? The seemingly inevitable answer was that as the good old days receded further from his grasp, the mythic cowboy would finally abandon his hopes and ride away.

THE MYTHIC COWBOY AND THE COWBOY'S COUNTRY HAVE BEEN IN the process of dying and disappearing for more than a hundred years, and that steady decay has imbued the figure of the cowboy with a sadness and a poignancy that he would not have had if he and his world were assured of long survival. From the haggard trail hands to the matinee idols to the hard-hided rodeo stars, cowboys have always been shamelessly sentimental, and there is nothing like the prospect of one's own death, or the death of a *compadre,* or, perhaps worse, the death of a whole way of life, to spawn sentimental memories and mawkish regrets.

When the drovers imagined death, they described it in maudlin cowboy

Cowboys bury a fellow buckaroo in James Reynolds's painting, The White Man's Way. And in a Saturday Evening Post *cover illustration by Norman Rockwell, an oldtimer gets sentimental when he listens to a sad old cowboy song.*

Images of cowboys mounting up and riding away forever have been a part of the cowboy myth for more than a century. (B. A. King)

metaphors. In the song "The Last Roundup," a dying cowboy says he is:

Gonna saddle old Paint for the last time
And ride
To the faraway range of the boss in the sky,
Where the strays are counted and branded,
There goes I.
I'm headin' for the last roundup.

His departure is peaceful, his attitude toward it serene and accepting, perhaps because the heaven he is heading toward resembles the life he has always known. But the figure in "The Dying Cowboy" cannot imagine an afterlife. He can think only of his fear of dying utterly alone:

"By my father's grave there let mine be,
And bury me not on the lone prairie,"

"Oh bury me not—" And his voice failed there.
But we took no heed of his dying prayer;
In a narrow grave just six by three
We buried him there on the lone prairie.

His comrades have cows to move and cannot take his body home to be buried. When they bury the cowboy in that lonely, narrow grave, they are chilled by both the cold reality of his death and by the realization that their fates will be much like his.

But among the dozens of trail songs that have survived and are still sung in the waning years of the twentieth century, many more lament the passing of the cowboy life than mourn the deaths of the boys themselves. Almost as soon as it had taken shape, the cowboy's way of life seemed to be jeopardized by railroads and barbed wire, by stockyards and stock trucks, and by the endless loss of the range to the demands of civilization:

Through progress of the railroads our occupation's gone;
So we will put ideas into words, our words into a song.
First comes the cowboy, he is pointed for the West;
Of all the pioneers I claim the cowboys are the best;
You will miss him on the round-up, it's gone, his merry shout—
The cowboy has left the country and the campfire has gone out.

Many early songs like "The Campfire Has Gone Out" saw the demise of the cowboy as symbolic of the death of the West itself. If the cowboy was the West's foremost symbolic figure, then his death would inevitably imply the demise of his region and its ideals.

"My West passed utterly out of existence so long ago as to make it nearly a dream," Remington remarked in 1907. His cowboy paintings and illustrations had become nationally renowned, but he insisted that they were only images of men and a time that had entirely "marched off the board." Cowboy artist Charles M. Russell agreed that the West and its cowboys had undergone radical transformations, but when he penned this rhyme in 1917, he was confident that their memory would live on in words as well as paintings:

The West is dead my friend,
But writers hold the seed,
And what they sow
Will live and grow
Again to those who read.

Yet readers and moviegoers were continually reminded that the cowboys that fascinated them had already vanished or were about to do so soon. Novelist Owen Wister called the cowboy "the last American hero," and Zane Grey speculated that his horse operas were so popular because Americans were naturally interested in a disappearing part of their heritage. In the film *Tumbleweeds* (1925), William S. Hart and a group of riders stop at the top of a hill and watch a cattle herd disappear across a plain that is about to be opened up to homesteaders. "Boys, it's the last of the West," Hart says. It was the last of Hart's contributions to the mythic West as well; he retired from film-making when *Tumbleweeds* was completed.

The movie cowboys added a new dimension to the death imagery that had always been a part of the cowboy myth. Not only were the mythic cowboys and their wild West always in danger of disappearing, the cowboy stars themselves eventually died or retired, and in doing so they provided a palpable image of a disappearing cowboy. Millions of Americans were shocked and grieved by Tom Mix's death in a car crash in Arizona in 1940, and when Tex Ritter, who hadn't appeared on the screen in decades, died in 1974, he could still be eulogized by one fan as a cowboy who was gone but who would never be forgotten:

Gone did I say? No, not really. So much of him is with us still, and it will always be here to remind us of golden days. In [the] hearts of many millions Tex Ritter dwelt, and there he will always remain.

But the death America least wanted to bear was that of John Wayne, the last Hollywood actor to be almost exclusively identified by his cowboy roles. When Wayne, who had already battled cancer once, underwent open-heart surgery in 1978, he received more than a hundred thousand get-well cards and letters from people for whom he had become America's final cowboy hero.

Wayne's last film, *The Shootist*, directed by Don Siegel, had been released in 1976. In it Wayne portrayed western gunman John Bernard Brooks, who in 1901 has "plain plumb out-lived [his] time," and who is told he is dying of cancer. Before Brooks decides what would be the most fitting and honorable

"The cowboy has left the country and the campfire has gone out," said an early song. But today a few cowboys still inhabit the empty country. (Martin Schreiber)

way to go out of the world, he is befriended by a widow and her son (Lauren Bacall and Ron Howard), who operate the boardinghouse where he has come to die. Twice he defines his personal creed for them, saying:

> I won't be wronged, I won't be insulted, I won't be laid a hand on. I don't do these things to other people and I require the same of them.

It was as if Wayne himself, the consummate mythic cowboy, had seized one last opportunity to express his personal western golden rule before his long and incredible career was over. *The Shootist* was not a great film by any means, but it was a wonderfully fitting finale for the nation's most memorable cowboy actor. Like one of the tough and stoic characters he had so often portrayed, Wayne faced up to his own death by straightforwardly acting it out on screen. *The Shootist* was still in distribution across the country when John Wayne died of cancer on June 11, 1979.

AMERICANS TENDED TO PRESUME THAT THE FIGURE OF THE COWBOY WAS ABOUT TO die—even in the days when he first took shape—because it seemed impossible that his symbolic importance could be sustained amid the society's changing conditions and concerns. The cowboy represented a link with the frontier, but the frontier had vanished; he symbolized a kind of literal, physical freedom, but the continent had become filled with people and civilization had closed in around him; and he symbolized individual courage and action in an age when social strictures had grown rigid and complex. The mythic cowboy was hopelessly anachronistic. He didn't belong in the twentieth century, but he would not disappear. He continued to evoke images of a past that was presumed to be better than the present, but his role was limited to that nostalgic evocation. Whenever his observers wondered what would become of the cowboy in the strange and uncertain future, the most likely possibility seemed to be that he would finally recede into his own century by dying a quiet and honorable cowboy death.

Yet the mythic cowboy has been a tenacious and stubborn hombre. His façade has steadily changed as the decades have spun themselves out; but he has not died, and he has yet to march off the board. He has negotiated the sometimes tenuous transitions from disreputable cattle tender to six-gun hero to silk-shirted singer to callous outlaw to street-wise urban roughneck without surrendering his sense of pride or his capable and courageous image. In every one of his manifestations, the cowboy has known who he is and where he belongs—even if he only belongs on the back of a wandering horse. Every mythic cowboy of every era has understood himself, or at least accepted himself, and he has faced his world with confidence, ease, and a measure of humor. Those are the threads that have entwined all of our

The retirements of movie cowboys like Roy Rogers provided evidence that cowboys really did get old, die, or disappear. But Rogers preserves the memories of his career in his California museum, sometimes telling visitors he'll even be glad to sing "Happy Trails" as they drive away.

American cowboys, and they have played a critical role in keeping the figure of the cowboy among us.

America, like every society, has needed its myths and mythic figures, its reassuring stories and idealized examples. The cowboy emerged as a distinctively American symbol of action and ability, a man who belonged in the unique landscape of the American West and who thrived on its harsh conditions and its bold possibilities. The cowboy represented America's proudest image of itself, and the West was the symbolic terrain where we tried to fulfill our noble promises.

Yet some observers have argued that the West itself has been crippled by the constraints of its mythic stories, that it has myopically reveled in its history and its colorful folklore without ever getting down to the sober, clear-eyed business of creating a vibrant and successful contemporary society. Westerners have chosen to pretend to be carefree cowboys, they charge, ignoring the problems and perplexities of their own age in favor of the nostalgic securities of the mythic frontier. "The West does not need to explore its myths much further," wrote novelist and western historian Wallace Stegner:

> It has already relied on them too long. It has no future in exploiting its setting either, for too consistently it has tried to substitute scenery for a society. All it has to do is to be itself at the most responsible pitch, to take a hard look at itself and acknowledge some things that the myths have consistently obscured—been *used* to obscure.

Aspects of the cowboy myth have unquestionably been counterproductive to the formation of the kind of society Westerners once dreamed they could create. The myth has, for instance, focused far too much attention on the conquering of the land, the taming and subduing of it, than on the obligation to husband it carefully and to sustain its beauty and bounty. It has let the romantic image of the roaming cowboy obscure the critical importance of staking an emotional claim and assuming real responsibility for a given place, its people and problems, and its future. The cowboy myth has played a damning role in the way in which all Americans have grown at ease with violence and become numbed to its horror; it has obscured the awful reality of the genocide that was practiced on Native Americans; and it has offered a pitifully poor example of how men and women should interact in a society that preaches equality for all its people.

While these shortcomings are real and profound, and it is important that we recognize and finally confront each one of them, it is also important to note that those same serious and destructive effects demonstrate the power and influence that the cowboy myth has had. If the cowboy and his mythic stories had offered only a kind of enduring entertainment, an easy escape from reality, they could not have harmed or deluded us in the ways that they have done. Nor could they have given us pride and confidence, the assurance that we could succeed and the security of knowing who we are. Vibrant myths—myths that affect the ways in which people think and act—are not innocuous. They can be as destructive as they are useful; they can blind a society to its faults as well as reassure it of the importance of its goals.

Stegner is right: The American West should simply be itself, acknowledging its weaknesses and protecting its successes. But Stegner fails to recognize that in the West's true and vital heart pumps the blood of the mythic cowboy. The West can't forget its swarthy horseman because he, more than any other figure, is the symbolic ancestor of all its people. It is hard to imagine the contemporary, chaotic, urbanizing West devoid of the historical figure of the cowboy. And it is likewise difficult to imagine America itself without its mythic stories of the frontier West to tell. Mythic history is vital because it offers a clear, if not necessarily precise, explanation of how the society got from *then* to *now*. And despite all the dire warnings during the past century, the mythic cowboy has refused to die or disappear because he has always managed to anticipate or adjust to our transitions through time.

Two old cowpokes share a story about the golden days. (ALL: Jack Parsons/ FotoWest)

"WHEN WE CAN'T HAVE SOMETHING, WE RE-CREATE IT," SAID DIRECTOR SAM Peckinpah in an attempt to explain why the American film industry has for so long devoted so much attention to the stories of the frontier West. Artists in every medium have tried to re-create the elusive cowboy ever since they first paid attention to his symbolic possibilities a century ago, when the frontier era drew to a close and began to be missed.

Buffalo Bill Cody created a cowboy that emodied the traits of the first fearless frontiersmen; the dime novelists made a daring gunfighter out of the cowboy; and once Owen Wister's Virginian appeared, that gunfighter became a loner who upheld a rigid moral code. William S. Hart's cowboys were badmen who turned to good. And the matinee cowboys of the B-Western era were scrupulously good men who stayed good all the way. The singing cowboys transformed the rough and tough West into an idyllic playground set to strumming guitars and occasional full orchestration. Then John Wayne turned the cowboy into a "normal fella" who was nonetheless fiercely heroic; Clint Eastwood crafted an antiheroic cowboy whose heroism was only his survival; and John Travolta created a brand-new cowboy for the eighties—a suburban cowboy far removed from cattle or horses, open land or open minds, a reactionary roughneck who was a cowboy only because he pretended to be one.

For more than a hundred years we have re-created the lowly cowboy in paintings, books, photographs, and dirt-filled arenas where young men risk their necks in cowboy competitions; we have manufactured a cowboy music and a cowboy art. We dress like cowboys; we dance like cowboys; we smoke like cowboys—and we yearn for the better life of the good old days as only cowboys can.

Frederic Remington's melancholy painting, The Fall of the Cowboy, *implies that both fences and the cold weight of winter have made the cowboy's work bitter and hard and have endangered his survival.*

Frederic Remington

"There are only a few of us left now," wrote cowboy Teddy Blue Abbott. *"The rest have gone ahead across the big divide. I hope they find good water and plenty of grass. But wherever they are is where I want to go."* (William Coupon)

The figure of the cowboy is as ubiquitous as the sunrise and the growing grass; the Marlboro Man does not seem laughably out of place on a billboard suspended above the New Jersey turnpike, and a businessman in lizard-skin boots and a silver-belly Resistol hat attracts no attention on Madison Avenue. There are cowboys in Connecticut, cowboys in Kentucky, and even a few cowboys left in Colorado; yet many of the cowboy's observers still insist that he has all but disappeared.

Today's cowboys are presumed to be in as much mortal danger as they ever have been—perhaps even a little more—because this is the space age, after all. We get from place to place by leaving the land and crossing it in a sky crosshatched by vapor trails; the West is filled with cities and missile silos, strip mines and retirement resorts; Hollywood has all but abandoned the Western movie; and cattle are reared in enormous feedlots that systematically turn their muscle into meat and their dung into methane fuel.

But it's still a risky business to eulogize the last cowboy, in part because there are so many kinds of cowboys whose expiration date is in question. The horse opera cowboy seems fit and healthy: Writers like Louis L'Amour continue to produce Western sagas at an astonishing clip, and millions of readers continue to buy and read each new story set in a fanciful Western world. Rodeo continues to grow in popularity, and scrappy young kids from every corner of the country attend rodeo schools to learn how to ride on the back of a horrified horse. Dozens of artists paint hundreds of cowboy paintings that sell for thousands of dollars apiece—cowboys frozen reverently in a frontier time, and contemporary cowboys who still look like, and sit a horse like, the battered old boys who preceded them.

The Western sets at the Hollywood studios are quiet these days; some sets have even been dismantled. But for every critic who verifies that the Western film is dead, another will offer solid assurances that somebody, somewhere will always be making Western movies. "I think our fascination with movies like *Star Wars* is similar to the fascination with Buck Rogers and shows like *The Phantom Empire*," says septuagenarian Gene Autry. "I've been around long enough to see things move in cycles, and it just seems like the right time for a cowboy hero to emerge again.... I even think there's room for a singing cowboy today." Actor-director Robert Redford agrees with the venerable singing cowboy: "There's a mythical element to the Western that will always make it viable and important," Redford says, "regardless of how many are made."

Children still ride stick horses across the carpets and pretend they are bold buckaroos, and adults still pack up their Levis each summer and head for dude ranches where they act out similar fantasies. Cowboys still sell beer and barbecued potato chips; they preach the Gospel and play pedal-steel guitar in smoky honky-tonks. There is a cowboy in the White House; there are cowboys

on Capitol Hill; and there are still a few certified cowboys in the West at work punching certified cows.

Those wind-beaten, bow-legged boys whose lives are shaped by the caprice of weather, the smell of horse sweat, and the belligerence of stupid beeves continue to tend cattle in that outmoded way because cowboying is, for all its trials, damned pleasurable work that is infused with a romantic connection to land and the cycle of seasons and a mythic connection to the decades gone by. Men and women still work cattle because cattle still have to be worked, and those who eschew the agri-business accouterments and go at it on horseback do so consciously, gladly. They are a diminishing breed, to be sure; there are fewer working cowboys in the 1980s than there were in the 1960s; and when the new century begins to cut its course, there will probably be fewer still. And when people pay fleeting attention to those twenty-first century cowboys at work in the urban West, they will swear, no doubt, that they are a vanishing bunch, surely soon to die.

A few months before he died in April 1939, Teddy Blue commented about how the numbers of the old trail hands were dwindling and how the range era had sadly passed:

> There are lots of young fellows punching cows today but they can never take our place, because cowpunching as we knew it is a thing of the past.... They are good fellows, but they never will get a show to learn like we did.... Only a few of us are left now, and they are scattered from Texas to Canada. The rest have left the wagon and gone ahead across the big divide, looking for a new range. I hope they find good water and plenty of grass. But wherever they are is where I want to go.

Teddy Blue surely found the old cowpunchers, and together they must have encountered a rich new range that is thick with summer grasses. Always an optimist and hopelessly sentimental, Teddy Blue would never have pronounced his comrade cowpokes dead, nor announced that their western ways were gone for good. True to that maudlin cowboy tradition, he merely lamented that lives and lifestyles and landscapes couldn't remain what they once were, then quickly assumed that whatever became of them would be filled with more good than bad.

That, ultimately, is all we can do with all of our mythic cowboys—the boys in the pastures and the boys in the barrooms, the horsemen and heroes, the tenders of cattle, and the tenders of western dreams. We can wish that each of them were as wonderfully free and alive as he was when we first encountered him, as vital as memory tells us he must have been. Then we can watch as all the cowboys ride abreast into an uncertain future, toward what may finally be the last roundup, but what is probably just one of dozens more yet to come. There are always cattle and stories to be gathered, and mythic brands to be burned into their hairy hides.

Even at the end of the twentieth century, there are still cattle to be branded, and there are still a few cowboys at work in the pastures and asleep on the prairie-hard carpets. (John Running; LEFT: Bill Ellzey)

Credits &
Acknowledgments

Contemporary Photographers

John Running
PAGES 27, 42, 43, 256, 257, 261, 262, 263, 390, 405, 428

Martin Schreiber
FROM THE LAST OF A BREED, TEXAS MONTHLY PRESS (1982),
PAGES 266, 395, 420

Glenn Short
PAGE 29; BRUCE COLEMAN, INC., PAGE 197

Jim Smith
PAGE 221

Steve Smith
PAGES 346, 421

Tom Stack
/TOM STACK & ASSOC., PAGE 425

Charles Steiner
/INTERNATIONAL STOCK PHOTO, PAGE 48

Hans Teensma
PAGES 68, 68–69, 199

Stanley Tretick
PAGE 84

Stephen Trimble
PAGES 135, 150

Peter C. van Dyke
PAGE 311

Joe Van Wormer
/BRUCE COLEMAN, INC., PAGE 161

Laine Whitcomb
PAGE 47

Nancy Wood
PAGES 209, 212, 219, 345, 429

Jonathan Wright
/BRUCE COLEMAN, INC., PAGES 4, 28, 172–173, 180

Bill Wunsch
PAGES 365, 379, 423

John Youngblut
/THE STOCK MARKET, PAGES 220, 377

Picture Credits

PAGE 18–19: Buffalo Bill Historical Center, Cody, Wyoming

PAGE 30: Montana Historical Society, Helena, Montana

PAGE 34: Buffalo Bill Historical Center, Cody, Wyoming

PAGE 35: Denver Center Cinema, Denver, Colorado

PAGE 38: ©1972, Warner Bros. Inc.

PAGE 39: ©1980, Paramount Pictures Corporation

PAGE 54: ©1938, United Artists Corporation; Museum of Modern Art/Film Stills Archive, New York

PAGE 57: *Trappers Saluting the Rocky Mountains,* Alfred Jacob Miller, Buffalo Bill Historical Center, Cody, Wyoming

PAGE 58–59: ©1981, Universal Pictures

PAGE 60–61: *A Storm in the Rocky Mountains—Mt. Rosalie,* Albert Bierstadt, The Brooklyn Museum, Brooklyn, New York

PAGE 63: Collection of Paul and Teresa Harbaugh, Denver, Colorado

PAGE 66: Circus World Museum, Baraboo, Wisconsin

PAGE 67: Collection of Joe Wheeler, Keene, Texas

PAGE 70: *Embudo, New Mexico,* William Henry Jackson, Amon Carter Museum, Fort Worth, Texas

PAGE 71: ©1959, NBC

PAGE 74: *Cow Skull and Meadowlark,* O. C. Seltzer, The Thomas Gilcrease Institute of American History and Art, Tulsa, Oklahoma

PAGE 78: *A Deep Ford,* Frederic Remington, Volair Limited, Kent, Ohio

PAGE 79: ©1948, Monterey Productions; renewed 1975 by United Artists Corporation

PAGE 81: Nocona Boot Company, Ackerman McQueen Advertising, Inc.

PAGE 90–91: *Charros at the Roundup,* James Walker, Kennedy Galleries, New York

PAGE 96: *Cruising for Stock,* Frederic Remington, Volair Limited, Kent, Ohio

PAGE 99: *Charro Mexicano,* Lino Sanchez Y Tapia, The Thomas Gilcrease Institute of American History and Art, Tulsa, Oklahoma

PAGE 100: *A Mexican Buccaro,* Frederic Remington, Volair Limited, Kent, Ohio

PAGE 101: Montana Historical Society, Helena, Montana

PAGE 105: *The Cowboy,* Frederic Remington, Amon Carter Museum, Fort Worth, Texas

PAGE 114: ©1957, ABC

PAGE 121: *Across the Continent: "Westward the Course of Empire Takes its Way,"* Fanny F. Palmer, Amon Carter Museum, Fort Worth, Texas

PAGE 122–123: *Conquest of the Prairie*, Irving R. Bacon, Buffalo Bill Historical Center, Cody, Wyoming

PAGE 136, TOP: *Boom Town*, Thomas Hart Benton, Memorial Art Gallery of the University of Rochester, Rochester, New York

PAGE 140: ©1953, Paramount Pictures Corporation

PAGE 141, TOP: ©1962, Universal Pictures

PAGE 141, BOTTOM: ©1953, Paramount Pictures Corporation

PAGE 142: ©1962, MGM; Denver Center Cinema, Denver, Colorado

PAGE 143: ©1980, Paramount Pictures Corporation

PAGE 146–147: *The Last of the Buffalo*, Albert Bierstadt, Buffalo Bill Historical Center, Cody, Wyoming

PAGE 153: Collection of Joe Wheeler, Keene, Texas

PAGE 155: Collection of Paul and Teresa Harbaugh, Denver, Colorado

PAGE 156: *American Buffalo*, George Catlin, Buffalo Bill Historical Center, Cody, Wyoming

PAGE 158: The Kansas State Historical Society, Topeka, Kansas

PAGE 159: ©1953, Walt Disney Studios

PAGE 162: Brown Brothers, Sterling, Pennsylvania

PAGE 178–179: *His First Lesson*, Frederic Remington, Amon Carter Museum, Fort Worth, Texas

PAGE 186: Culver Pictures, New York

PAGE 187: Museum of Modern Art/Film Stills Archive, New York

PAGE 194: *Buster Lee, 1929*, Ray Rector, from *Cowboy Life on the Texas Plains: The Photographs of Ray Rector*, College Station: Texas A & M University Press, 1982

PAGE 195: *"Wag" Blessing*, John Addison Stryker, from *The Rodeo of John Addison Stryker*, Austin, Texas: The Encino Press, 1977

PAGE 180: ©1933, Will James

PAGE 201: F. M. Steel Photograph Collection, Barker Texas History Center, The University of Texas, Austin, Texas

PAGE 204–205: ©1948, Monterey Productions; renewed 1975 by United Artists Corporation

PAGE 206: *Trouble with the Longhorns*, N. C. Wyeth, Buffalo Bill Historical Center, Cody, Wyoming

PAGE 208: *In a Stampede*, Frederic Remington, Volair Limited, Kent, Ohio

PAGE 211, BOTTOM: Texas State Archives, Austin, Texas

PAGE 217: Tom Lea, from *The Longhorns*, by J. Frank Dobie, Austin, Texas: University of Texas Press, 1941

PAGE 218, TOP: Brown Brothers, Sterling, Pennsylvania

PAGE 218, BOTTOM: ©1942, Will James

PAGE 231: Frederic Remington, Volair Limited, Kent, Ohio

PAGE 233: Collection of Paul and Teresa Harbaugh, Denver

PAGE 234–235: *The Song of the Talking Wire*, Henry F. Farny, The Taft Museum, Cincinnati, Ohio

PAGE 240: ©1951, renewed 1979 Columbia Pictures Industries

PAGE 241: ©1954, Linden Productions; United Artists Corporation

PAGE 242–243: *The Long Horn Cattle Sign*, Frederic Remington, Amon Carter Museum, Fort Worth, Texas

PAGE 244: Buffalo Bill Memorial Museum, Golden, Colorado

PAGE 245: Culver Pictures, New York

PAGE 248: Buffalo Bill Memorial Museum, Golden, Colorado

PAGE 250: ©1950, Universal Pictures

PAGE 254: ©1956, Warner Bros. Inc.

PAGE 255: ©1970, National General

PAGE 258, TOP: ©1944, 20th Century-Fox Film Corporation

PAGE 258, BOTTOM: ©1976, United Artists Corporation

PAGE 265: Photo Trends, New York, Color Realization by Sally Sleight, from *Esquire*, Robert Priest, Art Director

PAGE 268–269: *When Law Dulls the Edge of Chance*, Charles M. Russell, Buffalo Bill Historical Center, Cody, Wyoming

PAGE 270: Western History Collections, University of Oklahoma Library, Norman, Oklahoma

PAGE 271: Museum of Modern Art/Film Stills Archive, New York, ©1923, Fox Film Corporation

PAGE 272: ©1949, Magazine Enterprises

PAGE 273, TOP: *Death of a Gambler*, Charles M. Russell, Buffalo Bill Historical Center, Cody, Wyoming

PAGE 273, BOTTOM: Collection of Joe Wheeler, Keene, Texas

PAGE 275: ©1953, Universal Pictures

PAGE 278: ©1959, Armada Productions, Inc.

PAGE 279: ©1969, Paramount Pictures Corporation

PAGE 282: Buffalo Bill Memorial Museum, Golden, Colorado

PAGE 283: Circus World Museum, Baraboo, Wisconsin

PAGE 284: ©1952, United Artists Corporation; Museum of Modern Art/Film Stills Archive, New York

PAGE 285, TOP: *Enter the Law*, E. C. Ward, The Thomas Gilcrease Institute of American History and Art, Tulsa, Oklahoma

PAGE 285, BOTTOM: ©1976, Marvel Comics Group

PAGE 290: ©1956, Warner Bros. Inc.

PAGE 293: ©1953, MGM, from *Rocky Mountain Magazine*, Hans Teensma, Art Director

PAGE 294: Buffalo Bill Historical Center, Cody, Wyoming

PAGE 300–301: *In Without Knocking*, Charles M. Russell, Amon Carter Mueseum, Fort Worth, Texas

PAGE 302: ©1969, Campanile Productions, Inc. and 20th Century-Fox Film Corporation

PAGE 303: American Heritage Center, University of Wyoming, Laramie, Wyoming

PAGE 305, TOP: Norman Seeff, CBS Records

PAGE 307: Western History Collections, University of Oklahoma Library, Norman, Oklahoma

Text Credits

Bibliography

Edward Abbey. *The Brave Cowboy*. New York: Dodd, Mead, 1956.

E. C. (Teddy Blue) Abbott and Helena Huntington Smith. *We Pointed Them North: Recollections of a Cowpuncher*. New York: Farrar and Rinehart, 1939.

Andy Adams. *The Log of a Cowboy*. Boston: Houghton Mifflin, 1903.

C. Merton Babcock, ed. *The American Frontier*. New York: Holt, Rinehart and Winston, 1965.

Gretchen M. Bataille and Charles L. Silet, eds. *The Pretend Indians*. Ames: Iowa State University Press, 1980.

E. Douglas Branch. *The Hunting of the Buffalo*. Lincoln: University of Nebraska Press, 1962. (Reprint)

Dee Brown. *Bury My Heart at Wounded Knee*. New York: Holt, Rinehart and Winston, 1971.

Buffalo Bill and the Wild West. Brooklyn: Brooklyn Museum, 1981.

Walter Noble Burns. *The Saga of Billy the Kid*. New York: Ballantine, 1973. (Reprint)

Jenni Calder. *There Must Be a Lone Ranger*. New York: McGraw-Hill, 1977.

Benjamin Capps. *The Indians*. New York: Time-Life Books, 1973.

Agnes Morley Cleaveland. *No Life for a Lady*. Boston: Houghton Mifflin, 1941.

Henry Steele Commager. *The West*. New York: Promontory Press, 1976.

Elizabeth Bacon Custer. *Boots and Saddles*. Norman: University of Oklahoma Press, 1961. (Reprint)

David Dary. *Cowboy Culture: A Saga of Five Centuries*. New York: Knopf, 1981.

J. Frank Dobie. *Cow People*. Boston: Little, Brown, 1964.

J. Frank Dobie. *The Longhorns*. Boston: Little, Brown, 1941.

J. Frank Dobie. *The Mustangs*. Boston: Little, Brown, 1952.

John R. Erickson. *The Modern Cowboy*. Lincoln: University of Nebraska Press, 1981.

William K. Everson. *A Pictorial History of the Western Film*. Secaucus, N.J.: Citadel Press, 1969.

Dexter W. Fellows and Andrew A. Freeman. *This Way to the Big Show*. New York, 1934.

George N. Fenin and William K. Everson. *The Western: From the Silents to the Seventies*. New York: Grossman, 1973.

Austin Fife and Alta Fife, eds. *Ballads of the Great West*. Palo Alto, Calif.: American West, 1970.

William H. Forbis. *The Cowboys*. New York: Time-Life Books, 1973.

Pat Garrett. *The Authentic Life of Billy the Kid, Noted Desperado of the Southwest*. Norman: University of Oklahoma Press, 1965. (Reprint)

John Graves. *From a Limestone Ledge*. New York: Knopf, 1980.

Horace Greeley. *An Overland Journey*. London: MacDonald, 1965. (Reprint)

Zane Grey. *Nevada: A Romance of the West*. New York: Harper and Brothers, 1928.

Zane Grey. *Riders of the Purple Sage*. New York: Grossett & Dunlap, 1912.

Zane Grey. *30,000 on the Hoof*. New York: Harper and Brothers, 1940.

Zane Grey. *The Thundering Herd*. New York: Grosset & Dunlap, 1925.

Fred Groves. *The Buffalo Runners*. Garden City, N.Y.: Doubleday, 1968.

Douglas Kent Hall. *Let 'Er Buck*. New York: Dutton, n.d.

Charles W. Harris and Buck Rainey, eds. *The Cowboy: Six-Shooters, Songs and Sex*. Norman: University of Oklahoma Press, 1976.

E. Richard Hart, ed. *That Awesome Space*. Salt Lake City, Utah: Westwater Press, 1981.

W. H. Hutchinson. "Virgins, Villains, and Varmints," *The Rhodes Reader*. Norman: University of Oklahoma Press, 1957.

Helen Hunt Jackson. *A Century of Dishonor*. New York: Harper & Row, 1965. (Reprint)

Teresa Jordan. *Cowgirls: Women of the American West*. Garden City, N.Y.: Doubleday, 1982.

Sandra Kauffman. *The Cowboy Catalog*. New York: Clarkson N. Potter, 1980.

Rosemary Kent. *The Genuine Texas Handbook*. New York: Workman, 1981.

Jane Kramer. *The Last Cowboy*. New York: Harper & Row, 1977.

Howard R. Lamar, ed. *Reader's Encyclopedia of the American West*. New York: Crowell, 1977.

Louis L'Amour. *Shalako*. New York: Bantam, 1962.

Elizabeth Atwood Lawrence. *Rodeo: An Anthropologist Looks at the Wild and the Tame*. Knoxville: University of Tennessee Press, 1982.

John Leakey. *The West That Was*. Lincoln: University of Nebraska Press, 1958. (Reprint)

Peter Livingston. *The Complete Book of Country Swing and Western Dance*. Garden City, N.Y.: Doubleday, 1981.

Roscoe Logue. *Under Texas and Border Skies*. Amarillo, Texas: Russell Stationery, 1935.

Thomas McGuane. *An Outside Chance*. New York: Farrar, Straus & Giroux, 1980.

T. C. McLuhan, ed. *Touch the Earth*. New York: Promontory Press, 1971.

Larry McMurtry. *Horseman, Pass By*. New York: Harper & Row, 1961.

Larry McMurtry. *In a Narrow Grave*. Austin, Texas: Encino Press, 1968.

John G. Mitchell. *The Hunt*. New York: Knopf, 1980.

N. Scott Momaday. *The Way to Rainy Mountain*. Albuquerque: University of New Mexico Press, 1969.

Michael Ondaatje. *The Collected Works of Billy the Kid*. New York: Berkley, 1975.

Margaret L. Rector, ed. *The Photographs of Ray Rector*. Introduction by John Graves. College Station: Texas A&M University Press, 1982.

Joyce Gibson Roach. *The Cowgirls*. Houston: Cordovan Corporation, 1977.

Joseph G. Rosa. *The Gunfighter*. Norman: University of Oklahoma Press, 1969.

Don Russell. *The Lives and Legends of Buffalo Bill*. Norman: University of Oklahoma Press, 1960.

Bob St. James. *On Down the Road*. Englewood Cliffs, N. J.: Prentice-Hall, 1977.

Mari Sandoz. *Love Song to the Plains*. Lincoln: University of Nebraska Press, 1966. (Reprint)

William W. Savage, Jr. *The Cowboy Hero*. Norman: University of Oklahoma Press, 1979.

William W. Savage, Jr., ed. *Cowboy Life: Reconstructing an American Myth*. Norman: University of Oklahoma Press, 1975.

Jack Schaefer. *Shane*. Boston: Houghton Mifflin, 1949.

Charles A. Siringo. *A Texas Cow Boy*. Chicago: Umbdenstock, 1885.

Richard Slotkin. *Regeneration Through Violence*. Middletown, Conn.: Wesleyan University Press, 1973.

Henry Nash Smith. *Virgin Land*. Cambridge, Mass.: Harvard University Press, 1950.

Marshall Sprague. *The Mountain States*. New York: Time-Life Books, 1967.

Wallace Stegner. *The Sound of Mountain Water*. New York: Dutton, 1980.

Stephen Tatum. *Inventing Billy the Kid*. Albuquerque: University of New Mexico Press, 1982.

Owen Wister. *The Virginian*. New York: Harper and Brothers, 1902.

(Elliott McDowell)

Filmography

Apache, 1954, Robert Aldrich
The Aryan, 1916, William S. Hart
Barbarosa, 1982, Fred Schepisi
Billy the Kid, 1930, King Vidor
Billy the Kid Returns, 1938, Joe Kane
Bless the Beasts and Children, 1971, Stanley Kramer
Bonnie and Clyde, 1968, Arthur Penn
Broken Arrow, 1950, Delmer Daves
Buffalo Bill and the Indians, 1976, Robert Altman
Buffalo Bill Rides Again, 1947, B. B. Ray
Buffalo Bill on the U.P. Trail, 1926, Frank S. Mattison
Butch Cassidy and the Sundance Kid, 1969, George Roy Hill
Cheyenne Autumn, 1964, John Ford
The Covered Wagon, 1923, James Cruze
The Cowboys, 1972, Mark Rydell
The Culpepper Cattle Co., 1972, Dick Richards
Davy Crockett: King of the Wild Frontier, 1954, Norman Foster
Destry Rides Again, 1939, George Marshall
Duel in the Sun, 1946, King Vidor
Electric Horseman, 1979, Sydney Pollack
A Fistful of Dollars, 1967, Sergio Leone
For a Few Dollars More, 1967, Sergio Leone
Fort Apache, 1948, John Ford
The Good, the Bad, and the Ugly, 1968, Sergio Leone
The Green Berets, 1968, John Wayne
The Gunfighter, 1950, Henry King
The Hazards of Helen, 1914, Helen Holmes
Hell's Hinges, 1916, William S. Hart
High Noon, 1952, Fred Zinneman
How the West Was Won, 1963, John Ford
Hud, 1963, Martin Ritt
Indian Massacre, 1912, Thomas Ince
An Indian Wife's Devotion, 1911, William Selig
Junior Bonner, 1972, Sam Peckinpah
The Kid from Texas, 1950, Kurt Neuman
The Left-Handed Gun, 1948, Arthur Penn
Little Big Man, 1970, Arthur Penn
The Lone Ranger, 1956, Stuart Heisler
Lonely Are the Brave, 1962, David Miller
The Man Who Shot Liberty Valance, 1961, John Ford
The Misfits, 1961, John Huston
Monte Walsh, 1970, William A. Fraker
My Darling Clementine, 1946, John Ford
One-Eyed Jacks, 1961, Marlon Brando
The Outlaw, 1943, Howard Hawks/Howard Hughes

Paint Your Wagon, 1969, Joshua Logan
Parade of Buffalo Bill's Wild West, 1898, Thomas Edison
Pat Garrett and Billy the Kid, 1973, Sam Peckinpah
Ramona, 1910, D. W. Griffith
Red River, 1948, Howard Hawks
Ride the High Country, 1962, Sam Peckinpah
Rio Bravo, 1959, Howard Hawks
The Searchers, 1956, John Ford
Shane, 1953, George Stevens
She Wore a Yellow Ribbon, 1949, John Ford
The Shootist, 1976, Don Siegel
Sioux Ghost Dance, 1894, Thomas Edison
Son of Billy the Kid, 1949, Ray Taylor
The Sons of Katie Elder, 1965, Henry Hathaway
A Squaw's Love, 1911
Stagecoach, 1939, John Ford
To the Last Man, 1933, Henry Hathaway
True Grit, 1970, Henry Hathaway
Two Rode Together, 1961, John Ford
Urban Cowboy, 1980, James Bridges
The Westerner, 1940, William Wyler
The Wild Bunch, 1969, Sam Peckinpah
Will Penny, 1967, Tom Gries
Winchester '73, 1950, Anthony Mann

(Jay Dusard)

Index

(Chuck O'Rear/West Light)

(B. A. King)

(Martin Schreiber)

(Steve Smith)

(Michael Lichter)

(Bill Wunsch)

(Ernst Haas)

(Tom Stack/Tom Stack & Assoc.)

(Douglas Kent Hall/FotoWest)

(Susan Felter)

(John Running)

(Nancy Wood)

(Kurt Markus)

PAGES 406-407: *Douglas Kent Hall/FotoWest*
PAGE 408: *Skeeter Hagler*

The text was set in Kennerley by TGA Communications, Inc.
New York, New York.
The book was printed on 150 gsm. R 400 paper
by Amilcare Pizzi s.p.a. arti grafiche, Milan, Italy.
Bound in Italy by Amilcare Pizzi.